KB185991

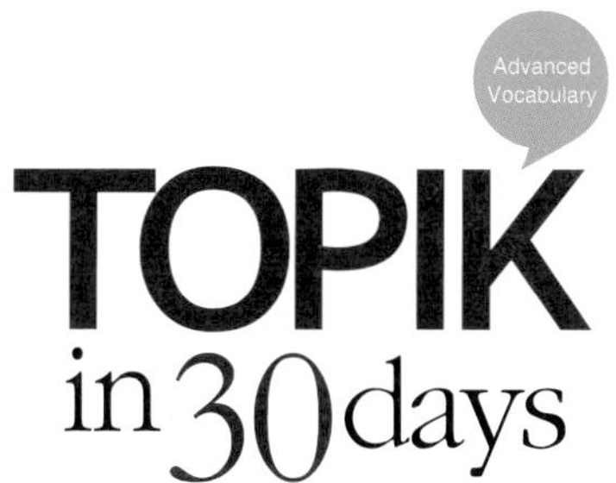

Kim Joo Yeon · Moon Sun Mi
Yoo Jae Seon · Choi You Ha

TOPIK in 30 days - Advanced Vocabulary

초판 인쇄 2024년 2월 14일
초판 발행 2024년 2월 23일

지은이 김주연 · 문선미 · 유재선 · 최유하
번역 Janice Jung
펴낸이 박찬익
펴낸곳 ㈜박이정 **주소** 경기도 하남시 조정대로45 미사센텀비즈 8층 F827호
전화 031)792-1193, 1195 **팩스** 02)928-4683 **홈페이지** www.pjbook.com
이메일 pijbook@naver.com **등록** 2014년 8월 22일 제2020-000029호
제작처 한영문화사

ISBN 979-11-5848-673-0 13710

* 책값은 뒤표지에 있습니다.

Contains more than 2200 words that are highly possible to appear in the upcoming TOPIK after analyzing the past tests.

Advanced Vocabulary

TOPIK in 30 days

김주연 · 문선미 · 유재선 · 최유하

self-vocabulary booklet and mp3 files included

교재 집필자 약력

김주연

건국대학교 국어국문학과 박사, 연세대학교 외국어로서의 한국어교육 석사

현 | 건국대학교 국어국문학과 강사, 건국대학교 언어교육원 한국어과정 강사

저서 | 『한국어 1』 건국대학교 출판부, 『한국어 3』 건국대학교 출판부,
『함께 배우는 건국 한국어 1』 건국대학교 출판부, 『토픽 필수 문법 150 중급』 한글 파크,
『New TOPIK I 필수문법 101 초급』 한글 파크, 『TOPIK II 중급어휘 30일 완성』 박이정

문선미

연세대학교 외국어로서의 한국어교육 석사

현 | 일본 릿쿄대학 한국어 겸임 강사

저서 | 『한국어 5』 건국대학교 출판부, 『토픽 필수 문법 150 중급』 한글 파크,
『New TOPIK I 필수문법 101 초급』 한글 파크, 『TOPIK II 중급어휘 30일 완성』 박이정

유재선

연세대학교 외국어로서의 한국어 교육 석사

현 | 서울대학교 언어교육원 한국어과정 강사

저서 | 『서울대 한국어 4』 투판즈, 『토픽 필수 문법 150 중급』 한글 파크,
『New TOPIK I 필수문법 101 초급』 한글 파크, 『TOPIK II 중급어휘 30일 완성』 박이정

최유하

연세대학교 외국어로서의 한국어교육 석사

현 | 건국대학교 언어교육원 한국어과정 강사

저서 | 『한국어 5』 건국대학교 출판부, 『함께 배우는 건국 한국어 5,6』 건국대학교 출판부,
『토픽 필수 문법 150 중급』 한글 파크, 『New TOPIK I 필수문법 101 초급』 한글 파크,
『TOPIK II 중급어휘 30일 완성』 박이정

<TOPIK in 30 days> is a textbook for foreigners who are preparing for the TOPIK- advanced level. It is suitably organized for learners to easily acquire new words that frequently appear on TOPIK and make them able to check their improved capability by solving the review questions.

Many students have trouble preparing for the TOPIK. It is because of the following reasons. First, a textbook that contains a list of required words to prepare for the TOPIK- advanced level does not exist. Also, there is no textbook that helps students study effectively by themselves. In order to solve these problems, this book has selected the words that must be acquired before taking test, and made a list to help students to easily proceed on their learning.

After closely analyzing questions from the past TOPIK exam, we have selected the words that have most frequently appeared on the test. Then, we have organized these words into a 30day curriculum and made it possible for the students to go over these words in 30 days. Moreover, the related word for every word is also attached together so that it can help students to better prepare for the test. Also, we provide a section where students can review the words that they know and can check their comprehension.

We wish foreign students positive results by preparing for the test effectively in this 30 day short period by using this book.

Thanks to numerous foreign students who gave precious advice and translator who translated the textbook into English and also to the people who gave a final review. Also, we appreciate the staffs in 박이정 publisher who put their efforts to complete this TOPIK textbook.

2021.11. authors

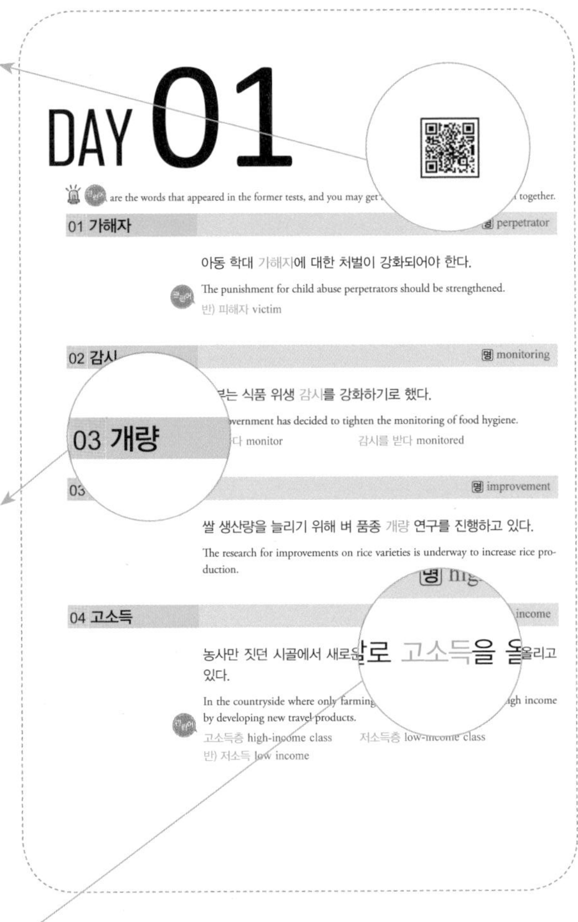

정확한 발음 확인
Check the accurate pronunciation

제시어와 예문의 발음을 확인하고 익힐 수 있도록 한국인의 발음을 수록하였습니다. MP3형태로 www.pjbook.com에서 직접 다운로드 받을 수 있습니다.

Includes Korean's voice of pronunciation of given words and example sentences in order to check and master them. Files are available to download from the www.pjbook.com site.

출제 빈도별 우선 순위 어휘
Words organized based on high frequency

토픽에 출제된 어휘들을 빈도순으로 엄선하고, 30일치 학습 분량으로 나눠 제시하였습니다. 빈도가 가장 높은 중요 단어들부터 제시함으로써 학습의 효율성을 높였습니다.

Thoroughly selected the words from past exams based on the frequency, and provided 30 days of curriculum. Increased the efficiency of learning by putting more frequently appeared words in the earlier part of the book.

암기력을 높이는 예문
Sample sentences section

제시어의 뜻을 가장 잘 드러낼 수 있는 예문을 해석과 함께 제시하였습니다. 제시어와 함께 예문을 외우면 실제 생활에서도 유용하게 쓸 수 있을 것입니다.

Provides the best sample sentences that clearly shows the suggested meaning together with Korean translation. By memorizing the given word and the sample sentence together, you can also use this in your daily life.

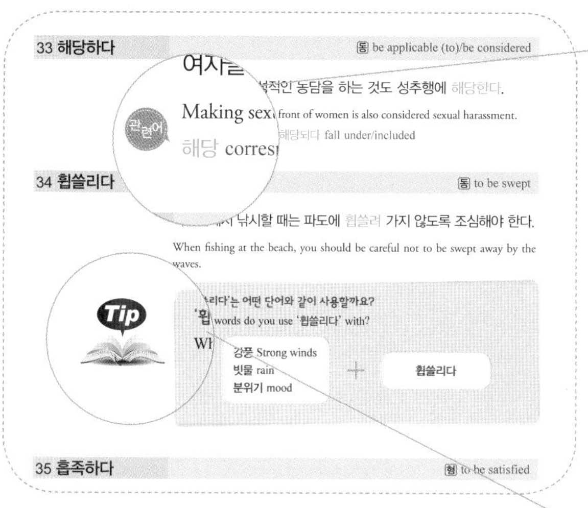

33 해당하다
동 be applicable (to)/be considered
여자들 앞에서 성적인 농담을 하는 것도 성추행에 해당한다.
Making sexual jokes in front of women is also considered sexual harassment.
관련어
해당되다 fall under/included
34 휩쓸리다
동 to be swept
바닷가에서 낚시할 때는 파도에 휩쓸려 가지 않도록 조심해야 한다.
When fishing at the beach, you should be careful not to be swept away by the waves.
Tip
'휩쓸리다'는 어떤 단어와 같이 사용할까요?
What words do you use '휩쓸리다' with?
강풍 Strong winds
빗물 rain
분위기 mood
휩쓸리다
35 흡족하다
형 to be satisfied

관련 어휘
Related words

제시어와 의미상 관련이 있거나 형태상 관련이 있는 어휘들입니다. 함께 외우면 토픽에서 고득점을 받을 수 있을 것입니다.

Words that are related with the given words by meaning or forms. It will help you get a high score in the test if you memorize them together.

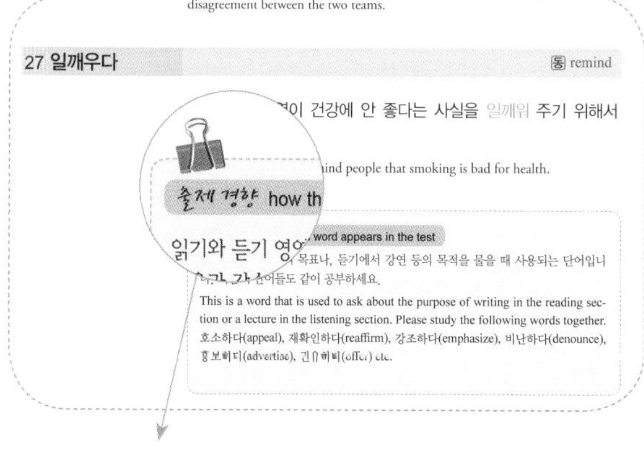

disagreement between the two teams.
27 일깨우다
동 remind
흡연이 건강에 안 좋다는 사실을 일깨워 주기 위해서
to remind people that smoking is bad for health.
출제 경향 how the word appears in the test
읽기와 듣기 영역에서 글의 목표나, 듣기에서 강연 등의 목적을 물을 때 사용되는 단어입니다. 다음 단어들도 같이 공부하세요.
This is a word that is used to ask about the purpose of writing in the reading section or a lecture in the listening section. Please study the following words together.
호소하다(appeal), 재확인하다(reaffirm), 강조하다(emphasize), 비난하다(denounce), 홍보하다(advertise), 권유하다(offer) etc.

어휘 정보
Words information

제시어와 혼동하기 쉬운 어휘와의 비교, 제시어와 함께 쓰이는 어휘 제시, 제시어에 대한 더 자세한 정보 등을 실었습니다.

These will have more detailed information about the given words.

출제 경향
Explanation of the latest question trends

제시어가 토픽에서는 어떤 방식으로 출제되었는지 혹은 출제될 가능성이 있는지를 설명했습니다. 그리고 제시어가 토픽 지문에서 주제로 활용되었을 때 자주 사용되는 표현이나 문법을 제시했습니다.

Explains how the given words appear in the actual TOPIK test or how probable the words will appear in the future test. Also, added the frequently used expressions or applied grammar when the given words are used as a topic in the test.

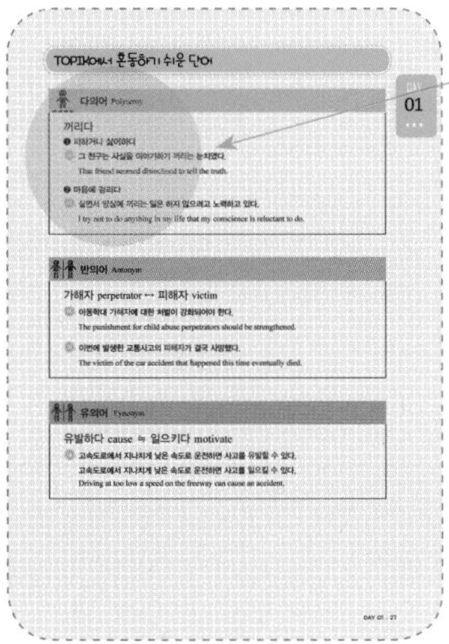

TOPIK에서 혼동하기 쉬운 단어

DAY 01

다의어 Polysemy

꺼리다

❶ 피하거나 싫어하다

그 친구는 사실을 이야기하기 꺼리는 눈치였다.
That friend seemed disinclined to tell the truth.

❷ 마음에 걸리다

살면서 양심에 꺼리는 일은 하지 않으려고 노력하고 있다.
I try not to do anything in my life that my conscience is reluctant to do.

반의어 Antonym

가해자 perpetrator ↔ 피해자 victim

아동학대 가해자에 대한 처벌이 강화되어야 한다.
The punishment for child abuse perpetrators should be strengthened.

이번에 발생한 교통사고의 피해자가 결국 사망했다.
The victim of the car accident that happened this time eventually died.

유의어 Synonym

유발하다 cause ≒ 일으키다 motivate

고속도로에서 지나치게 낮은 속도로 운전하면 사고를 유발할 수 있다.
고속도로에서 지나치게 낮은 속도로 운전하면 사고를 일으킬 수 있다.
Driving at too low a speed on the freeway can cause an accident.

DAY 01 · 27

TOPIK에서 혼동하기 쉬운 어휘
Easily confused TOPIK words

토픽에 출제된 유의어, 반의어, 다의어를 예문과 함께 제시해 설명했습니다.

This part explain synonyms, antonyms, and polysemy appeared in the past TOPIK tests along with the sample sentences.

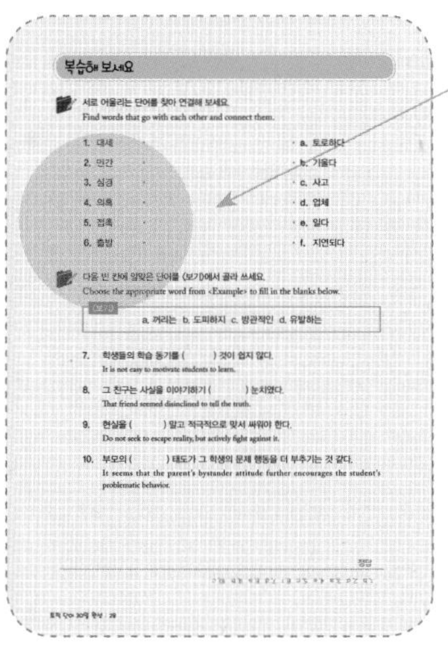

복습해 보세요

서로 어울리는 단어를 찾아 연결해 보세요.
Find words that go with each other and connect them.

1. 대세 · · a. 토로하다
2. 민간 · · b. 기울다
3. 심경 · · c. 사고
4. 의혹 · · d. 업체
5. 접촉 · · e. 일다
6. 출발 · · f. 지연되다

다음 빈 칸에 알맞은 단어를 〈보기〉에서 골라 쓰세요.
Choose the appropriate word from <Example> to fill in the blanks below.

보기: a. 꺼리는 b. 도피하지 c. 방관적인 d. 유발하는

7. 학생들의 학습 동기를 (　　) 것이 쉽지 않다.
It is not easy to motivate students to learn.

8. 그 친구는 사실을 이야기하기 (　　) 눈치였다.
That friend seemed disinclined to tell the truth.

9. 현실을 (　　) 말고 적극적으로 맞서 싸워야 한다.
Do not seek to escape reality, but actively fight against it.

10. 부모의 (　　) 태도가 그 학생의 문제 행동을 더 부추기는 것 같다.
It seems that the parent's bystander attitude further encourages the student's problematic behavior.

정답

토픽 단어 30일 완성 · 28

일일 복습
Daily review

그 날 그 날 학습한 어휘를 학습자 스스로 확인할 수 있도록 구성된 복습입니다.

Review that can let the learners check their comprehension of the words on a daily basis.

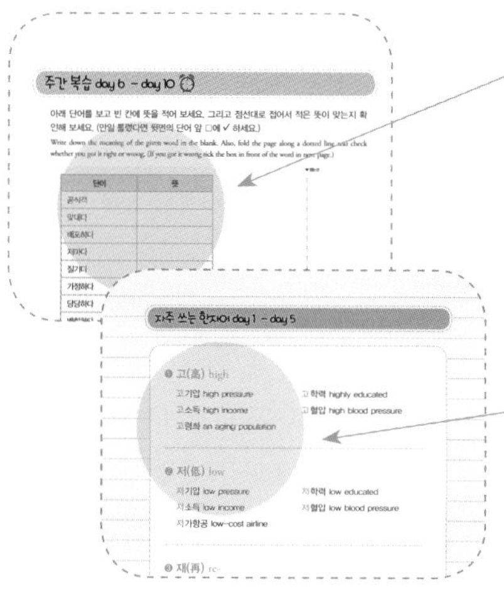

주간 복습
Weekly review

5일마다 제시되는 복습으로 그동안 학습한 어휘를 어느 정도 기억하는지 확인할 수 있도록 구성했습니다.

Review that is provided every 5 days, and is organized to let the learners check how much they remember the words they have learned.

토픽 고급 기출 한자어
Korean words of Chinese origin from past tests

토픽에 출제된 한자어를 알기 쉽게 제시했습니다.

Korean words of Chinese origin from past tests are presented in this part.

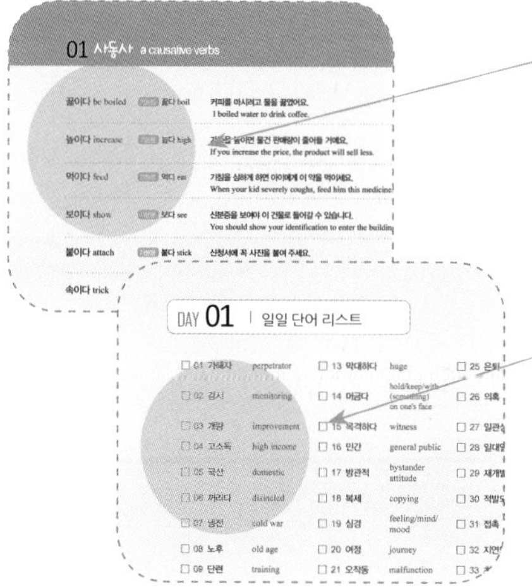

부록
Appendix

토픽에 자주 기출된 핵심 사동사, 피동사, 속담 및 관용표현으로 구성되었습니다.

Part that includes key causative verbs, passive verbs, and proverbs that frequently appeared in the past tests.

단어장
Self-vocabulary booklet

간단하게 잘라서 만들 수 있는 단어장입니다. 시험 전 간편하게 들고 다닐 수 있도록 만들어 보세요!

Provides a booklet that can simply be made only by cutting few pages from the book. Highly required to make one and easily repeat it in your daily life.

차례
Table of Contents

DAY
11 - 20

TOPIK 시험 안내

1. TOPIK 시험 목적

- 한국어를 모국어로 하지 않는 재외동포 · 외국인의 한국어 학습 방향 제시 및 한국어 보급 확대
- 한국어 사용능력을 측정 · 평가하여 그 결과를 국내 대학 유학 및 취업 등에 활용

2. TOPIK 응시대상

한국어를 모국어로 하지 않는 재외동포 및 외국인으로서

- 한국어 학습자 및 국내 대학 유학 희망자
- 국내외 한국 기업체 및 공공기관 취업 희망자
- 외국 학교에 재학중이거나 졸업한 재외국민

3. TOPIK 유효기간

- 성적 발표일로부터 2년간 유효

4. TOPIK 주관기관

- 교육부 국립국제교육원

5. TOPIK 시험의 주요 활용처

- 외국인 및 재외동포의 국내 대학(원) 입학 및 졸업
- 국내/외 기업체 및 공공기관 취업
- 영주권/취업 등 체류비자 취득
- 정부초청 외국인 장학생 프로그램 진학 및 학사관리
- 국외 대학의 한국어 관련 학과 학점 및 졸업요건

6. 시행시기

- 연간 총 6회 실시

시기		시행 지역	미주 · 유럽 · 아프리카	아시아 · 오세아니아	한국
상반기	2월경	국내	–	–	일요일
	4월경	국내 외	토요일	일요일	일요일
	5월경	국내	–	–	일요일
하반기	7월경	국내	토요일	일요일	일요일
	10월경	국내 외	토요일	일요일	일요일
	11월경	국내	–	–	일요일

7. 시험의 등급

- 시험 수준 : TOPIK I, TOPIK II
- 시험 등급 : 6개 등급(1급~6급)
- 획득한 종합점수를 기준으로 판정되며, 등급별 분할 점수는 아래와 같습니다.

구분	TOPIK I		TOPIK II			
	1급	2급	3급	4급	5급	6급
등급 결정	80~139	140~200	120~149	150~189	190~229	230~300

8. 문항 구성

• 시험 수준별 구성

시험수준	교시	영역	문제 유형	문항수	배점	총점
TOPIK I	1교시	듣기	선택형	30	100	300
		읽기	선택형	40	100	
TOPIK II	1교시	듣기	선택형	50	100	300
		쓰기	서답형	4	100	
	2교시	읽기	선택형	50	100	

• 문제 유형

- 선택형 문항(4지선다형)
- 서답형 문항(쓰기 영역)
  - 문장완성형(단답형) : 2문항
  - 작문형: 2문항(200~300자 정도의 중급 수준 설명문 1문항, 600~700자 정도의 고급 수준 논술문 1문항)

9. 시험 시간표

시험수준	교시	영역	한국			배점
			입실 완료 시간	시작	종료	
TOPIK I	1교시	듣기, 읽기	09:20 까지	10:00	11:40	100
TOPIK II	1교시	듣기, 쓰기	12:20 까지	13:00	14:50	110
	2교시	읽기	15:10 까지	15:20	16:30	70

10. 응시료(한국기준)

- TOPIK I : 40,000원
- TOPIK II : 55,000원

TOPIK 시험 안내

11. 쓰기 영역 작문 문항 평가 범주

문장번호	평가범주	평가내용
51-52	내용 및 과제 수행	- 제시된 과제에 맞게 적절한 내용으로 썼는가?
	언어사용	- 어휘와 문법 등의 사용이 정확한가?
53-54	내용 및 과제 수행	- 주어진 과제를 충실히 수행하였는가? - 주제에 관련된 내용으로 구성하였는가? - 주어진 내용을 풍부하고 다양하게 표현하였는가?
	글의 전개 구조	- 글의 구성이 명확하고 논리적인가? - 글의 내용에 따라 단락 구성이 잘 이루어졌는가? - 논리 전개에 도움이 되는 담화 표지를 적절하게 사용하여 조직적으로 연결하였는가?
	언어사용	- 문법과 어휘를 다양하고 풍부하게 사용하며 적절한 문법과 어휘를 선택하여 사용하였는가? - 문법, 어휘, 맞춤법 등의 사용이 정확한가? - 글의 목적과 기능에 따라 격식에 맞게 글을 썼는가?

12. 등급별 평가 기준

문장번호	평가범주	평가내용
TOPIK I	1급	- 자기 소개하기, 물건 사기, 음식 주문하기 등 생존에 필요한 기초적인 언어 기능을 수행할 수 있으며 자기 자신, 가족, 취미, 날씨 등 매우 사적이고 친숙한 화제에 관련된 내용을 이해하고 표현할 수 있다. - 약 800개의 기초 어휘와 기본 문법에 대한 이해를 바탕으로 간단한 문장을 생성할 수 있다. 또한 간단한 생활문과 실용문을 이해하고, 구성할 수 있다.
	2급	- 전화하기, 부탁하기 등의 일상생활에 필요한 기능과 우체국, 은행 등의 공공시설 이용에 필요한 기능을 수행할 수 있다. - 약 1,500~2,000개의 어휘를 이용하여 사적이고 친숙한 화제에 관해 문단 단위로 이해하고 사용할 수 있다. - 공식적 상황과 비공식적 상황에서의 언어를 구분해 사용할 수 있다.

문장번호	평가범주	평가내용
TOPIK II	3급	- 일상생활을 영위하는 데 별 어려움을 느끼지 않으며 다양한 공공시설의 이용과 사회적 관계 유지에 필요한 기초적 언어 기능을 수행할 수 있다. - 친숙하고 구체적인 소재는 물론, 자신에게 친숙한 사회적 소재를 문단 단위로 표현하거나 이해할 수 있다. - 문어와 구어의 기본적인 특성을 구분해서 이해하고 사용할 수 있다.
TOPIK II	4급	- 공공시설 이용과 사회적 관계 유지에 필요한 언어 기능을 수행할 수 있으며, 일반적인 업무 수행에 필요한 기능을 어느 정도 수행할 수 있다. 또한 뉴스, 신문 기사 중 비교적 평이한 내용을 이해할 수 있다. 일반적인 사회적 · 추상적 소재를 비교적 정확하고 유창하게 이해하고 사용할 수 있다. - 자주 사용되는 관용적 표현과 대표적인 한국 문화에 대한 이해를 바탕으로 사회 · 문화적인 내용을 이해하고 사용할 수 있다.
TOPIK II	5급	- 전문 분야에서의 연구나 업무 수행에 필요한 언어 기능을 어느 정도 수행할 수 있으며 정치, 경제, 사회, 문화 전반에 걸쳐 친숙하지 않은 소재에 관해서도 이해하고 사용할 수 있다. - 공식적 · 비공식적 맥락과 구어적 · 문어적 맥락에 따라 언어를 적절히 구분해 사용할 수 있다.
TOPIK II	6급	- 전문 분야에서의 연구나 업무 수행에 필요한 언어 기능을 비교적 정확하고 유창하게 수행할 수 있으며 정치, 경제, 사회, 문화 전반에 걸쳐 친숙하지 않은 주제에 관해서도 이해하고 사용할 수 있다. - 원어민 화자의 수준에는 이르지 못하나 기능 수행이나 의미 표현에는 어려움을 겪지 않는다.

Guidance for TOPIK

1. TOPIK Purpose of test

- To guide those learning Korean as a second language and promote more widespread us of the Korean language
- To assess individual proficiency in the Korean language and allow test-takers to use the test results in filing college applications, job applications, etc.

2. TOPIK Eligibility

- Overseas Korean or non-Korean whose first language is not Korean and who:
  - is currently learning Korean or wishes to study at a Korean college;
  - wishes to work for a Korean company or public agency based in or outside Korea.
  - Korean national who is currently studying at or has graduated from a school abroad

3. TOPIK Validity Period(TOPIK Score)

- Valid for two years from the announcement of the test score

4. TOPIK Management Organization

- Ministry of Education National Insitute for International Education

5. TOPIK Potential Uses

- serving as admission and graduation standard for universities in Korea.
- applying for companies and public institutions in Korea and abroad.
- obtaining Visa for qualifications of permanent residency and employment, etc.
- taking courses under Global Korean Scholarship(GKS) Program
- serving as substitute credits and requirements of graduation for Korean majors in overseas universities.

6. Exam Dates

- Tests held 6 times a year
  - The above test dates are subject to change according to the area or affiliate institution's circumstances.

Date		Area	The Americas/Europe/Africa	Asia	Korea
First Half Year	February	Korea	-	-	Sunday
	April	Korea/ Overseas	Saturday	Sunday	Sunday
	May	Korea	-	-	Sunday
Second Half Yeay	July	Korea	Saturday	Sunday	Sunday
	October	Korea/ Overseas	Saturday	Sunday	Sunday
	November	Korea	-	-	Sunday

7. Test Levels and Sublevels

- Levels: TOPIK I, TOPIK II
- Sublevels: 6 sublevels (Sublevels 1 to 6)
- The level and sublevel is determined based on the total score obtained as follows.

<table>
<tr><th rowspan="2"></th><th colspan="2">TOPIK I</th><th colspan="4">TOPIK II</th></tr>
<tr><th>Sublevel 1</th><th>Sublevel 2</th><th>Sublevel 3</th><th>Sublevel 4</th><th>Sublevel 5</th><th>Sublevel 6</th></tr>
<tr><td>Judgment criteria</td><td>80~139</td><td>140~200</td><td>120~149</td><td>150~189</td><td>190~229</td><td>230~300</td></tr>
</table>

8. Test Timetable

<table>
<tr><th>Level</th><th>Period</th><th>Section</th><th>Type</th><th>Number of questions</th><th>Points distribution</th><th>Maximum possible score</th></tr>
<tr><td rowspan="2">TOPIK I</td><td rowspan="2">1</td><td>Listening</td><td>Multiple choice questions</td><td>30</td><td>100</td><td rowspan="2">300</td></tr>
<tr><td>Reading omprehension</td><td>Multiple choice questions</td><td>40</td><td>100</td></tr>
<tr><td rowspan="3">TOPIK II</td><td rowspan="2">1</td><td>Listening</td><td>Multiple choice questions</td><td>50</td><td>100</td><td rowspan="3">300</td></tr>
<tr><td>Writing</td><td>Subjective questions</td><td>4</td><td>100</td></tr>
<tr><td>2</td><td>Reading omprehension</td><td>Multiple choice questions</td><td>50</td><td>100</td></tr>
</table>

- Question Types
  - Multiple choice (M/C) questions (4 choices)
  - Subjective questions (writing section)
    - · Complete-the-sentence questions (short answers): 2 questions
    - · Essay: 2 questions (one intermediate-level question requiring a response with about 200 to 300 characters and one advanced-level question requiring a response with about 600 to 700 characters)

9. Test Timetable

<table>
<tr><th rowspan="2"></th><th rowspan="2">Period</th><th rowspan="2">Section</th><th colspan="3">Korea</th><th rowspan="2">Duration (min)</th></tr>
<tr><th>Must enter the room by</th><th>Start</th><th>End</th></tr>
<tr><td>TOPIK I</td><td>1</td><td>Listening
Reading omprehension</td><td>09:20</td><td>10:00</td><td>11:40</td><td>100</td></tr>
<tr><td rowspan="2">TOPIK II</td><td>1</td><td>Listening
Writing</td><td>12:20</td><td>13:00</td><td>14:50</td><td>110</td></tr>
<tr><td>2</td><td>Reading omprehension</td><td>15:10</td><td>15:20</td><td>16:30</td><td>70</td></tr>
</table>

10. Registration fee (in Korea)

- TOPIK I : KRW 40,000
- TOPIK II : KRW 55,000

11. Evaluation Criteria for the Writing Section

Number of questions	Points distribution	
51-52	Content and task performance	- Was it written appropriately according to the given topic?
	Command of the language	- Was it written in a lexically and grammatically correct way?
53-54	Content and task performance	- Did the writer stay faithful to the given topic? - Is the content relevant to the topic? - Is the content rich with diverse expression?
	Structure and composition	- Was it written in a clear, logical way? - Was it properly divided into paragraphs? - Were transition/linking words used adequately to allow a smooth flow from one idea to the next?
	Command of the language	- Is it lexically and grammatically rich and diverse and did the writer make appropriate choices in terms of vocabulary and grammar? - Did the writer apply grammar rules and were the use of vocabulary and spelling accurate? - Did the writer write formally according to the purpose and function of writing?

12. Evaluation Criteria by Level/Sublevel

Level	Sublevel	Evaluation criteria
TOPIK I	1	The individual is capable of using basic language skills necessary for everyday activities, such as introducing him/herself, shopping, and ordering food, and understanding and expressing him/herself when conversing about him/herself, his/her family or pastimes, the weather, or other casual or familiar topics. The individual knows around 800 basic words and can form simple sentences with an understanding of basic grammar. He/she is also capable of understanding and forming practical sentences and simple sentences used in everyday life.
	2	The individual has the language skills necessary for everyday life, such as calling and asking for a favor, and for using the post office, bank, or public facilities. He/she knows some 1,500 to 2,000 words and can understand and compose paragraphs about a casual or familiar topic. He/she can also distinguish which linguistic form to use in formal and informal situations.

Level	Sublevel	Evaluation criteria
TOPIK II	3	The individual has no problem doing normal, day-to-day activities and has the basic language skills to use various public facilities and maintain interpersonal relationships. He/she can understand and express him/herself regarding not only familiar and specific topics but also familiar social issues in paragraphs. He/she is also capable of distinguishing the basic features of colloquial language and literary language and can understand and use the two forms of language him/herself.
	4	The individual has the language skills to use various public facilities and maintain interpersonal relationships and apply his/her skills to work situations to a certain extent. He/she can understand the news, news articles, etc. provided in relatively plain language. He/she can understand and express him/herself about a general social issue or abstract concept in a relatively accurate and fluent manner and about social and cultural issues based on frequently used idiomatic expressions and an understanding of Korean culture.
	5	The individual can use the language skills professionally or for research in a specialized field to a certain extent and understand and express him/herself regarding unfamiliar topics concerning politics, the economy, culture, and so on. He/she can appropriately use different forms of language according to the context and situation (e.g. formal/informal and colloquial/literary).
	6	The individual can use the language skills professionally or for research in a specialized field in a relatively accurate and fluent manner and understand and express him/herself regarding unfamiliar topics concerning politics, the economy, culture, and so on. While he/she may not be able to speak as a fluently as a native Korean speaker, he/she has no trouble expressing him/herself as intended.

Hey, everyone! There is a Korean saying, “A journey of 1000 miles begins with a single step.” It means that no matter how hard the task is, at some point you will reach your goal when you accomplish your task one by one every day.
How about well planning your schedule and settling down to your studies?
Now, let’s write down the days that you can study in the graph below.
Do not plan overwhelming tasks since you may give up while you are doing it.

Now, cheer up until you reach the high-level of TOPIK!

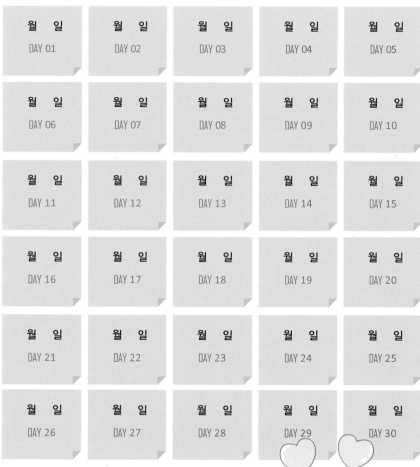

월 일 DAY 01	월 일 DAY 02	월 일 DAY 03	월 일 DAY 04	월 일 DAY 05
월 일 DAY 06	월 일 DAY 07	월 일 DAY 08	월 일 DAY 09	월 일 DAY 10
월 일 DAY 11	월 일 DAY 12	월 일 DAY 13	월 일 DAY 14	월 일 DAY 15
월 일 DAY 16	월 일 DAY 17	월 일 DAY 18	월 일 DAY 19	월 일 DAY 20
월 일 DAY 21	월 일 DAY 22	월 일 DAY 23	월 일 DAY 24	월 일 DAY 25
월 일 DAY 26	월 일 DAY 27	월 일 DAY 28	월 일 DAY 29	월 일 DAY 30

DAY 01

확인해 보세요

빨간 시트지로 가리고 단어의 뜻을 알면, □에 ✓ 해 보세요.

After covering up the words with red cover, please check(✓) the box (□) when you know the meaning of the word.

□ 01	가해자	perpetrator	□ 13	막대하다	huge	□ 25	은퇴	retirement
□ 02	감시	monitoring	□ 14	머금다	hold/keep/with (something) on one's face	□ 26	의혹	suspicion
□ 03	개량	improvement	□ 15	목격하다	witness	□ 27	일관성	consistency
□ 04	고소득	high income	□ 16	민간	general public	□ 28	일대일	one-on-one
□ 05	국산	domestic	□ 17	방관적	bystander attitude	□ 29	재개발	redevelopment
□ 06	꺼리다	disincled	□ 18	복제	copying	□ 30	적발되다	be caught
□ 07	냉전	cold war	□ 19	심경	feeling/mind/ mood	□ 31	접촉	be contact
□ 08	노후	old age	□ 20	여정	journey	□ 32	지연되다	delay
□ 09	단련	training	□ 21	오작동	malfunction	□ 33	초과	exceed
□ 10	대세	tide	□ 22	요건	requirement	□ 34	하마터면	almost
□ 11	도피하나	escape	□ 23	원료	ingredient	□ 35	확률	probability
□ 12	동참	participation	□ 24	유발하다	motivate			

DAY 01

 are the words that appeared in the former tests, and you may get a higher grade if you study them together.

01 가해자
명 perpetrator

아동 학대 가해자에 대한 처벌이 강화되어야 한다.

The punishment for child abuse perpetrators should be strengthened.

반) 피해자 victim

02 감시
명 monitoring

정부는 식품 위생 감시를 강화하기로 했다.

The government has decided to tighten the monitoring of food hygiene.

감시하다 monitor   감시를 받다 monitored

03 개량
명 improvement

쌀 생산량을 늘리기 위해 벼 품종 개량 연구를 진행하고 있다.

The research for improvements on rice varieties is underway to increase rice production.

04 고소득
명 high income

농사만 짓던 시골에서 새로운 여행 상품 개발로 고소득을 올리고 있다.

In the countryside where only farming was done, they are earning high income by developing new travel products.

고소득층 high-income class   저소득층 low-income class
반) 저소득 low income

05 국산

명 domestic

외국산 식재료를 국산으로 속여 판매하던 업체가 적발되었다.

The company that fradulently sold foreign food products as domestic ones was exposed.

반) 외국산 foreign goods 수입산 imported goods

06 꺼리다

동 disincled

그 친구는 사실을 이야기하기 꺼리는 눈치였다.

That friend seemed disinclined to tell the truth.

07 냉전

명 cold war

요즘 남편과 냉전 중이라서 서로 얼굴도 안 쳐다 본다.

I am in the middle of a cold war with my husband these days so we don't even look at each other's faces.

'냉전'은 무력을 사용하지 않고, 경제.외교 등으로 갈등하는 상태를 의미해요. 2차 세계 대전 이후 소련과 미국의 관계가 바로 '냉전'이었지요.

'냉전 (Cold War)' refers a state of conflict due to economic and diplomatic issues, instead of armed conflict. After World War II, the relationship between the Soviet Union and the United States was the '냉전 (Cold War)'.

08 노후

명 old age

젊었을 때 생각 없이 돈을 지출하다 보면 노후에 후회하게 될 것이다.

If you spend money without care when you are young, you will come to regret it at an old age.

노후자금
retirement savings

노후대비
retirement preparation

노후
Old age

노후연금
retirement pension

노후생활
retirement life

09 단련

명 training

그는 심신 단련을 위해서 매일 요가를 하고 있다.

He does yoga everyday for mental training.

단련하다 to train
단련되다 trained
단련시키다 to be trained

10 대세

명 tide

대세는 이미 우리에게 유리하게 바뀌었다.

The tide has already changed in our favor.

대세가 기울다 the tide has turned towards some thing

11 도피하다

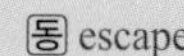

현실을 도피하지 말고 적극적으로 맞서 싸워야 한다.

Do not seek to escape reality, but actively fight against it.

도피 escape
도피 생활 escapist lifestyle
도피처 refuge

12 동참

명 participation

환경문제를 해결하기 위해서는 시민들의 동참이 필요하다.

Citizen participation is necessary to understand how to solve environmental problems.

동참하다 to participate

13 막대하다

형 huge

이번 해킹 사건으로 기업들이 막대한 손실을 입었다.

The hacking incident caused huge losses to companies.

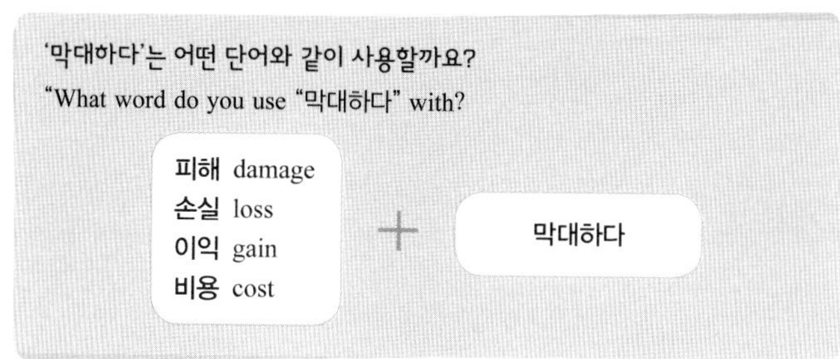

'막대하다'는 어떤 단어와 같이 사용할까요?
"What word do you use "막대하다" with?
피해 damage
손실 loss
이익 gain
비용 cost
+
막대하다

14 머금다

동 hold/keep/with (something) on one's face

그는 얼굴에 미소를 머금은 채 나를 쳐다봤다.

He looked at me with a smile on his face.

15 목격하다

동 witness

한강에서 일어난 사고를 목격한 사람을 찾고 있습니다.

We are looking for anyone who witnessed an accident in the Han River.

목격자 witness

16 민간

명 general public

이 치료법은 예전부터 민간에서 널리 사용되던 것이다.

This treatment has long been widely used in the general public.

민간 기관 nongovernmental organization

민간 업체 private sector

민간요법 folk remedy

17 방관적

명 bystander attitude

부모의 방관적인 태도가 그 학생의 문제 행동을 더 부추기는 것 같다.

It seems that the parent's bystander attitude further encourages the student's problematic behavior.

방관 look on idly　　방관하다 to look on idly

18 복제

명 copying

컴퓨터 프로그램의 불법 복제가 늘어나고 있다.

Illegal copying of computer programs is on the rise.

동물 복제 animal cloning　　복제하다 copying

복제되다 to be copied

19 심경

명 feeling/mind/mood

전쟁으로 인한 피해 영상을 보는내내 참담한 심경이었다.

While watching the video clip of the war damage, I was overwhlemed in a miserable feeling.

심경이 복잡하다 complicated feelings

심경을 토로하다 express one's mind

심경의 변화 change in one's feeling

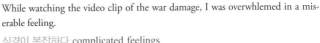

출제 경향 how this word appears in the test

토픽에는 인물의 심경을 묻는 질문이 항상 출제됩니다. 심경을 나타내는 다음 단어들을 공부해보세요.

In Topik, there are always questions about the character's feelings. Studythefollowingwordsthatexpressyourfeelings.

'참담하다(miserable)','난감하다(awkward)','어이없다'(ridiculous)','황당하다(absurd)','흐뭇하다(pleased)','허탈하다(empty),'홀가분하다(free)' etc.

20 여정

명 journey

1박 2일의 짧은 여정을 마치고 집으로 돌아오는 기차에 올랐다.

After a short journey of one night and two days, I got on the train returning home.

21 오작동

명 malfunction

기계의 오작동으로 인해 경고음이 울려서 사람들이 대피하는 혼란이 빚어졌다.

The alarm sounds rang due to a malfunction in the machine, causing coufusion while people evacutaed.

22 요건

명 requirement

컴퓨터 활용 능력은 취업할 때 필수 요건이라고 할 수 있다.

You can say that computer literacy is an essential requirement for employment.

23 원료

명 ingredient

천연 원료만을 이용해 음식을 만들었다는 광고가 거짓임이 드러났다.

The advertisement that they made food using only natural ingredients turned out to be false.

24 유발하다

동 motivate

학생들의 학습 동기를 유발하는 것이 쉽지 않다.

It is not easy to motivate students to learn.

유발 motivate　　유발되다 motivated

25 은퇴

명 retirement/cause

그 가수가 갑작스럽게 은퇴를 발표해서 많은 팬들이 슬퍼했다.

Many fans were sad because the singer suddenly announced his retirement.

26 의혹

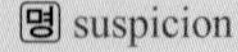
명 suspicion

일부 인스턴트 라면 회사들이 몸에 해로운 기름을 사용했다는 의혹이 일고 있다.

Suspicions have arisen that some instant ramen companies have used harmful oils for their bodies.

의혹이 생기다 Suspicions arise　의혹이 일다 suspicions erupt
의혹이 사라지다 suspicions disappear

27 일관성

명 consistency

아이들을 기를 때 부모는 옳고 그름에 대한 일관성을 유지해야 한다.

When raising children, parents must maintain consistency in their morals.

28 일대일

명 one-on-one

상담은 일대일로 진행되며, 상담 내용은 비밀 보장이 된다.

Counseling is conducted on a one-on-one basis, and the contents of the consultation are confidential.

일대일 면접 one-on-one interview
일대일 수업 one-on-one lesson

29 재개발

명 redevelopment

이 지역이 재개발로 지정이 되면서 원래 살던 사람들은 모두 이사를 가야 한다.

As the area is designated as redevelopment, all people who originally lived should move.

재개발하다 to redevelop　재개발되다 redeveloped
재개발 지역 redevelopment area

30 적발되다

동 be caught

시험을 볼 때 부정행위를 하다가 적발되면 0점 처리되니까 알고 있으세요.

Be aware that if you are caught cheating while taking an exam, you will get 0 points.

출제 경향 how this word appears in the test

토픽에서는 불법적인 행위를 적발하는 것과 관련된 신문 기사가 출제됩니다. 다음 표현들을 '적발'과 함께 공부해 보세요.

A newspaper articles related to the detection of illegal acts are present in the Topik test. Study the following expressions with 'caught'.

단속(crackdown), 밝혀지다(reveal), 정도가 심하다(in severe degree), N에 따르면 (according to N), 벌금(fines), 위반(violations) etc.

31 접촉

명 contact

지하철에서 가능한 다른 사람과의 신체적인 접촉을 피하려고 노력한다.

I try to avoid physical contact with others as possible on the subway.

접촉하다 to contact　　접촉되다 contacted

접촉 사고 minor collision

32 지연되다

동 delay

손님 여러분, 열차의 출발이 지연된 점 진심으로 사과 드립니다.

Dear passengers, I sincerely apologize for the delay in the departure of the train.

지연 delay　　지연하다 to delay

33 초과

명 exceed

내가 엘리베이터를 타자마자 정원 초과를 알리는 경보음이 울렸다.

As soon as I got on the elevator, an alarm rang to announce weight exceeded maximum capaicy

34 하마터면

부 almost

학교에 가는 길에 하마터면 교통 사고가 날 뻔 했다.

I almost had a car accident on the way to school.

35 확률

명 probability

위암 초기는 수술만 하면 생존 확률이 꽤 높은 편이에요.

In the early stages of gastric cancer, the probability of survival are quite high if surgery is performed.

TOPIK에서 혼동하기 쉬운 단어

다의어 Polysemy

꺼리다

❶ 피하거나 싫어하다

예 그 친구는 사실을 이야기하기 꺼리는 눈치였다.

That friend seemed disinclined to tell the truth.

❷ 마음에 걸리다

예 살면서 양심에 꺼리는 일은 하지 않으려고 노력하고 있다.

I try not to do anything in my life that my conscience is reluctant to do.

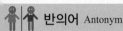

반의어 Antonym

가해자 perpetrator ↔ 피해자 victim

예 아동학대 가해자에 대한 처벌이 강화되어야 한다.

The punishment for child abuse perpetrators should be strengthened.

예 이번에 발생한 교통사고의 피해자가 결국 사망했다.

The victim of the car accident that happened this time eventually died.

유의어 Synonym

유발하다 cause ≒ 일으키다 motivate

예 고속도로에서 지나치게 낮은 속도로 운전하면 사고를 유발할 수 있다.

고속도로에서 지나치게 낮은 속도로 운전하면 사고를 일으킬 수 있다.

Driving at too low a speed on the freeway can cause an accident.

복습해 보세요

서로 어울리는 단어를 찾아 연결해 보세요.
Find words that go with each other and connect them.

1. 대세	a. 토로하다
2. 민간	b. 기울다
3. 심경	c. 사고
4. 의혹	d. 업체
5. 접촉	e. 일다
6. 출발	f. 지연되다

다음 빈 칸에 알맞은 단어를 〈보기〉에서 골라 쓰세요.
Choose the appropriate word from <Example> to fill in the blanks below.

〈보기〉
a. 꺼리는 b. 도피하지 c. 방관적인 d. 유발하는

7. 학생들의 학습 동기를 ( ) 것이 쉽지 않다.
It is not easy to motivate students to learn.

8. 그 친구는 사실을 이야기하기 ( ) 눈치였다.
That friend seemed disinclined to tell the truth.

9. 현실을 ( ) 말고 적극적으로 맞서 싸워야 한다.
Do not seek to escape reality, but actively fight against it.

10. 부모의 ( ) 태도가 그 학생의 문제 행동을 더 부추기는 것 같다.
It seems that the parent's bystander attitude further encourages the student's problematic behavior.

정답

1.b 2.d 3.a 4.e 5.c 6.f 7.d 8.a 9.b 10.c

DAY 02

확인해 보세요

빨간 시트지로 가리고 단어의 뜻을 알면, □에 ✓ 해 보세요.

After covering up the words with red cover, please check(✓) the box (□) when you know the meaning of the word.

- □ 01 개방적 open
- □ 02 개선하다 improve
- □ 03 고용 employment
- □ 04 국정 state affairs
- □ 05 끌어올리다 pull up
- □ 06 노리다 target
- □ 07 녹지 greenery
- □ 08 단서 clue
- □ 09 대수롭다 big deal
- □ 10 동향 to trend
- □ 11 동행 accompany
- □ 12 막론하다 regardless
- □ 13 면모 aspect/side
- □ 14 목차 table of contents
- □ 15 미화하다 glamorize
- □ 16 민감하다 sensitive
- □ 17 방범 crime prevention
- □ 18 복지 welfare
- □ 19 심화하다 deepen
- □ 20 역경 adversity
- □ 21 왕래 interaction/come and go
- □ 22 요령 trick/hang of it
- □ 23 원망 resentment
- □ 24 유보하다 to withhold
- □ 25 음성 audio
- □ 26 이견 disagreement
- □ 27 일깨우다 remind
- □ 28 입소문 word of mouth
- □ 29 재고 stock
- □ 30 전력 electricity
- □ 31 정년 retirement age
- □ 32 지장 harm/disrupt
- □ 33 촉박하다 to be tight on/pressed for (something)
- □ 34 회피하다 avoid
- □ 35 획일적 uniform

DAY 02

  are the words that appeared in the former tests, and you may get a higher grade if you study them together.

01 개방적 — 명 open

비판이 자유롭고 개방적인 사회야말로 건강한 사회라고 할 수 있다.

A society in which criticism is free and open is a healthy society.

02 개선하다 — 동 improve

교육 제도의 문제점을 개선하기 위해 다방면으로 노력해야 한다.

Efforts should be made in various ways to improve the problems of the education system.

개선 to improve　　개선점 improvement

03 고용 — 명 employment

장애인의 고용을 촉진하기 위한 정책이 필요하다.

Policies are needed to promote employment of persons with disabilities.

고용인 employee　　고용주 employer
피고용인 laborer　　고용하다 to hire

04 국정 — 명 state affairs

다양한 분야의 전문가와 국민들이 국정에 참여할 수 있는 기회가 많아졌다.

There are more opportunities for experts and citizens in various fields to participate in state affairs.

05 끌어올리다 — 동 pull up

강에서 침몰한 배를 끌어올리는 데 많은 시간이 걸렸다.

It took a lot of time to pull up the sunken ship out of the river.

06 노리다

동 target

독수리는 멀리서 참새를 노리다가 재빠르게 잡아 갔다.

The eagle targetted the sparrow from a distance and quickly caught it.

07 녹지

명 greenery

이 지역은 무분별한 개발로 인해 녹지가 거의 사라졌다.

The area has lost almost all greenery due to reckless development.

08 단서

명 clue

드디어 그 사건을 해결할 수 있는 결정적인 단서를 찾았다.

I finally found the decisive clue to solve the case.

09 대수롭다

형 big deal

대수롭지 않은 일이니까 너무 신경 쓰지 마세요.

It's not a big deal, so don't worry too much.

Tip

'대수롭다'는 주로 부정을 나타내는 표현과 같이 사용합니다.
'대수롭다' is often used for expressions of negative connotation.

대수롭지 않게 생각하다.
Think lightly of the situation

10 동향

명 trend

최근 연구 동향부터 살펴보기를 바란다.

Take a look at the latest research trends.

11 동행

명 accompany

산속에서 동행과 떨어져 혼자 가다가 사고가 났다.

An accident happened while I was separated from my companion in the mountains.

12 막론하다

동 regardless

이유여하를 막론하고 잘못을 저질렀으면 책임을 져야 한다.

Regardless of the reason, if you make a mistake, you should take responsibility.

'막론하다'는 어떤 단어와 같이 사용할까요?
What expression do you use the word '막론하다' with?

동서고금 all times and places
이유여하 what the reason may be
남녀노소 people of all ages and both sexes
국내외 home and abroad

\+ **막론하다**

13 면모

명 aspect/side

이번 여행에서 그의 인간적인 면모를 알게 되었다.

During this trip, I discovered his humanistic side

14 목차

명 table of contents

목차를 보면 전반적인 글의 내용을 파악할 수 있다.

The table of contents provides an overview of the content of the article.

15 미화하다

동 glamorize

이 소설은 실존했던 역사적 인물을 지나치게 미화하는 경향이 있다.

This novel tends to overly glamorize real historical figures.

미화 glamorization 미화되다 to be glamorized

출제 경향 how this word appears in the test

인물을 평가하는 것과 관련된 문제가 자주 출제되고 있습니다. 다음 단어와 함께 공부하세요.

Problems related to evaluating a person are frequently asked. Study with the following words.

미화하다(glamorize), 비하하다(disparage), 폄하하다(belittle), 과대평가하다(overestimate), 과소평가하다 (underestimate) etc.

16 민감하다

동 sensitive

내 피부는 너무 민감해서 화장품을 함부로 바꾸면 안 된다.

My skin is very sensitive, so I can't change my cosmetics arbitrarily.

민감 sensitive　　민감성 sensitivity

17 방범

명 crime prevention

그 지역은 방범 시설이 취약하여 범죄가 자주 일어난다.

That area has poor crime prevention system, so crimes occur often.

방범창 crime prevention window

방범 카메라 crime prevention camera

18 복지

명 welfare

동물 복지 농장에서 키운 닭이라서 건강에도 좋을 것입니다.

This chicken is raised in an animal-welfare farm so it will also be good for your health.

노후 복지 retirement welfare　　사회 복지 social welfare

19 심화되다

동 deepen

청년층의 고용 불안이 심화되고 있다.

Unemployment instability among young people is deepening.

심화 deepen　　심화하다 to deepen

심화 학습 intensive education

20 역경

명 adversity

그 사람은 지금까지 많은 역경이 있었지만 포기하지 않고 노력한 결과 지금의 성공을 이룰 수 있었다.

He had many adversity until now, but he was able to achieve the success he is today as a result of not giving up and working hard.

21 왕래

명 interaction/come and go

두 나라 간의 왕래가 잦다 보니 서로의 문화에 많은 영향을 주었다.

Frequent interaction between the two countries affected each other's culture a lot.

22 요령

명 trick/savvy/developed skill/hang of it

처음에 이 일을 시작할 때는 힘들었지만 자꾸 하다 보니 요령이 생겨서 이제는 어렵지 않게 할 수 있다.

When I started this work, it was difficult at first. But now I can do it with ease because over time I got the hang of it.

관련어

요령을 부리다 to use tricks

23 원망

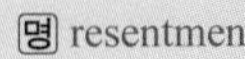

자신을 이해해 주지 않는 부모님에 대한 원망이 쌓여 갔다.

He grew resentful towards his parents for not understanding him.

원망하다 to resent　　원망스럽다 resentful

24 유보하다

동 to withhold

경기가 안 좋아 다음 달에 시작하려고 했던 사업을 당분간 유보하였다.

Due to the bad economy, we decided to withhold the business, which was supposed to start next month.

관련어

유보 withhold　　유보되다 to be withheld

25 음성

명 audio

이 번역 앱은 음성이 지원되니까 아주 편리하다.

This translation app is very convenient because it provides audio.

26 이견

명 disagreement

오랫동안 회의가 이어졌지만 두 팀의 이견을 좁히기 어려웠다.

Although the meeting continued for a long time, it was difficult to narrow the disagreement between the two teams.

27 일깨우다

동 remind

이 광고는 흡연이 건강에 안 좋다는 사실을 일깨워 주기 위해서 제작되었다.

This ad is designed to remind people that smoking is bad for health.

출제 경향 how this word appears in the test

토픽 읽기에서 글의 목표나, 듣기에서 강연 등의 목적을 물을 때 사용되는 단어입니다. 다음의 단어들도 같이 공부하세요.

This is a word that is used to ask about the purpose of writing in the reading section or a lecture in the listening section. Please study the following words together. 호소하다(appeal), 재확인하다(reaffirm), 강조하다(emphasize), 비난하다(denounce), 홍보하다(advertise), 권유하다(offer) etc.

28 입소문

명 word of mouth

이 식당은 가성비가 좋기로 입소문이 난 곳이다.

This restuarant is known to be good value by word of mouth.

29 재고

명 stock

창고에 지난 여름에 팔고 남은 옷이 재고로 남아 있다.

Clothing sold last summer is left in stock in the warehouse.

30 전력

명 electricity

여름이 되자 에어컨 사용 증가로 인해 전력의 소비가 급증하고 있다.

In summer, electricity consumption is rapidly increasing due to an increase in the use of air conditioners.

전력 부족 lack of power

전력 공급 supplying power

31 정년

명 retirement age

이 회사는 정년을 55세로 정했다.

The retirement age for this company is 55 years old.

정년하다 to retire　　정년퇴직 mandatory retirement

32 지장

명 harm/disrupt

작은아버지는 교통사고로 크게 다쳤지만 다행히 생명에는 지장이 없다.

My uncle was seriously injured in a car accident, but fortunately, there is no life-threatening harm.

지장을 초래하다 to disrupt　　지장이 있다 be interrupted

33 촉박하다

동 to be tight on/pressed for (something)

처음부터 다시 시작하기에는 시간이 너무 촉박하대요.

We are pressed for time to start over from the beginning.

34 회피하다

동 avoid

이렇게 큰 잘못을 하고 책임을 회피하면 어떻게 해요?

How could you make such a big mistake and avoid responsibility?

35 획일적

명 uniform

획일적인 기준이 아닌 다양한 기준과 관점에서 직원을 평가할 필요가 있다.

It is necessary to evaluate employees from a variety of criteria and perspectives rather than a uniform standard.

TOPIK에서 혼동하기 쉬운 단어

DAY 02 ★★★

다의어 Polysemy

재고

❶ 창고 등에 쌓여 있는 물건

예 창고에 지난 여름에 팔고 남은 옷이 재고로 남아 있다.

Clothing sold last summer is left in stock in the warehouse.

❷ 어떤 일이나 문제 등을 다시 생각하다.

예 이번 결정은 재고의 여지가 없다.

This decision cannot be reconsidered.

반의어 Antonym

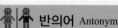

개방적 open ↔ **폐쇄적** closed

예 다양성을 인정하는 개방적인 사회로 바뀌어 가고 있다.

Society is changing to be an open society that recognizes diversity.

예 다양성을 인정하지 않는 폐쇄적인 사회는 발전할 수 없다.

A closed society that does not recognize diversity cannot improve.

유의어 Synonym

민감하다 sensitive ≒ **예민하다**

예 내 피부는 너무 민감해서 화장품을 함부로 바꾸면 안 된다.

내 피부는 너무 예민해서 화장품을 함부로 바꾸면 안 된다.

My skin is very sensitive, so I can't change my cosmetics arbitrarily.

복습해 보세요

자연스러운 문장이 되도록 완성해 보세요.
Try to complete the sentence in a natural way.

1. 교육 제도의 문제점을 ㄱㅅㅎㄱ 위해 다방면으로 노력해야 한다.
   Efforts should be made in various ways to improve the problems of the education system.

2. 이번 여행에서 그의 인간적인 ㅁㅁ를 알게 되었다.
   During this trip, I discovered his humanistic side.

3. 이 광고는 흡연이 건강에 안 좋다는 사실을 ㅇㄲㅇ 주기 위해서 제작되었다.
   This ad is designed to remind people that smoking is bad for health.

4. 그 지역은 ㅂㅂ 시설이 취약하여 범죄가 자주 일어난다.
   That area has poor crime prevention system, so crimes occur often.

5. 이유여하를 ㅁㄹㅎㄱ 잘못을 저질렀으면 책임을 져야 한다.
   Regardless of the reason, if you make a mistake, you should take responsibility.

6. 경기가 안 좋아 다음 달에 시작하려고 했던 사업을 당분간 ㅇㅂㅎㄷ.
   The business, which was supposed to start next month, was temporarily with held for the time being due to the bad economy.

자연스러운 문장이 되도록 둘 중에서 알맞은 단어를 고르세요.
Choose the proper word that fits the sentence more naturally.

7. 드디어 그 사건을 해결할 수 있는 결정적인 (a. 단서를 / b. 고용을) 찾았다.
   I finally found the decisive clue to solve the case.

8. 이 회사는 (a. 정년을 / b. 전력을) 55세로 정했다.
   The retirement age for this company is 55 years old.

9. 내 피부는 너무 (a. 미화해서 / b. 민감해서) 화장품을 함부로 바꾸면 안 된다.
   My skin is very sensitive, so I can't change my cosmetics arbitrarily.

10. (a. 획일적인 / b. 개방적인) 기준이 아닌 다양한 기준과 관점에서 직원을 평가할 필요가 있다.
    It is necessary to evaluate employees from a variety of criteria and perspectives rather than a uniform standard.

정답

1. 개선하기 2. 면모 3. 일깨워 4. 방범 5. 막론하고 6. 유보했다 7. a 8. a 9. b 10. a

DAY 03

확인해 보세요

빨간 시트지로 가리고 단어의 뜻을 알면, □에 ✓ 해 보세요.

After covering up the words with red cover, please check(✓) the box (□) when you know the meaning of the word.

□ 01	가부장적	patriarchal (something)	□ 13	무료하다	bored	□ 25	이왕이면	might as well
□ 02	가하다	put	□ 14	무안하다	to be embarrassed	□ 26	임종	death/passing
□ 03	격려하다	encourage	□ 15	무중력	zero gravity	□ 27	자초지종	full account
□ 04	공권력	law enforcement	□ 16	밀접하다	close	□ 28	재활	rehabilitation
□ 05	규제	regulation	□ 17	배제하다	to exclude/ rule out	□ 29	제도적	institutional (something)
□ 06	남용하다	abuse	□ 18	분쟁	conflict/ dispute	□ 30	제멋대로	as one pleases
□ 07	농산물	agricultural/ farm products	□ 19	불황	recession/ depression	□ 31	진열되다	on display
□ 08	달리하다	be different(from)	□ 20	역대	best/ worst ever	□ 32	친환경	eco-friendly (something)
□ 09	닳다	to run/ wear out/down	□ 21	열등감	sense of inferiority	□ 33	해당하다	be applicable(to)/ be considered
□ 10	돈독하다	close/friendly	□ 22	위반하다	to violate/ break (a law)	□ 34	휩쓸리다	to be swept
□ 11	늑섬	score	□ 23	유일무이	the one and only/sole	□ 35	흡족하다	to be satisfied
□ 12	만사	everything	□ 24	의료	healthcare/ medical care			

are the words that appeared in the former tests, and you may get a higher grade if you study them together.

01 가부장적

명 patriarchal (sonething)

한국에는 여전히 가부장적인 사고방식을 가진 사람들이 많다.

There are still many people with a patriarchal mindset in Korea.

가부장적 사고 patriarchal mindset

가부장 제도 patriarchal system

02 가하다

동 put

대기업은 자기 회사의 매출을 늘리기 위해 중소기업에 압력을 가하는 경우가 많다.

Large companies often put pressure on small and medium-sized companies to increase their sales.

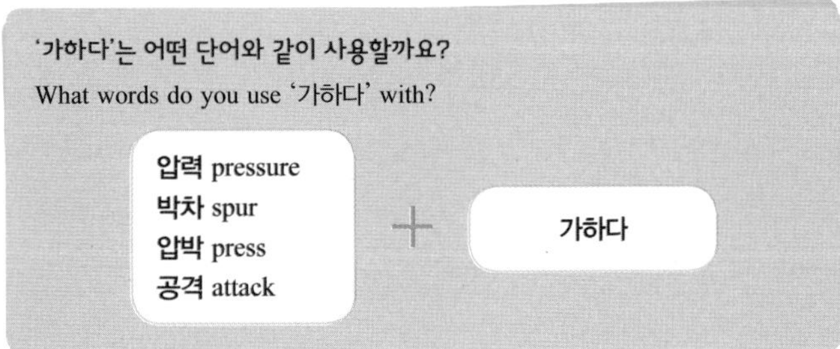

'가하다'는 어떤 단어와 같이 사용할까요?
What words do you use '가하다' with?
압력 pressure
박차 spur
압박 press
공격 attack
+
가하다

03 격려하다

동 encourage

열심히 일을 하는 직원들을 격려하기 위해 특별 보너스가 지급되었다.

A special bonus was given to encourage hard-working employees.

격려 encourage 격려사 words of encouragment

04 공권력

명 law enforcement/governmental power

많은 사람들이 시위에 참가하자 정부는 이를 진압하기 위해 공권력을 투입했다.

As more people joined the protest, the government sent in law enforcement to quell the demonstrations.

공권력을 강화하다 strengthen governmental power

05 규제

명 regulation

더 엄격해진 대출 규제 때문에 은행에서 돈을 빌리기가 어려워졌다.

It has become difficult to borrow money from banks due to stricter lending regulations.

규제를 강화하다 strengthen regulation
규제하다 regulate
법적 규제 legal regulation

06 남용하다

동 abuse

높은 지위에 있는 사람이 자신의 권력을 남용하는 경우가 많다.

People in high positions often abuse their power.

공권력 남용 abuse of governmental power
약물 남용 drug abuse

07 농산물

명 agricultural/farm products/produce

다른 나라와의 무역을 통해 수입 농산물이 많이 들어 왔다.

Many imported agricultural products came in through trade with other countries.

08 달리하다

동 differ/be different (from)

그 사람과 나는 의견을 달리한다.

That person and I differ in opinions.

관련어

운명을 달리하다 reach the end of one's life

09 닳다

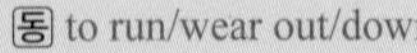

이 기계는 배터리가 빨리 닳아서 자주 충전해야 한다.

This machine has to charge frequently because its battery has run out quickly.

10 돈독하다

형 close/friendly

우리 애들은 유독 남매 간의 우애가 돈독하다.

Our children are especially close with each other

11 득점

명 score

오늘 경기에서는 양팀 모두 득점의 기회를 살리지 못했다.

Both teams failed to take a chance to score in today's game.

12 만사

명 everything

몸이 아프면 만사가 귀찮기 마련이다.

It is usual for everything to be troublesome when you are sick

13 무료하다

형 bored

사람들의 무료한 마음을 달래줄 컨텐츠들이 개발되고 있다.

Content that will soothe people's bored heart mind is being developed.

14 무안하다

형 to be embarrassed

그는 무안할 정도로 나를 빤히 쳐다보았다.

He stared at me so intently that it made me feel embarraased.

15 무중력

명 zero gravity/weightlessness

우주인들은 우주에 나가기 전에 무중력 상태에 적응하는 훈련을 실시한다.

Astronauts train for weightlessness before going into space.

16 밀접하다

형 close

전염병에 걸린 사람과 밀접하게 접촉했을 경우, 우선 검사를 받아 보는 것이 좋다.

If you have a close contact with an infectious disease, it is better to get tested first.

17 배제하다

동 to exclude/rule out

그가 살해되었을 가능성을 배제할 수 없다.

The possibility that he was murdered cannot be ruled out.

배제 rule out　　배제되다 to be excluded
배제시키다 to exclude

18 분쟁

명 conflict/dispute

이 곳은 국제 분쟁이 끊이지 않는 곳이다.

This is a place where international conflict never cease.

19 불황

명 recession/depression

코로나로 인해서 경기 불황이 심해지고 있다.

The recession is getting worse due to the COVID-19.

20 역대

명 best/worst ever

우리 팀은 이번 대회에서 역대 최고의 성적을 거두었다.

Our team had the best performance ever in this tournament.

21 열등감

명 sense of inferiority/inferiority complex

나보다 뛰어난 친구를 보면 열등감을 느낄 때가 있다.

There are times when I struggle with an inferiority complex when I see a friend who is better than me.

반) 우월감 sense of superiority/superiority complex

22 위반하다

동 to violate/break (a law)

교통 속도를 위반하여 십 만원의 벌금을 내야 했다.

He had to pay a fine of 100,000 won for breaking the traffic speed.

'위반하다'는 어떤 단어와 같이 사용할까요?
What expression do you use the word '위반하다' with?

계약 contract
규제 regulation
법규 law
속도 speed
신호 signal

\+ 위반하다

23 유일무이

명 the one and only/sole

김 이사님은 우리 회사에서 이사가 된 유일무이한 여성이다.

Director Kim is the one and only woman who has become a director in our company.

24 의료

명 healthcare/medical care

환자를 치료하느라 고생하는 의료진들에게 감사의 선물이 도착했다.

A gift of gratitude arrived for the medical staff who were struggling to treat the patient.

의료 행위 Medical Practice　　의료 보험 Healthcare Insurance
의료 기기 Healthcare Devices　　의료 봉사 Healthcare Volunteer

25 이왕이면

부 might as well

어차피 해야 할 숙제니까 이왕이면 빨리 끝내는 게 낫다.

I might as well finish it as soon as possible because it's homework to do anyway.

26 임종

명 death/passing/pass away

부모님의 임종을 지키지 못한 것이 늘 후회가 된다.

I always regret not being present at my parents' deathbed.

임종하다 to pass away

27 자초지종

명 full account/complete story

무슨 일이 있었는지 자초지종을 이야기해 봐.

Tell me the full account of what happened

자초지종을 묻다 ask about the complete story

28 재활

명 rehabilitation

그 선수는 어깨 수술 후 재활 운동에 집중하고 있다.

The player is focusing on rehabilitation exercise after the shoulder surgery.

재활하다 to rehabilitate　　재활 훈련 rehabilitation exercise

재활 치료 rehabilitation treatment

29 제도적

명 institutional (something)

직장을 잃은 사람이 다시 취업할 수 있도록 직업 교육 등의 제도적 지원이 필요하다.

Institutional support such as vocational education is needed to help those who have lost their jobs get a job again.

제도적 장치 institutional strategies

제도적 뒷받침 institutional support

30 제멋대로

부 as one pleases

단체 생활을 하는데 그렇게 제멋대로 행동하면 안 된다.

One cannot always act as one pleases when living in a group setting.

31 진열되다

통 on display

빵 가게 한편에는 여러 종류의 잼이 진열되어 있었다.

There were many kinds of jam on display at one side of the bakery.

진열 displayed　　진열하다 to display

32 친환경

명 eco-friendly (something)

오늘부터 설거지할 때 친환경 세제를 사용하기로 했다.

Starting today, we will use eco-friendly detergent when washing dishes.

친환경적 environmental friendly/eco-friendly/organic

33 해당하다

동 be applicable (to)/be considered

여자들 앞에서 성적인 농담을 하는 것도 성추행에 해당한다.

Making sexual jokes in front of women is also considered sexual harassment.

해당 correspond to　　해당되다 fall under/included

34 휩쓸리다

동 to be swept

바닷가에서 낚시할 때는 파도에 휩쓸려 가지 않도록 조심해야 한다.

When fishing at the beach, you should be careful not to be swept away by the waves.

'휩쓸리다'는 어떤 단어와 같이 사용할까요?
What words do you use '휩쓸리다' with?

강풍 Strong winds
빗물 rain
분위기 mood

\+ 휩쓸리다

35 흡족하다

형 to be satisfied

선생님은 큰 목소리로 인사하는 학생들의 모습에 흡족한 표정을 지었다.

The teacher had a satisfied look, watching the way the students greeted with loud voices.

TOPIK에서 혼동하기 쉬운 단어

DAY 03 ★★★

다의어 Polysemy

닳다

❶ 물건을 오래 써서 없어지다.

예 이 기계는 배터리가 빨리 닳아서 자주 충전해야 한다.

This machine has to charge frequently because its battery has run out quickly.

❷ 물건을 오래 써서 낡다.

예 형에게 물려받은 옷이라 그런지 빨리 닳는 것 같다.

The clothes seems to get worn out quickly because it was handed down from my brother.

반의어 Antonym

불황 recession/depression ↔ 호황 (economic) boom, prosperity

예 전자책의 증가로 출판계가 불황을 겪고 있다.

The publishing industry is experiencing a recession due to the increase in e-books.

예 무더위가 지속되자 에어컨 업체가 호황을 맞고 있다.

As the sweltering heat continues, air conditioning companies are booming.

유의어 Synonym

배제하다 to exclude ≒ 제외하다

예 이번 일은 부장님을 배제하고 진행하였다.

이번 일은 부장님을 제외하고 진행하였다.

This work was carried out without the manager.

복습해 보세요

자연스러운 문장이 되도록 완성해 보세요.
Try to complete the sentence in a natural way.

1. 개인적인 감정은 ㅂㅈㅎㄱ 말씀해 주십시오.
   Please refrain from expressing your personal feelings.

2. 부모님께서는 내가 힘들 때마다 ㄱㄹㅎ 주셨다.
   My parents encouraged me whenever I was having a hard time.

3. 그녀는 자녀들이 사이좋게 노는 모습을 ㅎㅈㅎㄱ 지켜보았다.
   She watched with satisfaction the children playing together.

4. 다음 조건에 ㅎㄷㅎㄴ 사람만 신청할 수 있습니다.
   Only those who meet the following conditions may apply.

자연스러운 문장이 되도록 둘 중에서 알맞은 단어를 고르세요.
Choose the proper word that fits the sentence more naturally.

5. 그는 취업을 하고 나서야 형에 대한 (a. 열등감 / b. 공권력)에서 벗어날 수 있었다.
   It was only after he got a job that he was able to break free from his inferiority complex towards his older brother.

6. 그 후보자는 선거법을 (a. 남용해서 / b. 위반해서) 벌금을 물게 되었다.
   The candidate was fined for violating election laws.

7. 국토 (a. 분쟁 / b. 재활) 지역에는 전쟁이 끊이지 않는다.
   Wars never end in territorial disputes.

8. 수입과 수출에 대한 (a. 불황 / b. 규제)가 완화되었다.
   Restrictions on imports and exports were relaxed.

정답

1. 배제하고 2. 격려해 3. 흐뭇하게 4. 해당하는 5. a 6. b 7. a 8. b

DAY 04

확인해 보세요

빨간 시트지로 가리고 단어의 뜻을 알면, □에 ✓ 해 보세요.

After covering up the words with red cover, please check(✓) the box (□) when you know the meaning of the word.

- □ 01 가사 household chores
- □ 02 간결하다 concise
- □ 03 격리 quarantine/isolation
- □ 04 공사장 construction site
- □ 05 균형 balance
- □ 06 납득하다 accept/understand
- □ 07 누리꾼 netizen
- □ 08 달구다 heat (up)
- □ 09 담담하다 unruffled/calm
- □ 10 돋보이다 to stand out
- □ 11 들락거리나 frequently went in and out
- □ 12 만연하다 be pervasive/rampant
- □ 13 무릅쓰다 risk
- □ 14 무언 unspoken (something)
- □ 15 무한 infinity
- □ 16 밀착시키다 to bring closer
- □ 17 배출 emission/discharge
- □ 18 분해하다 to disassemble/take (sth) apart
- □ 19 비관적 pessimism
- □ 20 역량 capability
- □ 21 열성 enthusiasm (for)
- □ 22 위법 illegal
- □ 23 유입 inflow/influx
- □ 24 의류 clothing
- □ 25 이윤 profit
- □ 26 임하다 assume
- □ 27 자본주의 capitalism
- □ 28 작심삼일 a short-lived resolve
- □ 29 쟁점 (controversial) issue
- □ 30 제시하다 to propose/present
- □ 31 제한하다 to restrict/limit
- □ 32 진출 advancement/inroad
- □ 33 침체 recession/depression
- □ 34 해박하다 comprehensive/extensive
- □ 35 휴전 ceasefire/truce

DAY 04

are the words that appeared in the former tests, and you may get a higher grade if you study them together.

01 가사

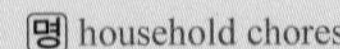

직장에서 일을 하고 퇴근 후에는 가사를 돌보느라 힘들어하는 맞벌이 가정이 많다.

There are many dual-income families who have a hard time taking care of household chores after work.

가사 분담 share household chores

02 간결하다

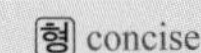

글을 쓸 때는 불필요한 내용을 길게 쓰는 것보다 필요한 내용만 간결하게 쓰는 것이 좋다.

When writing an article, it is better to write only the necessary content concisely than to write long unnecessary content.

'간결하다'와 '간단하다'는 비슷하게 보이지만 사용하는 상황이 달라요.
'간결하다(concise)' and '간단하다'(simple) look similar, but the situation is different.

예 간결한 디자인, 간결한 표현 (불필요한 것이 없이 깔끔하다)
consice design, concise expression (straightfoward and clean)

간단한 방법, 간단한 구조 (단순하고 쉽다)
simple method, simple structure (uncomplicated and easy)

03 격리

명 quarantine/isolation

전염병을 막기 위해 감염자의 격리가 시급하다.

The isolation of the infected is urgent in order to stop the contagious disease.

격리 치료 quarantined　　자가 격리 self-quarantine
격리하다 to quarantine　　격리되다 to be quarantined

04 공사장

명 construction site

방학에 학비를 벌기 위해 공사장에서 일하는 대학생들도 있다.

There are college students who work on construction sites to pay for tuition during vacations.

05 균형

명 balance

요즘 사람들은 일과 생활의 균형을 중요하게 생각한다.

These days, people consider work-life balance important.

균형이 잡히다 be well-balanced 균형을 잡다 to balance
균형을 맞추다 to strike a balance
반) 불균형 unbalanced

06 납득하다

동 accept/understand

이번 대회에서 나보다 실력이 낮은 참가자가 우승을 했다는 것을 납득할 수 없다.

It is hard to accept that a player who is lower than me won the championship.

납득이 가다 satisfy/persuade oneself

07 누리꾼

명 netizen

네티즌이라는 외국어 대신 누리꾼이라는 순한국어를 사용하는 사람들이 늘고 있다.

An increasing number of people are using the word '누리꾼 (nurikkun)' because it is purely Korean, instead of netizen which is a foreign word.

출제 경향 how this word appears in the test

인터넷과 관련된 용어가 자주 출제되고 있어요.
Internet-related vocabularies are often tested these days.
후기, 댓글, 악플, 웹사이트, 앱, 모바일 등의 관련 단어도 확인해 보세요.
Check out the related words : 후기(reviews), 댓글(comments), 악플(malicious/negstive comments), 웹사이트(website), 앱(apps), 모바일(mobile) etc.

08 달구다
동 heat (up)

프로그램 제작진은 가십성 얘기로 분위기를 달구었다.

The program crew heated up the atmosphere by talking about gossip.

09 담담하다
형 unruffled/calm/composed

저출산과 고령화 문제에 대해 20–30대 청년들의 반응은 의외로 담담하다.

The response of young people in their 20s and 30s to the low birth rate and aging population is surprisingly unruffled.

10 돋보이다
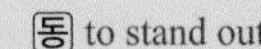
동 to stand out

이번 경기에서는 특히 골키퍼의 활약이 돋보였다.

In this match, the goalkeeper in particular stood out.
독창성이 돋보이다 creativity/originality stands out

11 들락거리다
동 frequently went in and out

어제 먹은 음식 때문인지 하루종일 화장실을 들락거렸다.

Maybe because of the food I ate yesterday, I frequently went in and out the bathroom all day.

12 만연하다
동 be pervasive/rampant

우리 사회에 만연하고 있는 물질주의가 문제다.

The problem is materialism that is pervasive in our society.

13 무릅쓰다
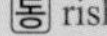
동 risk

그녀는 바이러스에 감염될 지도 모르는데 위험을 무릅쓰고 간호를 했다.

She risked her life to take care of sick even though she might become infected with the virus.

DAY
04
★★★

14 무언

명 unspoken (something)

회사를 그만두라는 무언의 압박에 시달리고 있다.

I'm suffering under unspoken pressure to quit the company.

15 무한

명 infinity/nonstop

사장님은 같은 내용의 잔소리를 무한 반복하고 있었다.

The boss keeps repeating the same nagging nonstop.

무한하다 unlimited
반) 유한 limited

16 밀착시키다

동 to bring closer

가구를 벽에 지나치게 밀착시키면 곰팡이가 생길 수 있으니 조금 공간을 만들어 두어야 한다.

If you put the furniture too close to the wall, mold can form, so leave a little space.

밀착 close contact　　밀착되다 stick to
밀착하다 close/cling to

17 배출

명 emission/produce/discharge/expulsion

오전에 있었던 가스 배출 사고로 5명의 인명 피해가 발생했다.

Five people were injured in the gas emission accident that occurred in the morning.

배출하다 to produce/emit　　배출되다 to be emitted
배출시키다 to emit/discharge/expel

18 분해하다

동 to disassemble/take (sth) apart

그는 어렸을 때 모든 전자제품을 분해하는 취미가 있었다.

As a child, he had a hobby of disassembling all electronics.

차량 분해 vehicle disassembly

19 비관적

명 pessimism

젊은이들은 미래에 대해 비관적인 태도를 가지고 있다.

Young people have a pessimistic attitude toward the future.

비관에 빠지다 to sink into pessimism 비관하다 to be pessimistic

20 역량

명 capability

청소년들의 잠재력과 역량을 강화하기 위한 프로그램을 개발하고 있다.

We are developing programs to strengthen the potential and capabilities of young people.

21 열성

명 enthusiasm (for)

동생은 최근 시작한 사업에 열성을 보이고 있다.

My younger brother is enthusiastic about his recent business.

열성적 enthusiastic/zealous

22 위법

명 illegal

쓰레기를 함부로 버린 위법 사례가 적발되었다.

A case of illegal dumping of garbage was discovered.

위법성 illegality 위법 사례 case of violation

위법 행위 illegal/unlawful act

23 유입

명 inflow/influx

인구의 급격한 유입으로 극심한 교통 문제가 발생했다.

The rapid influx of population caused severe traffic problems.

유입하다 to bring in 유입되다 flow into/be introduced

24 의류

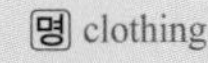

명 clothing

사용하지 않는 의류를 기부하면 필요한 사람들에게 전달됩니다.

If you donate unused clothing, it will be delivered to the people in need.

25 이윤

명 profit

기업은 이윤을 얻기 위해 존재한다.

Businesses exist to make a profit.

이윤을 추구하다 seek profit

26 임하다

동 assume/take (a type of attitude)

저 선수는 누구보다 진지하게 경기에 임하고 있다.

That player is taking the game more seriously than anyone else.

27 자본주의

명 capitalism

자본주의 체제에서는 기업가들이 자유로운 경쟁을 할 수 있다.

In a capitalism, entrepreneurs can compete freely.

28 작심삼일

명 a short-lived resolve

영어 공부를 시작했는데 이번에도 작심삼일로 끝나 버렸다.

I started studying English, but this attempt ended as a short-lived resolve again.

단단히 먹은 마음이 사흘을 못 간다는 뜻으로 새해 결심을 하거나 계획을 세운 후에 지키지 못했을 때 자주 말해요.

This word refers to the fact that a firmly made up mind often can't last three days. It is often used when one fails to follow a New Year's resolve or a plan.

29 쟁점

명 (controversial) issue

이번 이혼 소송의 최대 쟁점은 재산 분할이었다.

The main issue in the divorce case was the division of property.

쟁점으로 떠오르다 rise as an issue

30 제시하다

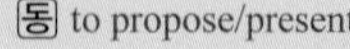

그가 제시한 아이디어가 최종적으로 선택되었다.

The idea he proposed was finally chosen.

제시 suggest/propose　　제시되다 to be suggested/proposed

31 제한하다

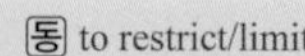

강력 범죄자가 배달 서비스 업종에 취업하는 것을 제한하는 법이 발의되었다.

A law has been proposed to restrict violent criminals from finding jobs in the delivery service sector.

관련어

제한 속도 speed limit

32 진출

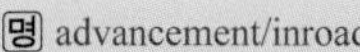

여성의 사회 진출이 늘면서 맞벌이 부부의 비율도 증가하고 있다.

As more women enter into society, the ratio of double-income couples is also increasing.

관련어

진출하다 to advance/enter

33 침체

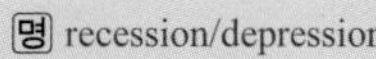

5년 간의 경기 침체로 젊은 세대의 실업률이 높은 편이다.

The unemployment rate of the younger generation is high due to the five-year economic downturn.

침체기 slump/period of economic stagnation

침체에 빠지다 sink into recession

34 해박하다

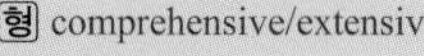

이 책의 저자는 인문학과 경제학을 넘나드는 해박한 지식으로 유명하다.

The author of this book is famous for his extensive knowledge that crosses the humanities and economics.

35 **휴전** 명 ceasefire/truce

한국과 북한은 휴전 상태이다.

South and North Korea remain in a state of ceasefire

TOPIK에서 혼동하기 쉬운 단어

다의어 Polysemy

가사

❶ 집안에서 하는 일

예 직장에서 일을 하고 퇴근 후에는 가사를 돌보느라 힘들어하는 맞벌이 가정이 많다.

There are many dual-income families who have a hard time taking care of household chores after work.

❷ 노래, 오페라 등에서 부르기 위해 쓴 글

예 그 노래는 가사가 시처럼 아름다워서 노벨문학상을 받았다.

The song was awarded the Literature Nobel Prize because the lyrics were beautiful like po etry.

반의어 Antonym

달구다 heat (up) ↔ 식히다 to cool

예 프로그램 제작진은 가십성 얘기로 분위기를 달구었다.

The program crew heated up the atmosphere by talking about gossip.

예 가십성 기사로 과열된 분위기를 식힐 필요가 있다.

You need to cool off the overheated atmosphere with gossip articles.

유의어 Synonym

제한하다 to restrict ≒ 통제하다

예 정부에서 그 회사 자동차의 수입을 제한하였다.

정부에서 그 회사 자동차의 수입을 통제하였다.

The government controlled the import of the company's cars.

복습해 보세요

서로 어울리는 단어를 찾아 연결해 보세요.
Find words that go with each other and connect them.

1. 이윤을	a. 가다
2. 쟁점으로	b. 맞추다
3. 균형을	c. 빠지다
4. 침체에	d. 추구하다
5. 납득이	e. 떠오르다

다음 빈 칸에 알맞은 단어를 〈보기〉에서 골라 쓰세요.
Choose the appropriate word from <Example> to fill in the blanks below.

〈보기〉

a. 해박한 b. 담담하게 c. 돋보이는 d. 제한하자

6. 나이를 ( ) 서비스를 이용하는 사람들이 대폭 감소했다.
The age limit has significantly reduced the number of people using the service.

7. 이 유튜버는 ( ) 뷰티 노하우로 인기가 많다.
This YouTuber is popular for her comprehensive beauty know-how.

8. 요즘은 간결함이 ( ) 인테리어 스타일을 추구하는 사람이 많다.
Nowadays, many people are looking for an interior style that stands out for simplicity.

9. 그는 그동안 힘들었던 일을 ( ) 고백했다.
He calmly confessed the hardships he had endured.

정답

1.d 2.e 3.b 4.c 5.a 6.d 7.a 8.c 9.b

Memo

DAY 05

확인해 보세요

빨간 시트지로 가리고 단어의 뜻을 알면, □에 ✓ 해 보세요.

After covering up the words with red cover, please check(✓) the box (□) when you know the meaning of the word.

	No.	단어	Meaning
□	01	가상	virtuality
□	02	갈다	replace
□	03	격식	formality
□	04	공산품	industrial products
□	05	극단적	extreme
□	06	납부	payment
□	07	누비다	travel, go around
□	08	담보	guarantee
□	09	대책	(counter) measure
□	10	돌발	unexpected/ burst
□	11	들추다	expose/lift
□	12	만장일치	unanimity
□	13	무모하다	reckless
□	14	무용지물	uselessness
□	15	무형	intangible
□	16	밀폐되다	be sealed/ enclosed
□	17	배타적	exclusive/ intolerant/
□	18	비례하다	be proportional
□	19	양해	understanding/ excuse
□	20	열악하다	poor/ inadequate
□	21	우세하다	superior/ exceed
□	22	위상	status/position
□	23	유전	heredity/ genetic
□	24	의약품	medical supplies
□	25	이전하다	to relocate/ move
□	26	이직	change of job
□	27	입시	entrance exam
□	28	잡음	static
□	29	저리다	to ache/ to be numb
□	30	제작하다	produce
□	31	조난	distress
□	32	진취적	enterprising
□	33	침해	invasion/ violation
□	34	해약하다	to cancel/ terminate
□	35	흐릿하다	cloudy/blurry

 are the words that appeared in the former tests, and you may get a higher grade if you study them together.

01 가상

명 virtuality/virtual(something)

지진을 대비하기 위해 가상 훈련을 실시했다.

Virtual training was conducted to prepare for an earthquake.

가상 현실 virtual reality　　　가상 공간 cyberspace/virtuyal space

02 갈다

동 replace

리모컨이 작동을 안 할 때는 오래된 배터리를 갈면 된다.

You can replace the old battery when the remote control does not work.

'갈다'는 '바꾸다'와 바꿔서 사용할 수 있어요. 하지만 '다른 것으로 교환하다' 뜻일 때만 가능하다는 것을 조심하세요.

Sometimes you can use the word '갈다 (replace)' and '바꾸다 (change)' interchangably. However, one must remember that '갈다' can only be used to express when you exchange an item to something else.

낡은 부품을 새 부품으로 바꾸었다. (= 갈았다)

I changed the old parts into new ones. (= replaced)

상황이 달라짐에 따라 낡은 사고방식을 바꿔야 한다. (갈아야 한다 X)

As the situation changes, the old way of thinking should be changed. (replaced X)

03 격식

명 formality

결혼식에 참석할 때는 격식을 차린 옷차림을 해야 한다.

You must dress formally when attending a wedding.

격식을 갖추다 be formal/observe formalities

DAY 05 ★★★

04 공산품

명 industrial products

최근 불황의 영향으로 공산품을 제조하는 회사들이 난항을 겪고 있다.

Companies that manufacture industrial products are experiencing difficulties due to the influence of the recent recession.

05 극단적

명 extreme/radical(something)

너무 극단적인 긍정론은 오히려 일을 그르칠 수가 있다.

Too extreme positivity can cause things to go wrong.

극단적 대립 extreme conflict/confrontation

06 납부

명 payment

공과금 납부 기한을 지키지 않으면 수수료를 낼 수 있다.

If you do not meet the utility bill payment deadline, you may be charged a fee.

세금 납부 tax payment　　납부금 payment

납부하다 to pay

07 누비다

동 travel, go around/about

나는 유명한 사람이 되어 전세계를 누비면서 살고 싶다.

I want to become a famous person and travel all over the world.

08 담보

명 collateral/security, guarantee, mortagage (for a property)

주택을 담보로 잡히고 대출을 받았다.

I took out a mortgage on my house and took out a loan.

09 대책

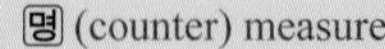
명 (counter) measure

민간 차원에서 조속히 대책을 마련해야 한다.

Measures should be taken as soon as possible at the private level.

대책을 세우다 make a plan

대책을 강구하다 consider a countermeasure

10 돌발

명 unexpected/burst

아이들은 돌발 행동을 할 수 있으므로 주의해야 한다.

Be careful with children, as they can act in an unexpected burst.

11 들추다

동 expose/reveal, lift

사생팬들이 연예인의 사생활을 들추어 무리를 빚고 있다.

Sasaeng fans who stalk their idols obsessively are causing trouble by exposing celebrities' private affairs.

12 만장일치

명 unanimity

그 법안은 이번 국회에서 만장일치로 통과되었다.

The bill was passed in unanimity in the National Assembly.

13 무모하다

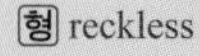
형 reckless

인간의 무모한 도전이 발전의 역사를 만들었다.

Humanity's reckless challenges have made a history of development.

무모한 시도 reckless/foolhardt attempt

14 무용지물

명 uselessness

무료 쿠폰이 있는데 사용 기간이 지났으니 무용지물이다.

There is a free coupon, but it is useless because the expiration date has passed.

15 무형

명 intangible

판소리는 한국의 대표적인 무형 문화재이다.

Pansori is a one of the main examples of an intangible cultural asset of Korea.

반) 유형 tangible

출제 경향 how this word appears in the test

문화재와 관련된 문제가 자주 출제되고 있어요.

Issues related to cultural heritage are frequently asked.

Also check related words : 무형문화재 (intangible cultural property), 유형문화재 (tangible cultural property), 문화재환수 (cultural property return), 문화재기부 (cultural property donation), 문화재대여 (cultural property rental), and 문화재복원 (cultural property restoration) etc.

16 밀폐되다

동 be sealed/enclosed

나는 밀폐된 공간에 들어가면 가슴이 답답하고 숨 쉬기가 힘들어진다.

When I enter an enclosed space, my chest becomes stuffy and hard to breathe.

밀폐 enclosed　　밀폐하다 to close off

17 배타적

명 state of being exclusive/intolerant

타 문화에 대해 배타적인 태도를 갖지 않도록 주의해야 한다.

One should be careful not to be intolerant of other cultures.

18 비례하다

동 be proportional

소비와 지출이 항상 비례하는 것은 아니다.

Spending and spending are not always proportionate.

19 양해

명 understanding/consent/excuse

사장님의 양해를 얻어 오늘 쉴 수 있었다.

I was able to rest today because my boss was being understanding.

양해하다 to excuse/be understanding 양해를 구하다 ask to be excused

DAY 05 ★★★

20 열악하다

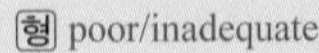
형 poor/inadequate

전쟁으로 인해 열악한 교육 환경 속에서도 뜨거운 교육열은 식지 않았다.

Despite the poor educational environment due to the war, the enthusiasm for learning did not cool down.

21 우세하다

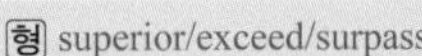
형 superior/exceed/surpass

우리 팀이 다른 팀보다 실력이 우세하다고 자만하다가는 큰코 다치기 십상이다.

If our team prides itself on being skillfully superior than other teams, we can end up regretting it later.

우세 superiority/predominance

22 위상

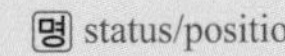
명 status/position

글로벌 시장에서 한국 문화 콘텐츠의 위상이 점점 높아지고 있다.

The status of Korean cultural content in the global market is rising.

23 유전

명 heredity/genetic

과학자들은 유전이 비만에 미치는 영향에 대해 연구하고 있다.

Scientists are studying the effect of genetics on obesity.

유전병 hereditary disease 유전자 genes
유전적 being hereditary/genetic

24 의약품

명 medicine/medical supplies

이 제품은 의약품이라기보다는 식품에 가깝다.

This product is more of a food than a medicine.

의약품을 판매하다 to sell medicine supplies
의약품을 지원하다 supply medicine supplies
의약품을 공급하다 provide medical supplies

25 이전하다

동 to relocate/transfer/move

계약이 끝나 가게를 이전해야 하는 문제로 고민이 많다.

I have a lot of worries about having to relocate the store because the contract is over.

이전 relocation　　이전되다 be moved/transferred/relocated

26 이직

명 change of job

지금 일하는 회사는 야근이 너무 많아 이직을 고려하고 있다.

The company I work for now has too many overtime hours, so I'm considering changing jobs.

이직하다 to change job　　이직률 turnover rate

회사 생활과 관련된 단어들을 기억하세요.
Remember the words related to corporate life.
취직(employment), 이직(job change), 승진(promotion), 해고(dismissal/fire), 발령(appointment/assignment), 출장(business trip)

27 입시

명 entrance exam

한국의 대학 입시는 11월에 치뤄진다.

Korean college entrance exams are held in November.

28 잡음

명 static, (white/background) noise

이 헤드폰은 잡음 제거 기능이 있어서 밖에서 음악을 자주 들으시는 분에게 좋습니다.

These headphones have a noise canceling function, which is great for those who often listen to music outside.

잡음이 들리다 to hear background noise

29 저리다

형 to ache/to be numb

오랫동안 바닥에 앉아 있었더니 다리가 저리다.

My legs are numb after sitting on the floor for a long time.

30 제작하다

동 to make/produce

이 의자는 제작하는 데에 한 달이 걸렸다.

It took about a month to build this chair

제작소 production/manufacturing office

제작자 producer/manufacturer

31 조난

명 distress

설악산에서 조난 당한 50대 남성이 무사히 구조되었다.

A man in his 50s who was in distress at Mt. Seorak was rescued safely.

32 진취적

명 enterprising/adventurous

진취적인 사고방식을 가진 사람이 성공할 가능성이 높다.

People with an enterprising mindset are more likely to be successful.

33 침해

명 invasion/violation

사생활 침해를 이유로 CCTV 설치에 반대하는 주민들이 있다.

There are residents who oppose the installation of CCTV because of invasion of privacy concerns.

인권 침해 human rights violations

34 해약하다

동 to cancel/terminate/close

보험을 중도에 해약하면 손해를 보기 때문에 가입 전에 신중히 생각해야 한다.

You should think carefully before signing up for an insurance plan because you will lose money if you cancel the plan midway.

적금 해약 installment savings cancellation

해약 요청 cancellation request

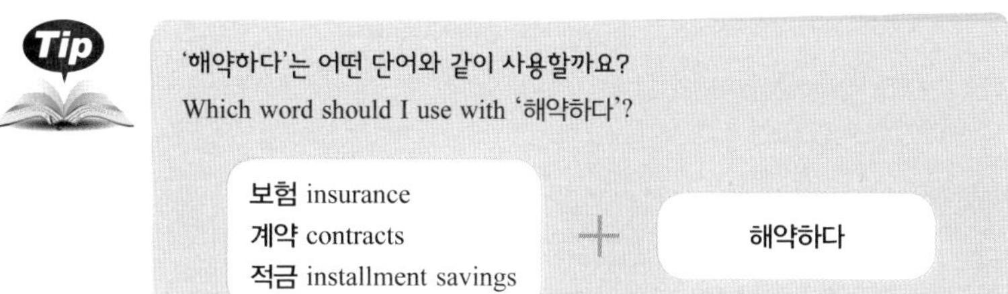

'해약하다'는 어떤 단어와 같이 사용할까요?

Which word should I use with '해약하다'?

보험 insurance
계약 contracts
적금 installment savings
\+ 해약하다

35 흐릿하다

형 cloudy/blurry/vague

아침부터 날씨가 흐릿하더니 오후부터 비가 내리기 시작했다.

It was cloudy in the morning and it started raining in the afternoon.

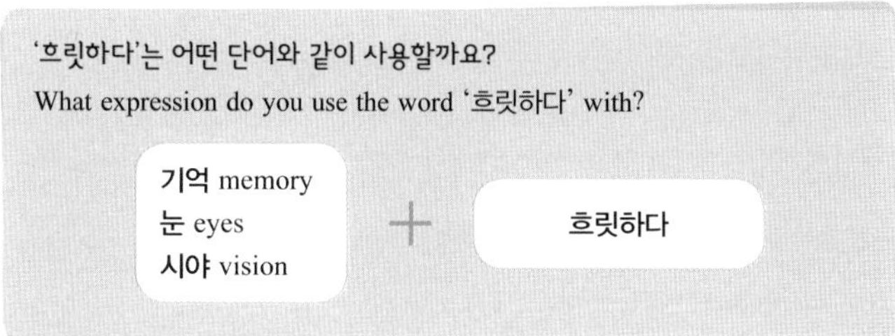

'흐릿하다'는 어떤 단어와 같이 사용할까요?

What expression do you use the word '흐릿하다' with?

기억 memory
눈 eyes
시야 vision
\+ 흐릿하다

TOPIK에서 혼동하기 쉬운 단어

다의어 Polysemy

이전하다

❶ 장소나 주소를 다른 데로 옮기다.

예 계약이 끝나 가게를 이전해야 하는 문제로 고민이 많다.

I have a lot of worries about having to relocate the store because the contract is over.

❷ 권리를 남에게 넘겨주거나 넘겨받다.

예 회사의 소유권을 다른 사람에게 이전했다.

The ownership of the company has been transferred to another person.

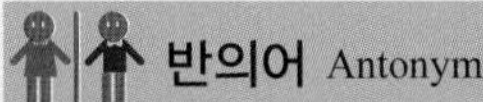

반의어 Antonym

흐릿하다 cloudy/blurry/vague ↔ 분명하다 clear

예 세월이 많이 지나서 그런지 그때의 기억이 흐릿하다.

Many years have passed, so the memories of that time are cloudy.

예 시간이 지났지만 아직도 그때를 분명하게 기억하고 있다.

I still remember that time very clearly even though time has passed.

유의어 Synonym

우세하다 superior/exceed/surpass ≒ 뛰어나다

예 상대 팀이 우리 팀보다 실력이 우세하다.

상대 팀이 우리 팀보다 실력이 뛰어나다.

The other team is skillfully superior than our teams.

복습해 보세요

자연스러운 문장이 되도록 완성해 보세요.
Try to complete the sentence in a natural way.

1. 서비스센터를 ㅇㅈㅎㄷㄴ 연락을 못 받았다.
   I didn't receive the news that the service center is relocating.

2. 보너스는 업무 성과에 ㅂㄹㅎㅅ 결정될 것입니다.
   The bonus decision will be proportional to the business performance.

3. 다른 나라의 문화에 대해 ㅂㅌㅈㅇ 인식을 갖지 말아야 한다.
   We should not have an intolerant stance towards the cultures of other countries.

4. 영화 촬영 현장이 생각보다 ㅇㅇㅎㅅ 놀랐다.
   I was surprised at the inadequate filming environment of the movie.

자연스러운 문장이 되도록 둘 중에서 알맞은 단어를 고르세요.
Choose the proper word that fits the sentence more naturally.

5. 친구의 (a. 돌발 / b. 무형) 행동에 깜짝 놀랐다.
   I was startled by my friend's sudden action.

6. 내년 (a. 입시 / b. 대책) 경향을 파악하기 위해서 설명회에 다녀왔다.
   I attended the briefing session to find out about the trends of next year's enterance exams.

7. 그는 매년 세금을 잘 내는 성실 (a. 납부자 / b. 유전자)로 상을 받았다.
   He pays his taxes well every year.

8. 다문화 사회에서 (a. 진취적 / b. 극단적)인 사고방식은 매우 위험하다.
   In modern society, extreme thinking is very dangerous.

정답

1. 이전한다는 2. 비례해서 3. 배타적인 4. 열악해서 5. a 6. a 7. a 8. b

자주 쓰는 한자어 day 1 - day 5

❶ 고(高) high

고기압 high pressure
고학력 highly educated
고소득 high income
고혈압 high blood pressure
고령화 an aging population

❷ 저(低) low

저기압 low pressure
저학력 low educated
저소득 low income
저혈압 low blood pressure
저가항공 low-cost airline

❸ 재(再) re-

재검토 review
재개발 redevelopment
재해석 reinterpretation
재충전 recharging
재교육 retraining
재생산 reproduction
재분배 redistribution
재혼 re-marriage

▲ 재충전 recharging

주간 복습 day 1 - day 5

아래 단어를 보고 빈 칸에 뜻을 적어 보세요. 그리고 점선대로 접어서 적은 뜻이 맞는지 확인해 보세요. (만일 틀렸다면 뒷면의 단어 앞 □에 ✓ 하세요.)

Write down the meaning of the given word in the blank. Also, fold the page along a dotted line and check whether you got it right or wrong. (If you got it wrong tick the box in front of the word in next page.)

▼접는선

단어	뜻
감시	
민감하다	
남용하다	
납득	
들추다	
도피하다	
면모	
무료하다	
돋보이다	
만장일치	
목격하다	
대수롭다	
배제하다	
밀착시키다	
밀폐되다	
복제	
노리다	
제멋대로	
역량	
조난	
오작동	
개선하다	
휩쓸리다	
제한하다	
해약하다	

※접어서 뜻이 맞는지 확인해보세요.

주간 복습 day 1 - day 5

빈 칸에 한국어 단어를 3번 적고 다시 외워 봅시다.

Write down the Korean word 3 times in the blank and try to memorize it again.

◀접는선

뜻	단어		
☐ monitoring	감시		
☐ sensative	민감하다		
☐ abuse	남용하다		
☐ accept/understand	납득		
☐ expose, lift	들추다		
☐ escape	도피하다		
☐ aspect/side	면모		
☐ bored	무료하다		
☐ to stand out	돋보이다		
☐ unanimously	만장일치		
☐ witness	목격하다		
☐ big deal	대수롭다		
☐ to exclude, rule out	배제하다		
☐ to bring closer	밀착시키다		
☐ be sealed/enclosed	밀폐되다		
☐ copying	복제		
☐ target	노리다		
☐ as one pleases	제멋대로		
☐ capability	역량		
☐ distress	조난		
☐ malfunction	오작동		
☐ improve	개선하다		
☐ to be swept	휩쓸리다		
☐ to restrict/limit	제한하다		
☐ to cancel/terminate	해약하다		

DAY 06

확인해 보세요

빨간 시트지로 가리고 단어의 뜻을 알면, □에 ✓ 해 보세요.

After covering up the words with red cover, please check(✓) the box (□) when you know the meaning of the word.

- □ 01 가식적 pretentious
- □ 02 감소 decline/reduction
- □ 03 격차 gap/disparity
- □ 04 공식적 official
- □ 05 극대화 maximization
- □ 06 낭패 trouble/failure
- □ 07 누출 leak
- □ 08 단축 shortneing
- □ 09 답례품 goodie bag
- □ 10 대처하다 to manage/respond
- □ 11 돌연변이 mutation
- □ 12 등장인물 characters
- □ 13 말단 end/terminal
- □ 14 맞대다 put together/face
- □ 15 무효 void
- □ 16 밑거름 (figurative) foundation
- □ 17 배포하다 distribute
- □ 18 범주 category
- □ 19 부재 absence
- □ 20 비중 importance/weight
- □ 21 어리둥절하다 puzzled
- □ 22 열의 enthusiasm
- □ 23 예리하다 keen/sharp
- □ 24 위생 hygiene/sanitation
- □ 25 유지하다 maintain
- □ 26 의외 surprise
- □ 27 이점 advantage/benefit
- □ 28 입양 adoption
- □ 29 장거리 long-distance
- □ 30 저마다 each
- □ 31 제한하다 to limit
- □ 32 죄책감 guilt
- □ 33 질기다 tough/durable
- □ 34 타격 blow/hit
- □ 35 행정부 administration

DAY 06

  are the words that appeared in the former tests, and you may get a higher grade if you study them together.

01 가식적

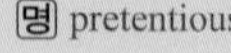

그 사람의 가식적인 웃음을 보면 무서울 때가 많다.

It's often scary to see his pretentious smile.

가식적인 태도 pretentious attitude

02 감소

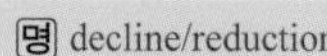

최근 국내 여행을 하는 여행객은 감소 추세를 보이고 있다.

Recently, the number of travelers traveling in Korea has been on the decline.

감소세 decline　　감소하다 to decrease

감소되다 be reduced

반) 증가 increase

'감소하다'는 '줄어들다'와 바꿔서 사용할 수 있어요.

'감소하다' can be used interchangeably with '줄어들다'

 정부의 노력으로 실업률이 감소하고 있다. (= 줄어들고 있다)

with the efforts of the government, the rate of unemployment is declining

03 격차

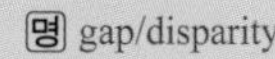

통신 수단의 발달은 도시와 시골의 격차를 줄였다는 평가를 받고 있다.

The development of communication means has been evaluated to have narrowed the gap between urban and rural areas.

소득 격차 income gap　　빈부 격차 wealth disparity

04 공식적

명 official

두 인기 배우가 결혼 소식을 공식적으로 발표했다

The two popular actors officially announced their wedding news.

05 극대화

명 maximization

운동 효과의 극대화를 위해 운동 전과 후에 먹는 음식을 조심해야 한다.

To maximize the effect of exercise, you should be careful about what you eat before and after exercise.

극대화하다 to maximized　　극대화되다 be maximized

06 낭패

명 trouble/failure

철저한 계획 없이 사업을 무작정 시작하면 낭패를 보기 쉽다.

If you start a business blindly without a thorough plan, it is easy run into trouble.

낭패를 보다 run into trouble

07 누출

명 leak

가스 누출 사고로 인해 많은 사람들이 죽고 다쳤다.

Many people were killed and injured in the gas leak accident.

가스 누출 gas leak

기밀 누출 leak out secrets/confidential information

08 단축

명 shortneing

오늘 학교에 코로나 확진자가 발생해서 단축 수업을 했다.

There was a confirmed case of COVID-19 at school today, so we had a shortened class.

단축하다 to shorten　단축되다 be shortened

단축시키다 to shorten

09 답례품

명 goodie bag

요즘은 결혼식 답례품으로 떡이나 와인, 홍삼의 주문이 늘고 있다

These days, people give out rice cake, wine or red girseng as wedding goodie bags.

10 대처하다

동 to manage/handle/deal/respond

돌발적인 상황에서 신속히 대처한 결과 인명 피해는 없었다.

No casualties were reported as a result of the rapid response in an unexpected situation.

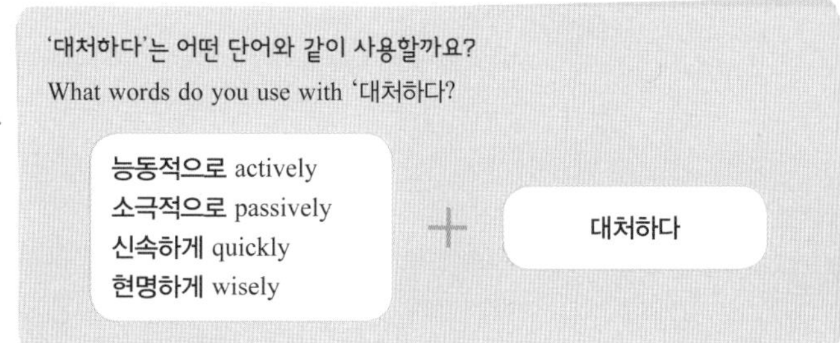

'대처하다'는 어떤 단어와 같이 사용할까요?
What words do you use with '대처하다'?
능동적으로 actively
소극적으로 passively
신속하게 quickly
현명하게 wisely
+
대처하다

11 돌연변이

명 mutation

유전자 돌연변이에 대한 연구가 성과를 내고 있다.

Research and progress are being made on genetic mutations.

12 등장인물

명 characters

이 소설은 등장인물의 섬세한 심리 묘사가 뛰어난 작품이다.

This novel has excellent psychological descriptions of the characters.

출제 경향 how this word appears in the test

연극이나 영화 등의 문화와 관련된 문제가 자주 출제되고 있어요.
Culture-related questions such as plays and movies are frequently asked.

연출, 감독, 대본, 창작 등의 관련 단어도 확인해 보세요.
Check out related words such as 연출(directing), 감독(directing), 대본(script), 창작(creation) etc.

13 말단

명 end/terminal/low-level

말단 공무원부터 시작해서 10년만에 고위직에 올랐다.

He rose to high level position in 10 years, starting with a low-level civil servant.

14 맞대다

동 put together/touch/face

그들은 밤새 머리를 맞대고 고민한 끝에 문제를 해결했다.

They put their heads together all night and solved the problem.

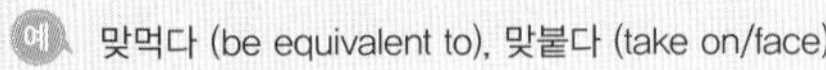

'맞-'이 붙으면 '마주 대하여 하는' 또는 '서로 엇비슷한'의 뜻을 나타내요.

If you add '맞–' to a word it means face to face' or 'similar to each other'

예 맞먹다 (be equivalent to), 맞붙다 (take on/face)

15 무효

명 void

골을 넣기 전 반칙이 인정돼서 이번 골은 무효 처리되었다.

The goal was void because a foul was recognized before scoring.

무효화 invalidation/nullification

16 밑거름

명 (literal) manure / (figurative) foundation

어떤 운동이든 반복 연습이 실력 향상의 밑거름이 된다.

Repeated practice is the foundation for improvement in any sport.

17 배포하다

동 distribute

연극 공연 입장권을 무료로 배포했지만 보러 온 사람이 얼마 없었다.

Admission to the play was distributed free of charge, but few people came to see it.

배포 distribution　　배포되다 be distributed

18 범주

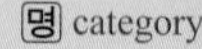
명 category

조사 결과를 다섯 가지 범주로 나누어서 분류했다.

The findings were divided into five categories.

범주에 속하다 fall within the category

19 부재

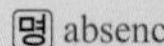
명 absence

가족 간의 대화 부재가 결국 이런 상황을 초래했다.

The lack of dialogue between family members eventually led to this situation.

정책 부재 absence of policy　　부재자 투표 absentee vote

20 비중

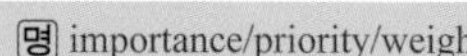
명 importance/priority/weight

정부는 경제 회복에 최우선적인 비중을 두고 있다.

The government puts a top priority on economic recovery.

비중을 차지하다 take up weight

비중 있게 다루다 to handle with importance/give weight to

21 어리둥절하다

형 puzzled/confused

그 소식을 듣고 아직도 영문을 몰라 어리둥절하다.

I'm still puzzled at the news.

22 열의

명 enthusiasm

김과장님은 자신이 맡은 일에 대한 열의가 대단하다.

Manager Kim is very enthusiastic about his work.

23 예리하다

형 keen/sharp

그 사람의 예리한 눈빛은 나의 거짓말을 이미 알고 있는 것 같았다.

His keen eyes seemed to already know my lie.

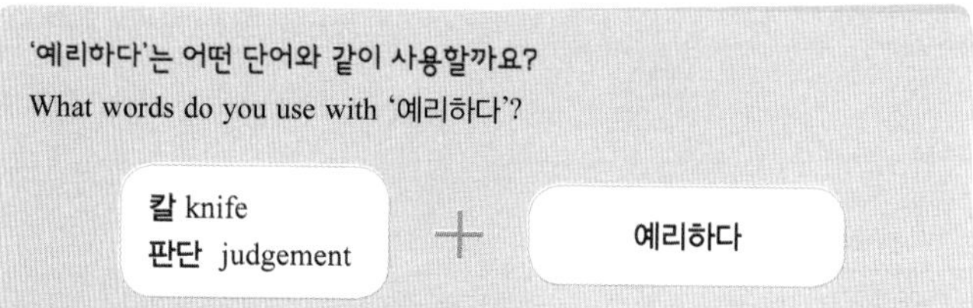

'예리하다'는 어떤 단어와 같이 사용할까요?
What words do you use with '예리하다'?
칼 knife
판단 judgement
+
예리하다

24 위생

명 hygiene/sanitation

전염병이 유행할 때는 개인 위생에 더 신경을 써야 한다.

You should pay more attention to personal hygiene when the epidemic is raging.

위생적 hygienic/sanitary　　비위생적 unsanitary

25 유지하다

동 maintain

건강을 유지하기 위해 바른 습관을 가지는 것이 중요하다.

It is important to keep the right habits to maintain your health

유지 maintenance　　유지되다 to be maintained

26 의외

명 surprise

민호 씨, 음식을 잘 먹을 줄 알았는데 의외네요.

Minho, I thought you would eat well, but I was surprised.

27 이점

명 advantage/benefit

그 지역이 발달한 데에는 위치적 이점이 컸다.

The region's development can mainly be attributed to its great location advantages.

28 입양

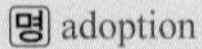 adoption

친구 부부는 아이 입양을 신청했지만 조건이 맞지 않아 할 수 없었다.

My friends applied to adopt a child, but couldn't because they didn't meet the conditions.

입양하다 to adopt　　입양되다 to be adopted

입양 가정 adoptive family

29 장거리

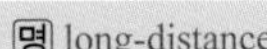 long-distance

장거리 운전은 아직 해 본 적이 없어서 이번에는 기차로 가려고요.

I haven't driven long distances yet, so I'm going to go by train this time.

장거리 달리기 long-distance running

30 저마다

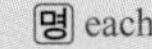 each

그곳에 모인 사람들은 저마다 고향을 떠나온 이유가 있었다.

Each of the people gathered there had a reason to leave their hometowns.

31 제한하다

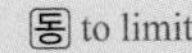 to limit

아이가 게임을 할 수 있는 시간을 1시간으로 제한하고 있다.

We are limiting the time the child can play games to one hour.

제한 limit　　제한되다 be limited

32 죄책감

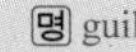 guilt

노벨은 자신이 개발한 다이너마이트가 무기로 사용되자 큰 죄책감을 느꼈다고 한다.

Nobel said he felt guilty when dynamite he developed was used as a weapon.

죄책감이 들다 to feel guilty

죄책감에 시달리다 to be haunted by guilt/to suffer under guilt

33 질기다

형 tough/durable

고기가 너무 질겨서 먹기가 힘들다.

The meat is too tough to eat.

34 타격

명 blow/hit

코로나 바이러스의 유행으로 항공업계와 여행업계는 큰 타격을 입었다.

The airline and travel industry have been hit hard by the COVID-19 virus outbreak.

관련어
정신적 타격 mental/psychological blow/shock
타격을 받다 take a hit

35 행정부

명 administration/the executive (branch)

국가 기관은 입법부, 행정부, 사법부로 구성되어 있다.

The national body consists of the legislature, the executive, and the judiciary branch.

TOPIK에서 혼동하기 쉬운 단어

다의어 Polysemy

질기다

❶ 물건이나 음식이 쉽게 끊어지지 않다.

예 고기가 너무 질겨서 먹기가 힘들다.

The meat is too tough to eat.

❷ 행동이나 일의 상태가 오래 끌거나 견디는 성질이 있다.

예 그와의 길고 질긴 인연을 이제는 끝내고 싶다.

I want to end my long and tough relationship with him.

반의어 Antonym

예리하다 keen/sharp ↔ 둔하다 dull, slow

예 그의 예리한 눈빛은 내 마음을 모두 아는 듯했다.

His keen gaze seemed to know all of my heart.

예 그는 걸음도 느리고 행동도 둔해서 사람들이 답답해한다.

Because he's both slow at walking and slow at action, people get frustrated at him.

유의어 Synonym

배포하다 distribute ≒ 배부하다

예 전국에 홍보용 책을 배포하였다.

전국에 홍보용 책을 배부하였다.

Promotional books were distributed throughout the country.

복습해 보세요

서로 어울리는 단어를 찾아 연결해 보세요.
Find words that go with each other and connect them.

1. 머리를	a. 차지하다
2. 죄책감에	b. 속하다
3. 비중을	c. 맞대다
4. 범주에	d. 대처하다
5. 능동적으로	e. 시달리다

다음 빈 칸에 알맞은 단어를 〈보기〉에서 골라 쓰세요.
Choose the appropriate word from <Example> to fill in the blanks below.

〈보기〉

a. 배포하기로 b. 예리한 c. 유지하기 d. 가식적인

6. 정부는 모든 국민들에게 마스크를 무료로 (   ) 하였다.
The government has decided to distribute masks free of charge to all citizens.

7. 회사 동료들과의 원만한 관계를 (   ) 위해서 노력하고 있다.
We strive to maintain a smooth relationship with our co-workers.

8. 그녀는 그의 (   ) 태도에 실망한 나머지 헤어지기로 결심했다.
Disappointed with his pretentious attitude, she decided to break up.

9. 은행 직원의 (   ) 판단으로 보이스피싱을 막을 수 있었다.
With the keen judgment of the bank staff, voice phishing was prevented.

정답

1.c 2.e 3.a 4.b 5.d 6.a 7.c 8.d 9.b

Memo

DAY 07

확인해 보세요

빨간 시트지로 가리고 단어의 뜻을 알면, □에 ✓ 해 보세요.

After covering up the words with red cover, please check(✓) the box (□) when you know the meaning of the word.

	No.	Word	Meaning		No.	Word	Meaning		No.	Word	Meaning
□	01	가정하다	assume/ suppose	□	13	명료하다	clear/articulate	□	25	이를테면	for example/ such as
□	02	개인주의	individualism	□	14	묵직하다	heavy	□	26	이정표	road sign/ milestone
□	03	견디다	endure/ withstand	□	15	바짝	extremely (close/dry/crisp)	□	27	입증하다	to prove
□	04	공유하다	to share	□	16	배회하다	to wander	□	28	장유유서	the younger should give precedence to the elder/elders first
□	05	근로	work/labor	□	17	범하다	make (a mistake)	□	29	저버리다	to betray
□	06	낱낱이	in detail/fully	□	18	비참하다	tragic/ miserable	□	30	조급하다	in a hurry
□	07	눈살	frown between one's eyebrows	□	19	어설프다	sloppy/clumpy	□	31	주도적	proactive
□	08	당당하다	to be confident	□	20	염두	mind	□	32	질리다	be frightened, be sick of
□	09	대체하다	replace	□	21	온난화	warming	□	33	타당성	validity
□	10	동감하다	agree	□	22	위조	forgery	□	34	허기	hunger
□	11	등재되다	be registered	□	23	유치하다	host	□	35	흥청망청	lavishly/ extravagantly
□	12	말문	speech	□	24	의지하다	rely				

 are the words that appeared in the former tests, and you may get a higher grade if you study them together.

01 가정하다

동 assume/suppose

최악의 상황을 가정해서 미리 준비하는 것이 필요하다.

It is necessary to assume the worst-case scenario and prepare in advance.

02 개인주의

명 individualism

요즘 젊은이들은 개인주의 성향이 강해서 개인의 권리와 자유를 무엇보다 중시한다.

Nowadays, young people have a strong tendency to individualism, so they value individual rights and freedom above all else.

개인 individual　　개인적 individual/personal

개인주의자 individualist

'개인주의'와 '이기주의'는 다른 뜻이에요.

'개인주의'는 '개인의 자유를 중요하게 생각하는 것'인 데 반해 '이기주의'는 '자신만 생각하고 다른 사람에게 피해를 주는 것은 신경쓰지 않는 것'을 의미해요.

'N주의' 형태의 단어를 많이 볼 수 있지요?

'개인주의' and '이기주의' have different meanings. '개인주의' places importances on one's own freedom, whereas '이기주의' only thinks of oneself without care for harming others. You can see the 'N주의' form a lot, right?

 이기주의 (egoism), 개인주의 (individualism), 채식주의 (vegetarianism)

03 견디다

동 endure/withstand/bear

동료들의 비웃음과 무시를 견디다 못해 퇴사를 결심했다.

Unable to withstand the ridicule and disrespect of my colleagues, I decided to resign.

04 공유하다

동 to share

결혼한 부부는 생활할 때 많은 것을 공유하면서 살게 된다.

Married couples share many things as they live together.

공유 경제 sharing economy

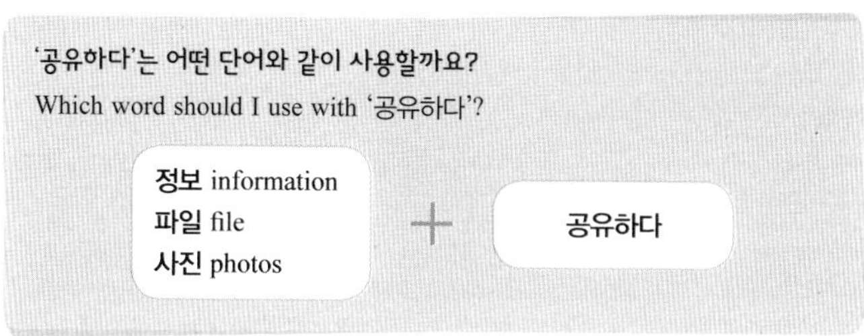

'공유하다'는 어떤 단어와 같이 사용할까요?
Which word should I use with '공유하다'?
정보 information
파일 file
사진 photos
+
공유하다

05 근로

명 work/labor

아이를 키우는 육아기에는 근로 시간을 단축할 수 있다.

Working hours can be shortened during the child-rearing period.

06 낱낱이

부 in detail/fully

경찰은 이 사건의 진상을 낱낱이 조사했다.

The police investigated the truth of this case thoroughly.

낱낱이 조사하다 investigate thoroughly

07 눈살

명 wrinkles/frown between one's eyebrows

따가운 햇살에 눈이 부셔서 눈살을 찌푸렸다.

I frowned because my eyes were blinded by the scorching sun.

08 당당하다

형 to be confident

나는 잘못한 것이 없기 때문에 법정에서도 당당하게 말할 수 있다.

I can speak confidently in court because I have done nothing wrong.

09 대체하다

동 replace

학기말 고사를 레포트로 대체할 것이다.

The final exam will be replaced by a report paper.

10 동감하다

동 agree

나는 그의 의견에 전적으로 동감한다.

I totally agree with his opinion.

동감 agreement

11 등재되다

동 be registered/entered

새로 발견된 유적지가 유네스코 세계 유산으로 등재되었다.

The newly discovered site has been registered as a UNESCO World Heritage Site.

12 말문

명 speech

그의 문자를 보고 하도 기가 막혀서 말문이 막혔다.

When I saw his text message, I was so stunned that I was speechless.

13 명료하다

형 clear/articulate

논문을 쓸 때는 전달하고자 하는 바를 명료하게 드러내는 것이 좋다.

When writing a paper, it is best to clearly articulate what you want to convey.

명료한 표현 clear expression

DAY
07
★★★

14 묵직하다

형 heavy

수술 후 배에 묵직한 통증이 찾아왔다.

After the surgery, I had a heavy pain in my stomach.

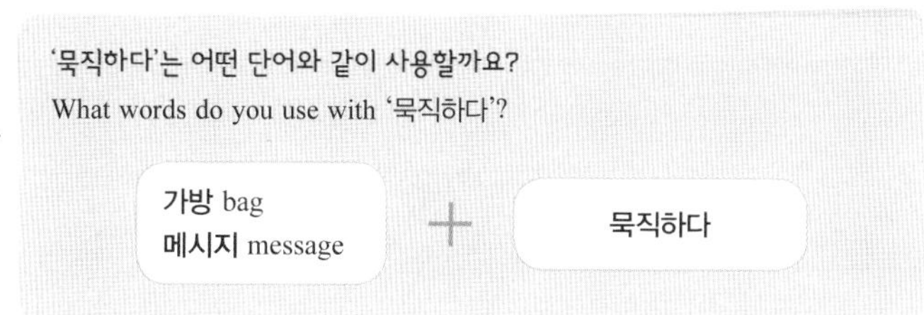

'묵직하다'는 어떤 단어와 같이 사용할까요?
What words do you use with '묵직하다'?

가방 bag
메시지 message
\+ 묵직하다

15 바짝

부 extremely (close/dry/crisp)

집이 너무 건조해서 입술이 바짝 말랐다.

My lips are extremely dry because the house is so dry.

16 배회하다

동 to wander

추운 겨울에 거리를 배회하던 노숙자가 사망하는 사건이 발생했다.

A incident occurred where a homeless wondering the streets in the cold winter died.

배회 loitering/wondering

17 범하다

동 make (a mistake)

장애인에 대한 이해 부족으로 큰 실례를 범한 듯하다.

It seems that I made a big mistake due to lack of understanding of the disabled.

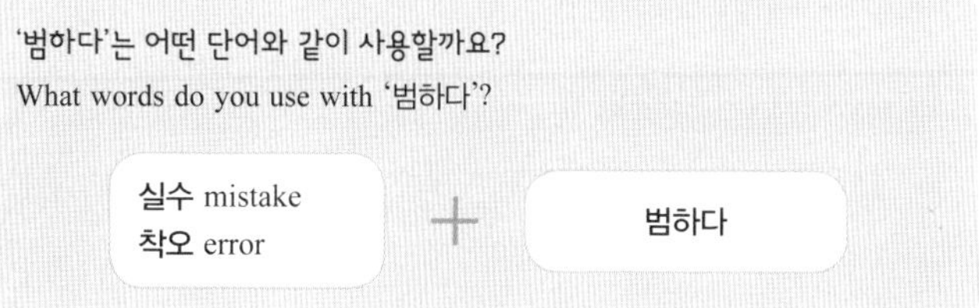

'범하다'는 어떤 단어와 같이 사용할까요?
What words do you use with '범하다'?

실수 mistake
착오 error
\+ 범하다

18 비참하다

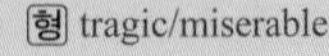
형 tragic/miserable

사고 현장의 비참한 모습은 상상하기조차 힘들었다.

It was hard to even imagine the tragic scene of the accident.

19 어설프다

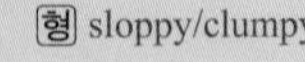
형 sloppy/clumpy

신인 배우라서 그런지 연기가 어설프다.

Perhaps because he is a new actor, his acting is clumsy.

20 염두

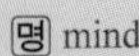
명 mind

나는 일하는 것이 좋기 때문에 아직 결혼은 염두에 두지 않고 있다.

I don't have marriage in mind yet because I love working.

21 온난화

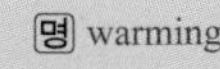
명 warming

지구 온난화가 심각해짐에 따라 여러 문제가 생기고 있다.

As global warming becomes more serious, several problems arise.

출제 경향 how this word appears in the test

환경과 관련된 문제가 자주 출제되고 있어요.

There are many enivronemtnal questions being asked.

지구온난화, 배기가스 일산화탄소, 대기오염, 수질오염, 토양오염, 해양오염 등 관련 단어를 꼭 확인하세요.

Be sure to check related words like 지구온난화 (global warming), 배기가스(exhaust gas), 일산화탄소 (carbon monoxide), 대기오염 (air pollution), 수질오염 (water pollution), 토양오염 (soil pollution), 해양오염 (marine pollution) etc.

22 위조

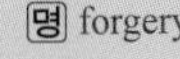
명 forgery

위조 여권을 가지고 출국하려던 범인이 공항에서 체포되었다.

A criminal who tried to leave the country with a fake passport was arrested at the airport.

위조 지폐 forged cash, fake bill　위조하다 to forge

위조되다 be forged

23 유치하다

동 host

평창은 동계 올림픽을 유치하기 위해 많은 노력을 했다.

Pyeongchang has put a lot of effort into hosting the Winter Olympics.

유치되다 be held

24 의지하다

동 rely

힘들 때 서로 의지하면서 지내도록 하자.

Let's rely on each other when times are tough.

25 이를테면

부 for example/such as

세상에는 논리적으로 설명할 수 없는 일들, 이를테면 귀신을 봤다거나 시간 여행을 했다고 주장하는 사람들이 있다.

Things that cannot be explained logically in the world, such as those that claim to have seen ghosts or traveled in time.

'예를 들어 말하자면'과 '다른 말로 하자면'의 두 가지 의미를 가지고 있어요.
"This word has the meanings of both '예를 들어 말하자면 (for example)' and '다른 말로 하자면 (to put in different terms)'."

26 이정표

명 road sign/milestone

운전할 때 이정표를 잘 볼 수 있어야 한다.

You should be able to see the signpost clearly when driving.

27 입증하다

동 to prove

그 사고가 상대편의 책임이라는 걸 입증할 수 있는 증거가 나왔다.

Evidence emerged to prove that the accident was the other party's responsibility.

입증 proof　　입증되다 be proven

DAY 07 ★★★

28 장유유서

명 the younger should give precedence to the elder/elders first

나이 든 사람을 공경하는 장유유서의 정신이 점점 사라져 가고 있다.

'Jang Yu Yu Seo' spirit of respecting older people is gradually disappearing.

29 저버리다

동 to betray/disappoint

그 가수는 팬들의 기대를 저버리지 않는 훌륭한 앨범을 만들어 다시 돌아왔다.

The singer is back with a great album that doesn't disappoint fans.

30 조급하다

형 in a hurry

마음이 조급하면 실수할 수 있으니 조금 차분해질 필요가 있다.

If you are in a hurry, you may make a mistake, so you need to calm down a little.

31 주도적

명 proactive

이번 학교 행사는 여학생들이 주도적으로 참여해서 진행하고 있다.

This school event is proactively led by female students.

주도권 leadership/intiatuve/upperhand 주도하다 to lead

32 질리다

동 be frightened, be sick of, be tired of

공포에 질린 주인공의 연기가 너무 실감났다.

The frightened performance of the protagonist was so realistic.

33 타당성

명 validity

이 기사는 논리적 타당성이 부족하다.

This article lacks logical validity.

타당하다 appropriate/valid/reasonable

34 허기

명 hunger

일할 때는 너무 정신이 없어서 허기도 느끼지 못했다.

When I was working, I was so busy that I did not feel hungry.

허기지다 famished

35 흥청망청

부 lavishly/extravagantly squander money

주식으로 큰 돈을 번 민수는 돈을 흥청망청 쓰기 시작했다.

Minsu, who made a lot of money from stocks, started to spend it lavishly

다의어 Polysemy

바짝

❶ 물기가 매우 마르는 모양

예 집이 너무 건조해서 입술이 바짝 말랐다.

My lips are extremely dry because the house is so dry.

❷ 매우 가까이 달라붙는 모양

예 여행지에서 일행을 놓칠 것 같아 바짝 따라붙었다.

On the trip, I was afraid I would miss my fellow travelers, so I followed them closely.

반의어 Antonym

조급하다 in a hurry ↔ 느긋하다 relaxed, at ease

예 약속 시간이 다가오는데 길이 막혀서 마음이 조급해졌다.

I felt rushed because the time of my appointment was approaching but there was a traffic jam.

예 우리 팀이 지고 있는데 감독은 느긋하게 바라보고 있다.

Our team is losing, but the coach is looking at it with ease.

유의어 Synonym

견디다 endure/withstand/bear ≒ 참다

예 동료들의 따돌림을 견디기가 힘들었다.

동료들의 따돌림을 참기가 힘들었다.

It was difficult to bear the bullying of colleagues.

복습해 보세요

자연스러운 문장이 되도록 완성해 보세요.
Try to complete the sentence in a natural way.

1. 퇴직했다고 ㄱㅈㅎㄱ 노후 생활에 대한 계획을 세워 보십시오.
   Assume you are retired and make plans for your retirement.

2. 전쟁이 끝나고 10년이 지났지만 국민들은 여전히 ㅂㅊㅎ 삶을 살고 있다.
   10 years have passed since the end of the war, but the people still live a miserable life.

3. 학교에 가기 싫어서 학교 근처를 ㅂㅎㅎㄴ 학생들이 많아졌다.
   Many students wander around the school because they do not want to go to school.

4. 요즘은 ㄷㄷㅎㄱ 공개 연애를 하는 연예인 커플이 늘어나고 있다.
   These days, more and more celebrity couples are confidently dating in public.

다음 빈 칸에 알맞은 단어를 〈보기〉에서 골라 쓰세요.
Choose the appropriate word from <Example> to fill in the blanks below.

〈보기〉
a. 입증되었다 b. 명료한 c. 유치하기 d. 대체할

5. 이 강의 채널은 깔끔하고 (　　　　) 강의로 인기를 끌고 있다.
   This lecture channel is gaining popularity for its clean and clear lectures.

6. 대통령은 올림픽을 (　　　　) 위해 세계 국가 정상들과 소통하고 있다.
   The president is communicating with world leaders to host the Olympics.

7. 이번 신제품 개발로 우리 회사의 기술력이 (　　　　).
   Our company's technological prowess has been proven with our new product development.

8. AI(인공지능)이 인간을 (　　　　) 수 없는 분야도 있다.
   There are areas where AI (Artificial Intelligence) cannot replace humans.

정답

1. 가정하고 2. 비참한 3. 배회하는 4. 당당하게 5. b 6. c 7. a 8. d

Memo

DAY 08

확인해 보세요

빨간 시트지로 가리고 단어의 뜻을 알면, □에 ✓ 해 보세요.

After covering up the words with red cover, please check(✓) the box (□) when you know the meaning of the word.

□	01 간과하다	overlook	□	13 명목	cause/pretext	□	25 이르다	to reach/ arrive
□	02 거슬리다	to be irrating	□	14 문득	suddenly/ all of a sudden	□	26 이주하다	to migrate/ move
□	03 견제하다	check, hold in check	□	15 박람회	fair/exhibition	□	27 입지	conditions, position
□	04 공정하다	fair/impartial	□	16 배후	someone behind the action	□	28 재개발	redevelopment
□	05 근무지	workplace	□	17 범행	crime	□	29 저작권	copyright
□	06 내면	inner side	□	18 상당하다	significant/ considerable	□	30 조마조마하다	nervous/ afraid
□	07 눈에 띄다	catch one's eye	□	19 어이없다	absurd	□	31 주되다	main/ principal
□	08 당락	outcome	□	20 염려	worry/concern	□	32 질의	question
□	09 대폭	significantly/ sharply	□	21 온전하다	sane/sound	□	33 탄생	birth
□	10 동결되다	be frozen/ stopped	□	22 위축되다	be daunted/ intimidated	□	34 허둥지둥	hurriedly, in a hurry
□	11 등지다	turn one's back on	□	23 유통되다	to be circulated/ distributed	□	35 흥행	hit/success
□	12 말미암다	due to	□	24 이기심	selfishness			

 are the words that appeared in the former tests, and you may get a higher grade if you study them together.

01 간과하다

동 overlook/ignore

아무리 효과가 좋은 약이라도 생길 수 있는 부작용을 간과해서는 안 된다.

No matter how effective the medicine is, side effects that can occur should not be overlooked.

02 거슬리다

동 to be irrating/bothersome/annoying

옆집에서 밤늦게 연주하는 악기 소리가 귀에 거슬린다.

The sound of musical instruments playing late at night next door bothers me.

'눈에 거슬리다'는 '마음에 안 들고 불쾌하다'는 뜻으로 자주 사용하는 관용 표현이에요.

'눈에 거슬리다 (to be bothersome/annoying)' is an idiom that's often used to mean '마음에 안 들고 불쾌하다 (I don't like it or feel uncomfortable)'

 다른 사람을 배려하지 않는 그의 태도가 눈에 거슬렸다.
His disrespect for others was annoying.

03 견제하다

동 check, hold in check

두 나라는 서로를 견제하고 있다.

The two countries are holding each other in check.

 견제를 받다 be checked out

04 공정하다

형 fair/impartial

이번 대회에서 심판이 공정하지 못한 판단을 했다고 비판을 받고 있다.

The referee is criticized for making unfair judgments in this competition.

공정성 fairness/equity　　공정 justice, impartiality

반) 불공정하다 to be unfair

05 근무지

명 workplace

이직하면서 근무지가 바뀌어서 아직 낯설다.

It's still unfamiliar because my workplace has changed as I moved.

근무자 worker　　근무하다 to work

06 내면

명 inner side

내가 모르는 나의 내면에는 그 친구를 부러워하는 마음이 있었던 것 같다.

It seems that there was a feeling of envy of that friend inside of me that I did not know.

07 눈에 띄다

동 be noticed/seen, catch one's eye

길거리에 개성 있는 옷차림을 한 사람들이 자주 눈에 띈다.

People in unique attire are often seen on the streets.

08 당락

명 outcome/success/result

이번 수능은 국어가 당락을 가를 것이라고 한다.

It is said that the Korean language will determine the outcome of this CSAT.

당락을 좌우하다 to determine the outcome

09 대폭

부 significantly/sharply/drastically

생필품의 소비자 가격이 대폭 인상되었다.

Consumer prices for daily necessities have increased significantly.

대폭 늘어나다 to increase significantly

10 동결되다

동 be frozen/stopped

회사 사정이 어려워짐에 따라 올해는 임금이 동결되었다.

As the company's situation became difficult, wages were frozen this year.

동결시키다 impose a freeze

11 등지다

동 turn one's back on

세상이 너를 등지더라도 나는 네 옆에 있을 것이다.

Even if the world turns against you, I will be by your side.

12 말미암다

동 due to

그의 부주의로 말미암아 다른 사람들이 피해를 입었다.

Others were harmed due to his negligence.

'(으)로 말미암아'의 형태로 사용되며 '(으)로 인하여'와 바꿔 쓸 수 있어요.

This word is used in the form of '(으)로 말미암아' and can be used interchangeably with '(으)로 인하여'.

작은 실수로 말미암아 큰 사고가 났다.
작은 실수로 인하여 큰 사고가 났다.
Both sentences mean 'A big accident occurred due to a small mistake.'

13 명목

명 cause/pretext/in the name of

동호회 지원 명목으로 받은 회비를 개인적으로 사용했다.

The membership dues received in the name of supporing the club were used for personal gains.

명목을 내세우다 assert/claim cause/pretexta
명목을 유지하다 maintain cause/pretext

14 문득

부 suddenly/all of a sudden

길을 걷다 문득 생각이 나서 엄마에게 전화를 했다.

I called my mom because I suddenly thought of her while walking on the street.

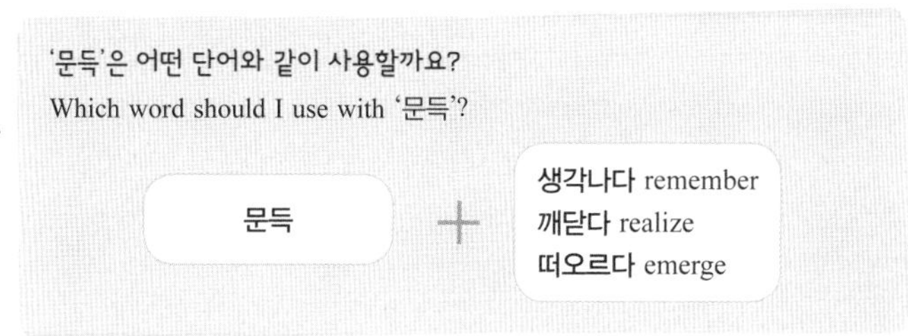

'문득'은 어떤 단어와 같이 사용할까요?
Which word should I use with '문득'?
문득
생각나다 remember
깨닫다 realize
떠오르다 emerge

15 박람회

명 fair/exhibition

이번주부터 학교에서 취업 박람회가 열린다고 한다.

It is said that there will be a job fair at school starting this week.

16 배후

명 someone behind the action

경찰은 이번 테러의 배후 세력을 찾기 위해 집중하고 있다.

Police are focusing on finding the people behind the attack.

17 범행

명 crime

그들은 함께 범행을 공모했다.

They conspired to commit the crime together.

범행 동기 motive of a crime
범행을 저지르다 to commit a crime

18 상당하다

형 significant/considerable

이 앱은 상당한 시간과 노력을 들인 끝에 개발되었다.

This app was developed after a considerable amount of time and effort.

19 어이없다

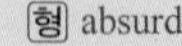
형 absurd

아버지께서는 정치 관련 기사를 읽고 어이없는 표정을 지으셨다.

My father read an article about politics and made an absurd expression on his face.

20 염려

명 worry/concern

주위의 염려에도 불구하고 내 친구는 새로운 사업을 시작하기로 결정했다.

Despite the concerns around her, my friend decided to start a new business.

염려하다 be concerned/worried

21 온전하다

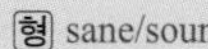
형 sane/sound

온전한 정신이라면 그런 말도 안 되는 선택을 할 리가 없다.

A sane mind cannot make such a ridiculous choice.

22 위축되다

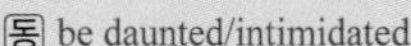
동 be daunted/intimidated

졸업 후 취업을 준비하는 기간이 길어지면서 심리적으로 많이 위축되는 것을 느낀다.

As the period of preparing for employment after graduation is extended, I feel psychologically shrinking.

위축 shrinking/withering

23 유통되다

동 to be circulated/distributed

시중에서 유통되고 있는 제품 중 일부를 선택해 안전 검사를 실시하였다.

Some of the products on the market were selected for safety inspection.

유통 distribution

- 유통업체 distribution company
- 유통망 distribution network
- 유통기한 expiration date
- 유통경로 distribution route

24 이기심

명 selfishness

자기만 생각하는 이기심을 버리고 다른 사람을 생각할 필요가 있다.

You need to stop being selfish and think about others.

25 이르다

동 to reach/arrive

선수들의 실수가 계속 되자 감독의 인내심도 한계에 이르렀다.

As the players' mistakes continued, the manager's patience also reached its limit.

형용사 '이르다'와 구별해야 해요.

The verb form of '이르다 (to reach)' is different from the adjective form '이르다 (early)'.

올해 첫눈은 다른 해에 비해 좀 이른 감이 있다.
The first snow of the year seems a bit earlier than the rest of the year.

26 이주하다

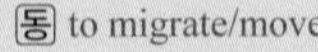 to migrate/move

1900년대 초부터 하와이 지역으로 한국인들이 이주하기 시작했다.

Koreans began to migrate to Hawaii in the early 1900s.

이주 migration　　이주민 immigrant

27 입지

명 conditions, position

그 지역은 교통면에서 공장 입지로 최고의 조건을 가지고 있었다.

The area had the best conditions for factory location in terms of transportation.

28 재개발

명 redevelopment

이 지역은 최근에 도시 재개발이 결정되었다.

This area has recently been decided for urban redevelopment.

29 저작권

명 copyright

많은 사람들이 자신이 저작권을 위반하는지도 모르는 경우가 많다.

Many people often don't even know they're violating copyright.

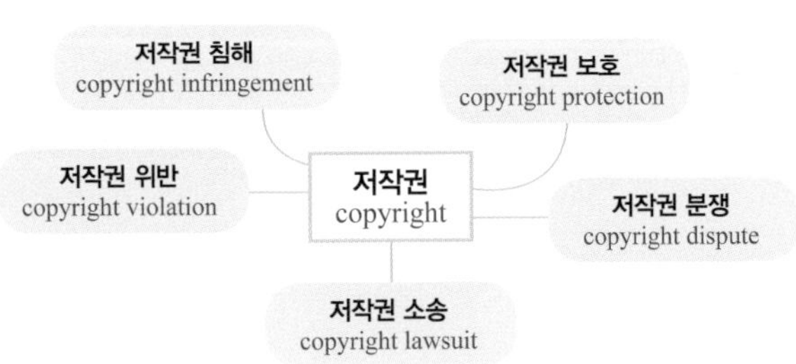

30 조마조마하다

형 nervous/afraid

수술 결과를 기다리는데 마음이 계속 조마조마했다.

I was nervous waiting for the results of the surgery.

31 주되다

[동] main/principal/major

이번 회의의 주된 내용은 온라인 수업을 활성화시키는 방안이다.

The main content of this conference is to revitalize online classes.

32 질의

[명] question

다음으로 질의응답 시간을 갖도록 하겠습니다.

Next, we will have a Q&A time.

33 탄생

[명] birth

제 직업은 새 생명의 탄생 현장을 볼 수 있어서 정말 보람 있어요.

My job is really rewarding to see the scene of the birth of a new life.

34 허둥지둥

[부] hurriedly, in a hurry/rush

언니는 약속 시간에 늦었다면서 허둥지둥 나갔다.

My sister went out hurriedly saying she was late for her appointment.

관련어 허둥지둥하다 hurry/rush

35 흥행

[명] hit/success

봉준호 감독의 이번 영화는 전세계적으로 흥행에 성공했다.

Director Bong Joon-ho's film was a box office hit worldwide.

흥행하다 to be a hit/sucess

TOPIK에서 혼동하기 쉬운 단어

다의어 Polysemy

동결되다

❶ 자산이나 돈의 사용이 금지되다.

예 회사 사정이 어려워짐에 따라 올해는 임금이 동결되었다.

As the company's situation became difficult, wages were frozen this year.

❷ 추위나 냉동으로 얼어붙다.

예 동결건조식품은 동결된 식품을 다시 건조시킨 것이다.

Freeze-dried foods are frozen foods that are dried again.

반의어 Antonym

탄생 birth ↔ 사망 death

예 아들의 탄생을 처음부터 끝까지 지켜보았다.

I watched the birth of my son from beginning to end.

예 경찰 조사가 끝났지만 사망 원인을 알 수 없었다.

Though the police investigation ended, the cause of death was unknown.

유의어 Synonym

공정하다 fair/impartial ≒ 공평하다

예 심판이 공정하지 못한 판단을 내렸다.

심판이 공평하지 못한 판단을 내렸다.

The referee made an unfair decision.

복습해 보세요

서로 어울리는 단어를 찾아 연결해 보세요.
Find words that go with each other and connect them.

1. 신경에 • • a. 이르다
2. 범행을 • • b. 거슬리다
3. 견제를 • • c. 좌우하다
4. 한계에 • • d. 공모하다
5. 당락을 • • e. 받다

다음 빈 칸에 알맞은 단어를 〈보기〉에서 골라 쓰세요.
Choose the appropriate word from <Example> to fill in the blanks below.

〈보기〉
a. 공정하게 b. 동결되자 c. 이주하고 d. 상당한

6. 몇 년째 연봉이 ( ) 이직하는 직원이 늘고 있다.
As salaries have been frozen for several years, the number of employees leaving has been increasing.

7. 그는 젊은 나이에 ( ) 부동산을 소유하고 있다.
He owns a considerable amount of real estate at a young age.

8. 도시 생활에 염증을 느낀 사람들이 대거 농촌으로 ( ) 있다.
A large number of people who feel tired of city life are migrating to rural areas.

9. 정부는 국민들로부터 세금을 ( ) 거두어 들여야 한다.
The government should fairly collect taxes from the people.

정답

1.b 2.d 3.e 4.a 5.c 6.b 7.d 8.c 9.a

Memo

DAY 09

확인해 보세요

빨간 시트지로 가리고 단어의 뜻을 알면, □에 ✓ 해 보세요.

After covering up the words with red cover, please check(✓) the box (□) when you know the meaning of the word.

	No.	Word	Meaning		No.	Word	Meaning		No.	Word	Meaning
□	01	간소하다	simple/plain	□	13	명백하다	to be clear	□	25	익명	anonymity
□	02	걷잡다	control	□	14	문명	civilization	□	26	자가	oneself
□	03	결단	decision	□	15	박탈하다	disqualify	□	27	재고	stock/ inventory
□	04	근원	root/cause/ source	□	16	번거롭다	inconvenient/ cumbersome	□	28	저조하다	low
□	05	급변하다	to rapidly change	□	17	법규	law	□	29	조만간	soon
□	06	내몰다	to drive/force	□	18	생소하다	unfamiliar	□	30	주목	attention
□	07	눈에 선하다	be fresh/live in one´s memory	□	19	어처구니	be absurb	□	31	주식	staple food
□	08	당면	current/ immediate	□	20	영광	honor/glory	□	32	터놓다	open one's heart
□	09	대피	evacuation	□	21	완쾌하다	recover completely	□	33	허름하다	shabby/poor
□	10	동경	admiration/ longing	□	22	위태롭다	risky/perilous	□	34	흐뭇하다	pleased
□	11	디디다	step on	□	23	유해	hazard, harm	□	35	희미하다	to be faint/ dim
□	12	맞아떨어지다	match	□	24	이득	profit				

DAY 09

  are the words that appeared in the former tests, and you may get a higher grade if you study them together.

01 간소하다

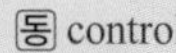 simple/plain

이번 생일은 친구들과 파티를 하지 않고 간소하게 보내고 싶다.

I want to spend this birthday simply without having a party with my friends.

간소화하다 to simplify   간소화되다 to be simplified

02 걷잡다

동 control

계속되는 실패로 인해 걷잡을 수 없는 좌절감에 빠지게 되었다.

Continuing failures have left me with an uncontrollable frustration.

이 단어는 '걷잡다'가 아니라 '걷잡을 수 없다' 형태로 사용해야 해요.

This word should be used in the form of '걷잡을 수 없다', instead of '걷잡다'.

 전염병에 감염되는 사람이 걷잡을 수 없이 증가하고 있다.

The number of people infected with infectious diseases is increasing out of control.

03 결단

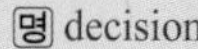 decision

그 사람은 한번 결단을 내린 일은 절대로 바꾸지 않는다.

That person never changes a decision once it's made

결단력 initiative/purpose/decision/determination

결단하다 to decide/determine

04 근원

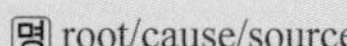 root/cause/source

스트레스는 만병의 근원이다.

Stress is the root cause of all illnesses.

05 급변하다

동 to rapidly change

외교를 잘하기 위해서는 급변하는 국제 정세를 잘 파악해야 한다.

In order to be good at diplomacy, we need to understand the rapidly changing international situation well.

급변 sudden change

06 내몰다

동 to drive/force/turn out

아이들을 학원으로만 내모는 현재의 교육은 문제가 많다.

The current education system that only drives out children to private after-school academies is problematic.

07 눈에 선하다

형 be fresh/live in one´s memory, linger before one´s eyes

어렸을 때 친구들과 놀던 고향이 아직도 눈에 선하다.

My hometown where I used to play with my friends as a child is still fresh in my memories.

08 당면

명 current/immediate/urgent

환경 문제는 우리들의 당면 과제다.

Environmental issues are our current challenge.

당면하다 to confront/face

09 대피

명 evacuation

태풍으로 피해를 입은 주민들이 대피 시설로 이주했다.

Residents affected by the typhoon moved to evacuation facilities.

대피소 shelter, refuge

대피하다 to evacuate

대피시키다 to evcuate others

10 동경
명 admiration/longing

그 곳에서 평생 동경의 대상이었던 사람을 만났다.

There, I met the one whom I had admired for a lifetime.

동경하다 to admire/yearn/long for

11 디디다
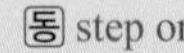
동 step on

이 길은 위험해서 발을 잘못 디디면 큰 사고가 날 수 있으니 조심해야 한다.

This road is dangerous, so you have to be careful as a wrong step can cause a serious accident.

'첫발을 디디다'는 관용 표현이에요. '어떤 일을 처음 시작한다는 뜻'이에요.
'첫발을 디디다' is an expression which means 'starting a new type of work'.

오늘은 사회인으로서 첫발을 디디는 날이다.
Today is the day I take my first steps as a member of society.

12 맞아떨어지다
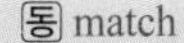
동 match

그 배우의 이미지와 배역이 잘 맞아떨어졌다.

The actor's image and his role matched well.

13 명백하다
형 to be clear

음주운전은 변명의 여지가 없는 명백한 잘못이다.

Drunk driving is a clear and inexcusable offense.

14 문명
명 civilization

세계 4대 문명은 모두 큰 강 주변에서 시작되었다.

The world's four major civilizations all started around a large river.

15 박탈하다

동 disqualify/deprive/deny

올림픽 위원회는 약물 사용이 밝혀진 선수의 자격을 박탈하였다.

The Olympic Committee disqualified athletes who were found to have used drugs.

박탈 deprivation　　박탈되다 to be disqualified/kicked out

박탈감 sense of deprivation

16 번거롭다

형 inconvenient/cumbersome

이 음식은 만들기가 너무 번거로워서 자주 안 먹게 된다.

This food is too cumbersome to make, so I don't eat it often.

17 법규

명 law

그는 교통 법규를 위반해서 벌금을 내야했다.

He broke traffic laws and had to pay a fine.

법규를 지키다 keep/obey the law

18 생소하다

형 unfamiliar

이 프로그램은 외국인들에게 생소한 한국 문화를 접하게 해 준다.

This program allows foreigners to experience unfamiliar Korean culture.

19 어처구니

명 be absurb

자기가 잘못해 놓고 오히려 화를 내니 어처구니가 없다

It's ridiculous that he's angry even though he is the one at fault here.

이 단어는 '어처구니가 없다'의 형태로 사용해요. '어처구니가 있다'라고는 사용하지 않으니 조심하세요.

This word is only used in the form of '어처구니가 없다 (to be absurd).' Be careful to never use it as '어처구니가 있다'.

DAY 09 ★★★

20 영광

명 honor/glory

저는 1등한 영광을 지금까지 저를 아끼고 도와주신 부모님에게 돌리고 싶습니다.

I would like to give the honor of winning the first place to my parents who have cared for and helped me.

21 완쾌하다

동 recover completely

빨리 완쾌하시기를 바랍니다.

I hope you recover completely soon.

완쾌되다 to recover completely
완쾌 complete recovery

22 위태롭다

형 risky/perilous/critical

당시 조선은 내부적인 혼란과 외부의 침략으로 매우 위태로운 상황이었다.

At that time, Joseon was in a perilous situation due to internal turmoil and external aggression.

23 유해

명 hazard, harm

아이들의 장난감에서 기준치 이상의 유해 물질이 검출되었다.

Hazardous substances above the standard limit were detected in children's toys.

유해성 harmfulness 유해하다 be harmful/detrimental

24 이득

명 profit

불법 도박 사이트를 운영하며 막대한 이득을 취한 일당이 체포됐다.

A group of people who made huge profits from running illegal gambling sites were arrested.

관련어

금전적 이득 financial gain 부당 이득 unfair profit
이득을 보다 gain profit

DAY
09
★★★

25 익명

명 anonymity (anonymous), pseudonym

익명의 제보를 받고 출동한 경찰들은 그를 체포했다.

Police, who were dispatched because of an anonymous report, arrested him.

익명성 anonymity

26 자가

명 oneself

전염병이 퍼진 후 해외에서 입국한 사람들은 2주 동안의 자가 격리를 해야 했다.

Those who entered the country after the pandemic spread had to self-quarantine for two weeks.

자가 진단 self-diagnosis

27 재고

명 stock/inventory

롱패딩의 재고가 쌓이자 기업들은 할인 판매를 하기로 결정했다.

As stocks of long padding piled up, companies decided to sell it at a discount.

재고 정리 clearance, inventory adjustment

28 저조하다

형 low

학교에서 계획한 행사에 학생들의 참여가 저조하다.

Students' participation in events planned by the school is low.

29 조만간

부 soon

바쁜 일이 끝나고 조만간 만나기로 했다.

We decided to meet soon after busy work.

30 주목

명 attention

그 가수는 흉내내기 힘든 댄스 실력으로 주목을 받고 있다.

The singer is attracting attention for his dance skills that are hard to imitate.

주목하다 pay attention

31 주식

명 staple food

한국인의 주식은 쌀이다.

The rice is the staple food of Koreans.

32 터놓다

동 open one's heart

미영이하고는 마음을 터놓고 지내는 사이이다.

Mi-young and I have a close relationship where we open up to one another.

33 허름하다

형 shabby/poor

이 식당은 보기에는 허름한 식당이지만 김치찌개 맛집으로 유명하다.

This restaurant looks shabby, but it is famous for its delicious kimchi stew.

34 흐뭇하다

형 pleased

부모님은 내가 피아노를 치고 있으면 항상 흐뭇한 모습으로 지켜보셨다.

My parents always watched me play the piano with a happy face.

35 희미하다

형 to be faint/dim

연필로 쓴 글씨는 너무 희미해서 잘 알아볼 수가 없었다.

The pencil handwriting was so faint that it was hard to recognize.

TOPIK에서 혼동하기 쉬운 단어

다의어 Polysemy

주식

❶ 끼니에 주로 먹는 음식

예 한국인의 주식은 쌀이다.

The rice is the staple food of Koreans.

❷ 회사의 자본을 구성하는 단위

예 나는 요즘 주식 투자를 위해 공부를 하고 있다.

Recently, I have been studying to invest in stocks.

반의어 Antonym

희미하다 to be faint/dim ↔ **뚜렷하다** clear, distinct

예 연필로 쓴 글씨는 너무 희미해서 잘 알아볼 수가 없었다.

The pencil handwriting was so faint that it was hard to recognize.

예 이 그림을 보면 두 화가의 차이점을 뚜렷하게 볼 수 있다.

This painting clearly shows the difference between the two artists.

유의어 Synonym

생소하다 unfamiliar ≒ **낯설다**

예 이 프로그램은 외국인들에게 생소한 한국 문화를 접하게 해 준다.

이 프로그램은 외국인들에게 낯선 한국 문화를 접하게 해 준다.

This program allows foreigners to experience unfamiliar Korean culture.

복습해 보세요

서로 어울리는 단어를 찾아 연결해 보세요.
Find words that go with each other and connect them.

1. 법규	a. 받다
2. 주목	b. 보다
3. 옷차림	c. 지키다
4. 기억	d. 허름하다
5. 이득	e. 희미하다

다음 빈 칸에 알맞은 단어를 〈보기〉에서 골라 쓰세요.
Choose the appropriate word from <Example> to fill in the blanks below.

〈보기〉
a. 걷잡을 b. 근원 c. 위태로운 d. 이득 e. 어처구니

6. 스트레스는 만병의 (   )이다.
Stress is the root cause of all illnesses.

7. 계속되는 실패로 인해 (   ) 수 없는 좌절감에 빠지게 되었다.
Continuing failures have left me with an uncontrollable frustration.

8. 자기가 잘못해 놓고 오히려 화를 내니 (   )이/가 없다
It's ridiculous that he's angry even though he is the one at fault here.

9. 불법 도박 사이트를 운영하며 막대한 (   )을/를 취한 일당이 체포됐다.
A group of people who made huge profits from running illegal gambling sites were arrested.

10. 당시 조선은 내부적인 혼란과 외부의 침략으로 매우 (   ) 상황이었다.
At that time, Joseon was in a perilous situation due to internal turmoil and external aggression.

정답

1.c 2.a 3.d 4.e 5.b 6.b 7.a 8.e 9.d 10.c

DAY 10

확인해 보세요

빨간 시트지로 가리고 단어의 뜻을 알면, □에 ✓ 해 보세요.

After covering up the words with red cover, please check(✓) the box (□) when you know the meaning of the word.

□ 01	간절하다	to be desperate	□ 13	명분	cause/ justificiation	□ 25	이름나다	to be famous for
□ 02	겪다	to experience	□ 14	문상	offer of condolences	□ 26	인건비	labor costs
□ 03	결말	ending	□ 15	반감	hostility/ animosity	□ 27	자각	self-awareness/ consciousness
□ 04	공해	pollution	□ 16	번번이	always, all the time	□ 28	재난	natural disaster
□ 05	금리	interest rate	□ 17	법률	law	□ 29	저하	fall, decline
□ 06	내비치다	express	□ 18	생계	livelihood	□ 30	조율하다	to tune, to coordinate
□ 07	눈여겨보다	pay attention to	□ 19	억누르다	to suppress	□ 31	질환	disease/illness
□ 08	당부	request	□ 20	영구적	permanent/ lasting	□ 32	짐작하다	to assume
□ 09	댓글	comments	□ 21	완화하다	to relax	□ 33	허물다	knock down
□ 10	동등하다	equal (to)	□ 22	위협	threat/harm	□ 34	허용되다	to be allowed/ permitted
□ 11	딜레마	dilemma	□ 23	유형	type, category	□ 35	희박하다	rare/sparse
□ 12	맞장구	chime in	□ 24	이르다	early			

DAY 10

 are the words that appeared in the former tests, and you may get a higher grade if you study them together.

01 간절하다

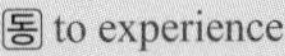 to be desperate

독거 노인들을 향한 도움의 손길이 간절합니다.

We desperately need a helping hand for the elderly living alone.

02 겪다

동 to experience

많은 어려움을 겪으면서도 그 아이는 강인한 정신력으로 결코 포기하지 않았다.

Despite experiencing many the difficulties, the child never gave up with a strong mentality.

'겪다'와 '경험하다'는 뭐가 다를까요?

'경험하다'는 다양한 상황에서 모두 쓰이지만 '겪다'는 보통 '어려움, 곤란, 갈등, 불편, 시련, 시행착오' 와 같은 부정적인 상황에서 자주 사용해요.

What is the difference between'겪다' and '경험하다'?

'경험하다' is used in all kinds of situations, but '겪다' is usually used in negative situations such as "어려움(hardship), 곤란(difficulty), 갈등(conflict), 불편(inconvenience), 시련(hardship), 시행착오(trial and error)'.

 이번 여행을 통해서 다양한 것을 경험할 수 있었다.

I was able to experience various things through this trip.

03 결말

명 ending

최근 보고 있는 드라마의 결말이 어떻게 될지 매우 궁금하다.

I'm very curious to see what the ending of the drama I'm currently watching will be.

결말이 나다 come to/reach a end

결말을 내다 bring to a conclusion/an end

DAY 10 ★★★

04 공해

명 pollution

환경 오염이 심해짐에 따라 대도시에서는 공해 문제를 해결하기 위해 노력하고 있다.

As environmental pollution gets worse, big cities are trying to solve pollution problems.

소음 공해 noise pollution

05 금리

명 interest rate

금리가 점차 오르고 있어서 대출을 받으려는 사람들이 감소하는 추세이다.

Interest rates are rising, so the number of people seeking loans is on the decline.

금리가 오르다 interest rates have risen

06 내비치다

동 express/indicate/hint at

김 과장님은 퇴사할 뜻을 내비쳤다.

Manager Kim expressed his intention to resign.

07 눈여겨보다

동 pay attention to/watch/observe/eye

김 사장님은 신입사원 채용 지원자들의 행동 하나하나를 눈여겨보았다.

President Kim paid attention to each and every action of applicants for new employee recruitment.

08 당부

명 request

최근 코로나 확진자가 많이 나오고 있는 시설 이용자들께 당부 말씀 드리겠습니다.

I would like to make a request to the users of the facilities with many recent COVID-19 cases.

09 댓글

명 comments

그 기사에 대해서 수천 개의 댓글이 달렸다.

Thousands of comments were written about that article

댓글을 달다 to write a comment

댓글을 올리다 to post a comment

10 동등하다

형 equal (to)

누구나 차별없이 동등한 기회를 가져야 한다.

Everyone should be granted equal opportunities without discrimination.

11 딜레마

명 dilemma

세계 경제가 코로나 딜레마에 빠져서 이러지도 저러지도 못하고 있다.

The world economy is stuck with the coronavirus dilemma, unable to do anything about it.

12 맞장구

명 chime in, agree/respond well

상대방이 말할 때 맞장구를 쳐주면 대화가 잘 풀린다.

If you chime in positively when the other person speaks, the conversation will work out well.

13 명분

명 cause/justificiation

전쟁을 하게 되면 명분과 실리를 모두 잃게 된다.

If you go to war, you lose both idealistic justification and practical benefit.

명분이 없다 have no justification/cause

14 문상

명 offer of condolences

오늘 퇴근 후 친구 어머님 장례식장에 문상을 가려고 한다.

I'm going to visit the funeral of my friend's mother to offer condolences after work today.

문상하다 offer condolences   문상객 mourner

15 반감

명 hostility/animosity

그는 이번 정부에 대해 반감을 가지고 있다.

He harbors hostile feeling towards the current administration.

16 번번이

부 always, all the time

아무리 신입 사원이라고 해도 이렇게 번번이 실수하는 것은 문제가 있다고 본다.

No matter how new you are, I think it's a problem to always make such mistakes.

17 법률

명 law

공동구매로 법률 상담을 진행하고 있다.

We are conducting legal consultation through joint purchase.

법률가 lawyer

18 생계

명 livelihood/living

그는 평생 가족의 생계를 위해 일해야 했다.

He had to work to earn a living for his family all his life.

생계형 범죄 survival crimes: crimes committed to survive

생계를 잇다 earn a living

19 억누르다

동 to suppress

감정을 억누르기만 하다가는 우울증에 걸리기 쉽다.

It is easy to get depression if you only suppress your emotions.

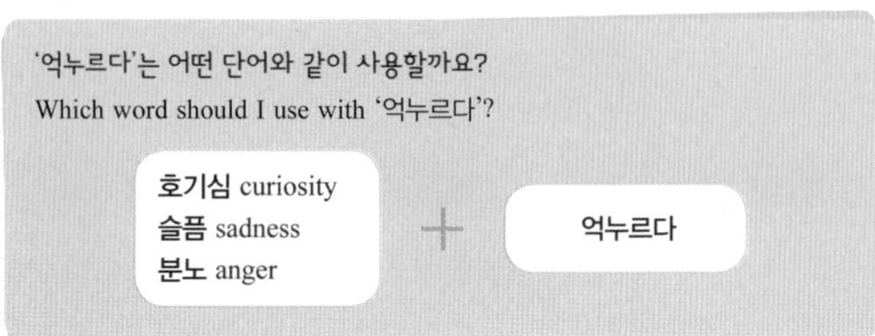

'억누르다'는 어떤 단어와 같이 사용할까요?
Which word should I use with '억누르다'?
호기심 curiosity
슬픔 sadness
분노 anger
+
억누르다

20 영구적

명 permanent/lasting

이 배터리는 영구적으로 사용할 수 있는 제품입니다.

This battery is a lasting product.

21 완화하다

동 to relax/ease/soften/alleviate

농산물 수입 제한을 완화함에 따라 다양한 수입 농산물들이 들어오고 있다.

Various imported agricultural products are coming in as restrictions on imports of agricultural products are relaxed.

관련어

완화되다 be eased/relaxed　　완화 relaxation, easing

22 위협

명 threat/harm

담배는 건강에 위협이 되기 때문에 되도록 끊어야 한다.

You should stop smoking as much as you can because it poses a health threat.

위협적 being threatening/menacing　　위협하다 to threaten

23 유형

명 type, category, pattern, form

내년부터 한국어 시험 유형이 바뀐다고 한다.

It is said that the format of Korean test will change from next year.

24 이르다

형 early

올 첫눈은 다른 해에 비해 좀 이른 감이 있다.

The first snow of this year seems a little earlier compared to in other years.

동사 '이르다'와 구별해야 합니다.
This word is different from the verb form of '이르다 (to reach)'.

선수들의 실수가 계속 되자 감독의 인내심도 한계에 이르렀다.
As the player's mistakes continued, the manager's patience also reached its limit.

25 이름나다

동 to be famous for

그 식당은 이 지역에서는 맛있기로 이름난 곳이에요.

The restaurant is famous for its deliciousness in this area.

26 인건비

명 labor costs

노동자들의 인건비가 증가하면 물건의 가격도 높아진다.

Increasing labor costs for workers also increases the price of goods.

27 자각

명 self-awareness/consciousness

그는 병이 진행되는 동안 전혀 자각 증세가 없었다고 한다.

He said he was completely unconscious of the symptoms during the course of the disease.

자각하다 to be aware of

28 재난

명 natural disaster

이번 태풍으로 피해가 특히 심했던 지역을 특별 재난 지역으로 지정했다.

Areas that were particularly affected by the typhoon were designated as special disaster areas.

재난을 피하다 avoid disaster
재난을 막다 prevent disaster

29 저하

명 fall, decline

시력 저하의 원인으로 과도한 스마트폰 사용이 지적되었다.

Excessive smartphone use was pointed out as the cause of the decline in eyesight.

저하되다 drop decline

30 조율하다

동 to tune, to coordinate/mediate/compromise/resolve

입장이 다른 두 팀의 의견을 조율하는 것이 힘들었다.

It was hard to coordinate the opinions of the two teams with different positions.

31 질환

명 disease/illness/problem

환절기에는 호흡기 질환 환자가 증가한다.

In-between seasons, the number of patients with respiratory diseases increases.

정신 질환 mental illness　　피부 질환 skin disease/problem
심장 질환 heart disease/problem

32 짐작하다

동 to assume

나는 그 사람의 말투를 듣고 외국인이라고 짐작했다.

I heard how the person spoke and assumed he was a foreigner.

짐작 assumption　　짐작되다 be assumed
짐작이 가다 can guess/assume

33 허물다

동 knock down/demolish/get rid of

우리 가족은 낡은 집을 허물고 새로 짓기로 했다.

Our family decided to demolish the old house and build a new one

건물을 허물다 demolish a building

34 허용되다

동 to be allowed/permitted

이 부근은 낚시가 허용되지 않는다.

Fishing is not permitted in this area

35 희박하다

형 rare/sparse/sli

DAY 10 ★★★

산악 지대는 인구 밀도가 희박하다.

The mountainous region has a sparse population.

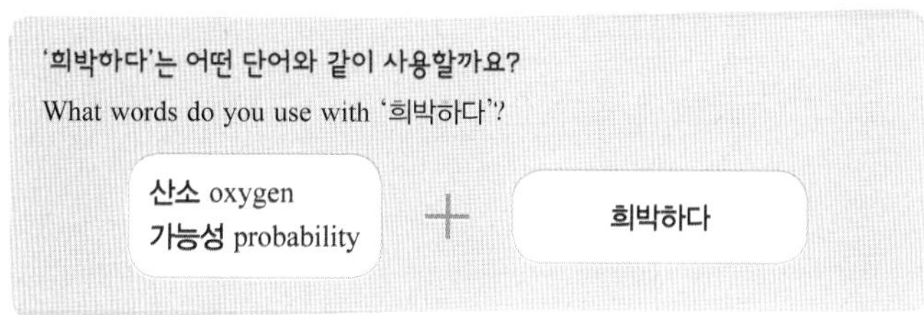

'희박하다'는 어떤 단어와 같이 사용할까요?
What words do you use with '희박하다'?
산소 oxygen
가능성 probability
+
희박하다

TOPIK에서 혼동하기 쉬운 단어

다의어 Polysemy

이르다

❶ 기준보다 빠르다.

예 올 첫눈은 다른 해에 비해 좀 이른 감이 있다.

The first snow of this year seems a little earlier compared to in other years.

❷ 어떤 정도에 미치다.

예 그 회사의 기술은 이미 최고 상태에 이르렀다.

The company's technology have already reached its peak.

❸ 어떤 장소에 도착하다.

예 기차가 종착역에 이르면 안내방송이 나온다.

When the train arrives at the final station, an announcement is made.

반의어 Antonym

완화하다 to relax/ease/soften/alleviate ↔ 강화하다 strengthe, tighten

예 농산물 수입 제한을 완화함에 따라 다양한 수입 농산물들이 들어 오고 있다.

IVarious imported agricultural products are coming in as restrictions on imports of agricul tural products are relaxed.

예 전염병이 확산되면서 입국 절차를 강화하기로 했다.

As the epidemic spreads, the immigration process has been tightened.

유의어 Synonym

이름나다 to be famous for ≒ 유명하다

예 그 식당은 이 지역에서는 맛있기로 이름난 곳이에요.

그 식당은 이 지역에서는 맛있기로 유명한 곳이에요.

The restaurant is famous for its deliciousness in this area.

복습해 보세요

자연스러운 문장이 되도록 둘 중에서 알맞은 단어를 고르세요.
Choose the proper word that fits the sentence more naturally.

1. 최근 보고 있는 드라마의 (a. 결말 / b. 댓글)이 어떻게 될지 매우 궁금하다.
   I'm very curious to see what the ending of the drama I'm currently watching will be.

2. 환경 오염이 심해짐에 따라 대도시에서는 (a. 공해 / b. 문상) 문제를 해결하기 위해 노력하고 있다.
   As environmental pollution gets worse, big cities are trying to solve pollution problems.

3. 그는 이번 정부에 대해 (a. 유형 / b. 반감)을 가지고 있다.
   He harbors hostile feeling towards the current administration.

4. 노동자들의 (a. 인건비 / b. 생계)가 증가하면 물건의 가격도 높아진다.
   Increasing labor costs for workers also increases the price of goods.

5. 이번 태풍으로 피해가 특히 심했던 지역을 특별 (a. 위협 / b. 재난) 지역으로 지정했다.
   Areas that were particularly affected by the typhoon were designated as special disaster areas.

서로 어울리는 단어를 찾아 연결해 보세요.
Find words that go with each other and connect them.

6. 금리	a. 완화되다
7. 슬픔	b. 오르다
8. 제한	c. 억누르다
9. 의견	d. 허물다
10. 건물	e. 조율하다

정답

1.a 2.a 3.b 4.a 5.b 6.b 7.c 8.a 9.e 10.d

❶ 화(化) -ization

온난화 global warming

세계화 globalization

디지털화 digitalization

❷ 세(稅) fee

관세 (customs/import) duty

소득세 income tax

수도세 water bill

주민세 residence tax

전기세 electric bill

❸ 최(最) most

최고 maximum, best

최대 the biggest, the largest

최신 the newest, the latest

최우선 first priority

최저 the lowermost, the minimum

최소 the smallest

최근 the nearest, the most recent

최후 the last, the end

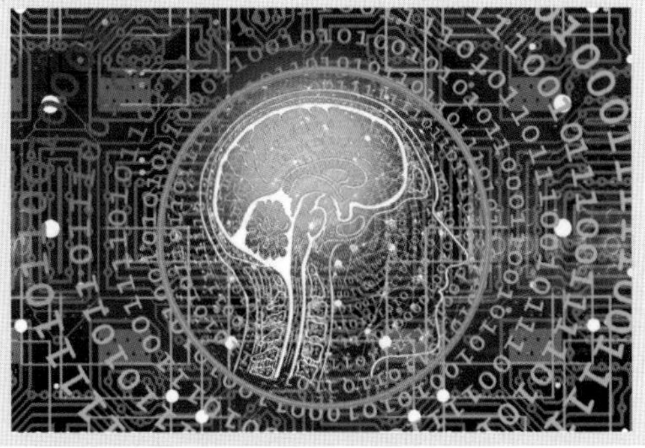

▲ 디지털화 digitalization

주간 복습 day 6 - day 10

아래 단어를 보고 빈 칸에 뜻을 적어 보세요. 그리고 점선대로 접어서 적은 뜻이 맞는지 확인해 보세요. (만일 틀렸다면 뒷면의 단어 앞 □에 ✓ 하세요.)

Write down the meaning of the given word in the blank. Also, fold the page along a dotted line and check whether you got it right or wrong. (If you got it wrong tick the box in front of the word in next page.)

▼접는선

단어	뜻
공식적	
맞대다	
배포하다	
저마다	
질기다	
가정하다	
당당하다	
배회하다	
주도적	
조급하다	
간과하다	
문득	
위축되다	
흥행	
저작권	
대피	
생소하다	
조만간	
희미하다	
터놓다	
공해	
억누르다	
유형	
허용되다	
희박하다	

※접어서 뜻이 맞는지 확인해보세요.

주간 복습 day 6 – day 10

빈 칸에 한국어 단어를 3번 적고 다시 외워 봅시다.

Write down the Korean word 3 times in the blank and try to memorize it again.

◀접는선

뜻	단어		
☐ official	공식적		
☐ put together/touch	맞대다		
☐ distribute	배포하다		
☐ each	저마다		
☐ tough/durable	질기다		
☐ assume/suppose	가정하다		
☐ to be confident	당당하다		
☐ to wander	배회하다		
☐ proactive	주도적		
☐ in a hurry	조급하다		
☐ overlook/ignore	간과하다		
☐ suddenly/ all of a sudden	문득		
☐ be daunted/ intimidated	위축되다		
☐ hit/success	흥행		
☐ copyright	저작권		
☐ evacuation	대피		
☐ unfamiliar	생소하다		
☐ soon	조만간		
☐ to be faint/dim	희미하다		
☐ open one's heart	터놓다		
☐ pollution	공해		
☐ to suppress	억누르다		
☐ type, category	유형		
☐ to be allowed/ permitted	허용되다		
☐ rare/sparse	희박하다		

DAY 11

확인해 보세요

빨간 시트지로 가리고 단어의 뜻을 알면, ☐에 ✓ 해 보세요.

After covering up the words with red cover, please check(✓) the box (☐) when you know the meaning of the word.

	No.	단어	Meaning
☐	01	간접	indirect
☐	02	견문	knowledge/ experience/
☐	03	결함	defect/fault
☐	04	과감하다	to be daring/ decisive
☐	05	금액	price
☐	06	내역	breakdown
☐	07	눈을 붙이다	get some sleep, take a little nap
☐	08	당사자	the person/ party directly involved
☐	09	덤벼들다	to lunge for
☐	10	동력	driving force/ power source
☐	11	딛다	step on, overcome
☐	12	매기다	score, set
☐	13	명상	meditation
☐	14	문헌	literature/ references
☐	15	반려견	pet dog
☐	16	번식하다	to reporduce
☐	17	법안	bill
☐	18	생태계	ecosystem
☐	19	언급	comment/ reference
☐	20	연료	fuel
☐	21	예산	budget
☐	22	위화감	sense of incompatibility
☐	23	유효	valid/available
☐	24	이념	ideology/ ideals
☐	25	이산화탄소	carbon dioxide
☐	26	인공위성	satellite
☐	27	자금	fund
☐	28	재능	talent
☐	29	저해	hindrance/ impairment (to)
☐	30	조작하다	to operate/ create
☐	31	주장하다	to claim/ assert
☐	32	집단	organization
☐	33	통과되다	to be passed
☐	34	허술하다	to be flimsy
☐	35	희생하다	to sacrifice

DAY 11

 are the words that appeared in the former tests, and you may get a higher grade if you study them together.

01 간접 명 indirect

독서를 통해서 간접 경험의 기회를 얻을 수 있다.

You can get a chance to experience indirectly through reading.

간접 광고 indirect advertismemt　　간접적 indirectly

반) 직접 direct

02 견문 명 knowledge/experience/horizon

여행을 하다 보면 다양한 사람들을 만남으로써 견문을 넓힐 기회가 많아진다.

As you travel, you have more opportunities to broaden your horizon by meeting various people.

견문을 넓히다 broaden one's horizon/enlarge one's experience

'견문'은 '보고 듣다'라는 의미가 있어요. 즉, 보고 들은 다양한 경험과 지식을 가리키는 단어예요.
'견문' means 'to see and hear'. In other words, it is a word that refers to various experiences and knowledge that have been seen and heard.

03 결함 명 defect/fault

우주인 선발 조건은 신체적 결함이 전혀 없어야 한다는 것이다.

A prerequisite to be selection as an astronaut is that there must be absolutely no physical defects.

기계 결함 machine fault/defect

04 과감하다 형 to be daring/decisive/bold/drastic

신중한 것도 좋지만 새로운 일을 할 때는 과감할 필요도 있다.

It's good to be cautious, but when trying new things, you need to sometimes be daring.

05 금액

명 price

제품에 써 있는 금액을 잘 확인하고 구매해야 한다.

You need to check the price on the product carefully before purchase.

06 내역

명 breakdown/details/history

매일 그날 소비한 지출 내역을 정리하면 돈을 계획적으로 사용할 수 있다.

You can plan your money by organizing the history of your daily spendings.

내역
breakdown

지출 내역
spending history

통화 내역
call history

사용 내역
details of use

입금 내역
deposit breakdown/history

07 눈을 붙이다

동 get some sleep, take a little nap

피곤할 때는 무리해서 일하는 것보다 잠깐 눈을 붙였다가 다시 시작하는 것이 효율적이다.

When you are tired, it is more efficient to take a little nap and then start again than to work too hard.

08 당사자

명 the person/party directly involved

이 문제는 당사자가 직접 나서서 해결해야 한다.

This issue must be resolved by the parties themselves.

09 덤벼들다

동 to lunge for/strike at/attack

그는 화가 나서 앞뒤 안 가리고 형에게 덤벼들었다.

He got so angry that he lunged to attack his brother without hesitation

DAY 11 ★★

10 동력

명 driving force/power source

이번 훈련이 우리 팀이 우승을 할 수 있는 동력이 되었다.

This training was the driving force for our team to win the championship.

동력 장치 power unit

11 딛다

동 step on, overcome

이제는 슬픔을 딛고 일어나야 할 때다.

It is time to overcome sadness and rise up.

12 매기다

동 score, set/determine something

말하기 평가는 두 명의 선생님이 점수를 매길 것입니다.

The speaking section will be scored by two teachers.

13 명상

명 meditation

눈을 감고 음악을 들으면서 명상을 하면 정신 건강에 좋다.

It is good for your mental health to meditate by closing your eyes and listening to music.

14 문헌

명 literature/references

조선 시대 문헌을 참고해 그 당시 복장에 대한 정보를 얻을 수 있었다.

It was possible to obtain information on the attire of the Joseon Dynasty by referring to the literature of that time.

15 반려견

명 pet dog

공동주택에서 반려견을 기르는 사람들이 늘어나면서 많은 문제가 발생하였다.

Many problems have arisen as the number of people raising dogs in apartment houses increase.

반려동물 pet animals 반려자 companion

16 번식하다

동 to reporduce/breed/flourish

이곳은 습도가 높아 세균이 번식하기에 최적의 장소이다.

This place has high humidity, making it the perfect location for bacteria to flourish.

관련어

번식 breeding/reproduction　　번식되다 being bred
번식시키다 to breed

17 법안

명 bill

DAY 11 ★★

1인 가구의 주거 정책을 위한 법안이 통과되었다.

A bill for single-person households' housing policy was passed.

법안을 검토하다 to review the bill

18 생태계

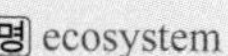

명 ecosystem

지구온난화가 생태계의 변화를 가져왔다.

Global warming brought a change to the ecosystem

생태계를 보호하다 to protect the ecosystem

19 언급

명 comment/reference

목격자임에도 불구하고 사건에 대해 언급을 회피하였다.

Despite being a witness, he declined to comment on the incident.

언급하다 to refer to/mention/comment
언급되다 refered to mentioned

20 연료

명 fuel

지구 온난화의 주범인 화석 연료를 대신할 수 있는 대체 연료를 개발 중이다.

Alternative fuels are being developed to replace fossil fuels, the main culprit of global warming.

21 예산

명 budget

서울시는 예산 부족으로 도로 신설 계획을 연기하기로 했다.

The Seoul Metropolitan Government decided to postpone its plan to build new roads due to a budget deficit.

22 위화감

명 sense of incompatibility

학교 안에서 학생들의 경제적 차이로 인해 위화감이 조성되는 경우가 있다.

There are some cases when financial differences between students can create a sense of incompatibility within the school.

23 유효

명 valid/available

토픽 같은 어학 자격증은 대부분 유효 기간이 2년이다.

Most language certificates such as TOPIK are valid for two years.

유효하다 to be valid

24 이념

명 ideology/ideals/philosophy

1950년에 일어난 한국 전쟁은 이념의 차이 때문에 발생한 전쟁이다.

The 1950 Korean War was a war caused by ideological differences.

이념적 ideaological

다양한 이념을 부르는 말을 정리해 두세요.
Review the words that call for various ideologies.
자본주의(capitalism), 사회주의(socialism), 공산주의(communism), 국가주의(nationalism), 민주주의(democracy) 등.

25 이산화탄소

명 carbon dioxide

전세계가 이산화탄소 배출을 줄이기 위해 노력해 나가야 한다.

The world should put effort into lowering carbon dioxide emissions.

26 인공위성

명 satellite

이 사진은 인공위성에서 지구의 모습을 찍은 사진입니다.

This picture is the view of Earth from a satellite.

인공위성을 쏘다 to launch a satellite

27 자금

명 fund

그는 사업을 위한 자금을 마련하고 있다고 했다.

He said he was raising funds for the business.

결혼 자금 marriage fund　　주택 자금 housing fund

28 재능

명 talent

우리 학교에는 음악에 재능이 있는 학생들이 많이 있다.

There are many musically-talented students in our school

29 저해

명 hindrance/impairment (to)

지나친 음주는 숙면의 저해 요인 중 하나이다.

Excessive drinking is one of the factors that impair sleep.

저해하다 to hinder/impair　　저해되다 to be hindered/impaired

30 조작하다

동 to operate/create, to forge/manipulate

이 기계를 조작할 수 있는 사람은 우리 회사에 두 명뿐이다.

There are only two people in our company who can operate this machine.

조작 fabrication/invention

31 주장하다

동 to claim/assert

그 사람은 지갑을 훔친 건 자신이 아니라고 주장했다.

That person claimed that he did not steal the wallet

32 집단

명 group

집단에 의해 이루어지는 왕따는 피해 학생에서 큰 상처를 남긴다.

Group bullying leaves a big scar on the life of the victim student.

집단적 collective

33 통과되다

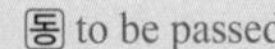
동 to be passed

음주 운전에 대한 처벌을 강화하는 법안이 국회에서 통과되었다.

A bill to tighten punishment for drunk driving has been passed by the National Assembly.

통과하다 to pass

34 허술하다

형 to be flimsy/poor/weak/lax

이런 허술한 논문으로 박사 학위를 받았다고요?

You received a doctorate with this poor thesis?

35 희생하다

동 to sacrifice

우리 부모님은 평생 자식을 위해 희생해 오셨다.

Our parents have been sacrificing for their children all their lives.

TOPIK에서 혼동하기 쉬운 단어

다의어 Polysemy

딛다

❶ 어려운 상황을 이겨 내다

예 이제는 슬픔을 딛고 일어나야 할 때다.

It is time to overcome sadness and rise up.

❷ 발을 올려놓거나 누르다

예 등산하다가 다리를 다쳤는데 땅을 딛고 일어서기 힘들다.

I hurt my leg while hiking, so it's hard to stand up by stepping from the ground.

DAY 11 ★★

반의어 Antonym

간접 indirect ↔ 직접 direct, (one)self

예 독서를 통해서 간접 경험의 기회를 얻을 수 있다.

You can get a chance to experience indirectly through reading.

예 내 친구는 다른 사람에게 일을 맡기는 것보다 자신이 직접 하는 것을 좋아한다.

My friend likes to do things himself rather than entrusting others with his job.

유의어 Synonym

덤벼들다 to lunge for/strike at/attack ≒ 덤비다

예 그는 화가 나서 앞뒤 안 가리고 형에게 덤벼들었다.

그는 화가 나서 앞뒤 안 가리고 형에게 덤볐다.

He got so angry that he lunged to attack his brother without hesitation.

복습해 보세요

자연스러운 문장이 되도록 완성해 보세요.
Try to complete the sentence in a natural way.

1. 여행을 하다 보면 다양한 사람들을 만남으로써 ㄱㅁ을 넓힐 기회가 많아진다.
   As you travel, you have more opportunities to broaden your horizon by meeting various people.

2. 말하기 평가는 두 명의 선생님이 점수를 ㅁㄱ 것입니다.
   The speaking section will be scored by two teachers.

3. 제품에 써 있는 ㄱㅇ을 잘 확인하고 구매해야 한다.
   You need to check the price on the product carefully before purchase.

4. 이곳은 습도가 높아 세균이 ㅂㅅㅎ기에 최적의 장소이다.
   This place has high humidity, making it the perfect location for bacteria to flourish.

5. 우리 부모님은 평생 자식을 위해 ㅎㅅ해 오셨다.
   Our parents have been sacrificing for their children all their lives.

다음 빈 칸에 알맞은 단어를 〈보기〉에서 골라 쓰세요.
Choose the appropriate word from <Example> to fill in the blanks below.

〈보기〉

a. 과감할 b. 간접 c. 재능 d. 위화감

6. 독서를 통해서 (　　　) 경험의 기회를 얻을 수 있다.
   You can get a chance to experience indirectly through reading.

7. 신중한 것도 좋지만 새로운 일을 할 때는 (　　　) 필요도 있다.
   It's good to be cautious, but when trying new things, you need to sometimes be daring.

8. 학교 안에서 학생들의 경제적 차이로 인해 (　　　)이/가 조성되는 경우가 있다.
   There are some cases when financial differences between students can create a sense of incompatibility within the school.

9. 우리 학교에는 음악에 (　　　)이/가 있는 학생들이 많이 있다.
   There are many musically-talented students in our school.

정답

1. 견문 2. 매길 3. 금액 4. 번식하 5. 희생 6. b 7. a 8. d 9. c

DAY 12

확인해 보세요

빨간 시트지로 가리고 단어의 뜻을 알면, □에 ✓ 해 보세요.

After covering up the words with red cover, please check(✓) the box (□) when you know the meaning of the word.

□ 01 간주하다 to regard/consider	□ 13 명성 fame	□ 25 인공적 artificial
□ 02 결합 union/combination	□ 14 물끄러미 to peer/gaze	□ 26 자급자족 self-sufficient
□ 03 계발 improvement	□ 15 반론 rebuttal	□ 27 재정적 financial
□ 04 과대평가 overestimation	□ 16 번창 prosperity, flourish	□ 28 적발하다 to catch/uncover
□ 05 급등 jump, sharp rise	□ 17 베테랑 veteran/expert	□ 29 조장하다 encourage/aggravate
□ 06 내쫓다 kick out	□ 18 서먹하다 to feel awkward/uncomfortable	□ 30 주최 host
□ 07 눈짓 look/glance	□ 19 언론 press/media	□ 31 차단하다 to block
□ 08 당선 election	□ 20 예상하다 to predict/expect	□ 32 터뜨리다 to pop/burst
□ 09 덮치다 to hit/strike	□ 21 욕구 desire/want	□ 33 투덜거리다 to complain
□ 10 동문서답 an irrelevant answer	□ 22 유교 Confucianism	□ 34 홀가분하다 to be lighthearted/carefree
□ 11 따갑다 sting/prick	□ 23 육지 land/mainland	□ 35 희한하다 to be rare/exotic
□ 12 매달리다 to cling/hang (on)	□ 24 이상 기후 abnormal climates	

DAY 12

 관련어 are the words that appeared in the former tests, and you may get a higher grade if you study them together.

01 간주하다

동 to regard/consider/deem

일부의 의견을 다수의 의견으로 간주해서는 안 된다.

The opinion of some should not be regarded as the opinion of the majority.

간주되다 to be considered

02 결합

명 union/combination

결혼은 두 사람의 정신적, 육체적 결합을 의미한다.

Marriage is the spiritual and physical union of two people.

결합하다 to unite/combine 결합되다 to be united

03 계발

명 improvement

교사는 학생의 잠재 능력 계발을 위한 교육을 해야 한다.

Education to improve student's potential talents should be taught by teachers.

'계발'과 '개발'은 어떻게 다를까요? '계발'은 '잠재된 능력을 발견해서 발전시킬 때' 사용할 수 있습니다.

What is the difference between '계발' and '개발'? '계발' can be used when 'discovering and improving a potential ability.'

예 아이들의 상상력을 계발해야 한다.
We need to improve the creativity of children.

'개발'은 '새로운 능력이나 지식을 발전시킬 때' 또는 '산업'이나 '자연 자원'과도 자주 쓰입니다.

'개발' is used when 'developing a new ability' or developing an 'industry' and 'natural resources.'

예 여가 시간에 자기 개발을 위해 노력해야 성공할 수 있다.
You can only succeed if you strive for self-improvement during your spare time.
신제품/새로운 산업을 개발하고 있다.
We are developing new products/new industries.

04 과대평가

명 overestimation

나에 대한 사람들의 과대평가가 부담스럽다.

I am burdened by people's overestimations of me.

과대평가를 하다 to overestimate

반) 과소평가 to underestimate

05 급등

명 jump, sharp rise, skyrocket

아파트 값 급등에 집 없는 서민들의 한숨 소리가 커지고 있다.

The sighs of ordinary people without homeownership are growing due to skyrocketing apartment prices.

급등하다 to jump/soar/rise

반) 급락 crash/plunge/plummet

06 내쫓다

동 kick out

나쁜 형 놀부는 착한 동생 흥부를 집에서 내쫓았다.

The evil brother Nolbu kicked the good brother Heungbu out of the house. (reference to a Korean folktale)

07 눈짓

명 look/glance/wink

그 사람은 나에게 아무 말도 하지 말라는 눈짓을 보냈다.

He gave me a glance not to say anything.

눈짓을 보내다 to send a glance

08 당선

명 election

대통령 당선 이후 우리 사회에 새로운 분위기가 형성되고 있습니다.

Since the election of the president, a new atmosphere has been forming in our society.

당선 작품 elected/selected work

당선되다 to be elected

DAY 12 ★★

09 덮치다

동 to hit/strike/sweep/attack

내게 불행이 덮쳤을 때 주변 사람들의 도움으로 헤쳐나올 수 있었다.

When misfortune struck me, I was able to get through it with the help of those around me.

10 동문서답

명 an irrelevant answer

언제 오냐는 질문에 날씨가 좋다고 동문서답하였다.

When asked about when I am going to arrive, I gave an irrelevant answer by replying that the weather is nice.

11 따갑다

형 sting/prick/hot/harsh/smart

그 배우는 뜨거운 인기와 따가운 비난을 동시에 받았다.

The actor received both hot popularity and stinging criticism.

12 매달리다

동 to cling/hang (on), to stick to, to beg

이제 와서 여자 친구에게 울며불며 매달려도 소용없다.

It's no use crying and clinging to your girlfriend now.

13 명성

명 fame

'기생충'을 계기로 한국 영화가 세계적으로 명성을 떨치고 있다.

Korean films are gaining worldwide fame with 'Parasite'.

14 물끄러미

부 to peer/gaze

아이의 자는 얼굴을 한참 동안 물끄러미 들여다보았다.

I peered into the child's sleeping face for a long time.

15 반론

명 rebuttal

변호사는 검사의 주장에 대해 반론을 제기하였다.

The lawyer provided a rebuttal to the prosecutor's claims.

16 번창

명 prosperity, flourish, success

사람들은 사업의 번창을 기원하며 고사를 지낸다.

People pray for the prosperity of their business and pass the ceremony.

번창하다 to flourish

17 베테랑

명 veteran/expert

수술 경험이 많은 베테랑이니까 걱정하지 마세요.

I'm a veteran of surgery, so don't worry.

18 서먹하다

형 to feel awkward/uncomfortable

취업한 지 얼마 안 돼서 아직 사람들과의 관계가 서먹하다.

It hasn't been long since I got the job, so my relationship with people is still a little awkward.

19 언론

명 press/media

정부는 언론의 자유를 보장해야 한다.

The government must ensure freedom of the press.

언론사 news media/jouralism   언론인 journalist/reporter

20 예상하다

동 to predict/expect

궂은 날씨 때문에 택배가 예상했던 날짜보다 늦게 도착했다.

Due to the bad weather, the package arrived later than expected.

예상 prediction

DAY 12 ★★

21 욕구

명 desire/want/craving/drive

그 광고는 소비자들의 구매 욕구를 자극하고 있다.

The advertisement is stimulating consumers' desire to purchase.

22 유교

명 Confucianism

조상들을 위해 제사를 지내는 것은 유교의 전통 중 하나이다.

Having a ritual for ancestors is one of the Confucian traditions.

23 육지

명 land/mainland/shore

섬을 육지와 연결하기 위한 다리 공사가 진행 중이다.

A bridge is being built to connect the island to the mainland.

24 이상 기후

명 abnormal climates

지구 온난화로 인해 세계 곳곳에서 이상 기후가 나타나고 있다.

Due to global warming, abnormal climates are appearing all over the world.

25 인공적

명 artificial

이 음식은 인공적인 맛이 너무 강해서 별로였다.

I didn't like this food because the artificial taste was too strong.

26 자급자족

명 self-sufficient

시골에 살면서 채소는 자급자족이 가능했지만 채소를 제외한 다른 먹거리는 다 구입해야 했다.

Living in the countryside, vegetables were self-sufficient, but they had to buy everything except vegetables.

자급자족하다 to be self-sufficient

27 재정적

명 financial

저는 대학원까지 부모님께 재정적 지원을 받았어요.

I received financial support from my parents all the way to graduate school.

재정적 부담 financial burden

28 적발하다

동 to catch/uncover

경찰이 불법으로 영업하던 술집들을 적발했다.

The police caught illegally operating bars.

적발 exposure　　적발되다 to be exposed/uncovered

DAY 12 ★★

29 조장하다

동 encourage/aggravate

정부의 이번 부동산 정책이 오히려 부동산 투기를 조장하고 있다.

The government's real estate policy is actually encouraging real estate speculation.

조장 incitement, instigation

30 주최

명 host

이번 축제에서는 주최 측이 생수를 무료로 제공하기로 했다.

At the festival, host organizers decided to provide free bottled water.

주최하다 to host

31 차단하다

동 to block

더운 여름에는 뜨거운 햇빛을 차단할 수 있게 커튼으로 창문을 가리는 것이 좋다.

In the hot summer, it is good to cover the windows with a curtain in order to block off the hot sunlight.

차단되다 to be blocked　　차단시키다 to block

32 터뜨리다

동 to pop/burst/explode/blossom

선생님이 무섭게 혼을 내자 학생은 울음을 터뜨렸다.

The student bursted into tears when the teacher scolded him in a scary manner.

33 투덜거리다

동 to complain

아이는 자기가 좋아하는 반찬이 하나도 없다고 투덜거렸다.

The child complained that there weren't any side dishes that he liked.

34 홀가분하다

형 to be lighthearted/carefree

중요한 프로젝트가 끝나서 홀가분한 마음으로 여행을 떠났다.

I went on the trip with a carefree heart because an important project was done.

35 희한하다

형 to be rare/exotic

전화기를 처음 발명했을 때 많은 사람들은 희한한 물건이라며 신기해했다.

When the telephone was first invented, many people were amazed, saying that is was an exotic item.

TOPIK에서 혼동하기 쉬운 단어

다의어 Polysemy

터뜨리다

❶ 감정을 크게 보여 주다

예 선생님이 무섭게 혼을 내자 학생은 울음을 터뜨렸다.

The student bursted into tears when the teacher scolded him in a scary manner.

❷ 물건이 부서지다

예 운동회 때 풍선을 터뜨리는 게임을 했다.

We played a game of popping balloons during the sports days.

DAY 12 ★★

반의어 Antonym

과대평가 overestimation ↔ 과소평가 underestimation

예 나에 대한 사람들의 과대평가가 부담스럽다.

I am burdened by people's overestimations of me.

예 소극적인 사람들은 자기의 능력을 실제보다 과소평가하는 경향이 있다.

Shy people tend to underestimate their abilities than they really are.

유의어 Synonym

내쫓다 kick out ≒ 쫓아내다

예 나쁜 형 놀부는 착한 동생 흥부를 집에서 내쫓았다.

나쁜 형 놀부는 착한 동생 흥부를 집에서 쫓아냈다.

The evil brother Nolbu kicked the good brother Heungbu out of the house. (reference to a Ko rean folktale)

복습해 보세요

서로 어울리는 단어를 찾아 연결해 보세요.
Find words that go with each other and connect them.

1. 눈짓	a. 따갑다
2. 햇볕	b. 차단하다
3. 재정적	c. 보내다
4. 마음	d. 부담
5. 소음	e. 홀가분하다

자연스러운 문장이 되도록 완성해 보세요.
Try to complete the sentence in a natural way.

6. 교사는 학생의 잠재 능력 ㄱㅂ을 위한 교육을 해야 한다.
Education to improve student's potential talents should be taught by teachers.

7. 아파트 값 ㄱㄷ에 집 없는 서민들의 한숨 소리가 커지고 있다.
The sighs of ordinary people without homeownership are growing due to skyrocketing apartment prices.

8. 이제 와서 여자 친구에게 울며불며 ㅁㄷㄹㄷ 소용없다.
It's no use crying and clinging to your girlfriend now.

9. 궂은 날씨 때문에 택배가 ㅇㅅㅎㄷ 날짜보다 늦게 도착했다.
Due to the bad weather, the package arrived later than expected.

10. 아이는 자기가 좋아하는 반찬이 하나도 없다고 ㅌㄷㄱㄹㄷ.
The child complained that there weren't any side dishes that he liked.

정답

1. c 2. a 3. d 4. e 5. b 6. 계발 7. 급등 8. 매달려도 9. 예상했던 10. 투덜거렸다

DAY 13

확인해 보세요

빨간 시트지로 가리고 단어의 뜻을 알면, □에 ✓ 해 보세요.

After covering up the words with red cover, please check(✓) the box (□) when you know the meaning of the word.

□ 01	갈등	conflict	□ 13	명심하다	keep in mind	□ 25	이성적	rational
□ 02	경기	economy	□ 14	물량	supply/volume	□ 26	인권	human rights
□ 03	공산주의	communism	□ 15	반목	hostility/feud	□ 27	자립	self-reliance
□ 04	과도하다	excessive	□ 16	벤처	venture	□ 28	재촉하다	to urge
□ 05	급속	rapidity, swiftness	□ 17	성취하다	to achieve/ accompany	□ 29	적정	optimum
□ 06	냉담하다	to be cold	□ 18	얼떨떨하다	to be dazed/ bewildered	□ 30	조정	adjustment
□ 07	눈치를 보다	to be self-conscious, to read the room	□ 19	예외	exception	□ 31	중소	small and medium
□ 08	대거	in a group, in great numbers	□ 20	우선순위	priority	□ 32	차분하다	to be calm
□ 09	도	limit, degree	□ 21	우여곡절	complications, twist and turns	□ 33	투표권	right to vote
□ 10	동반	company, together	□ 22	원자력	nuclear power	□ 34	허위	falsehood
□ 11	딱하다	pitiful, sad	□ 23	유권자	voters	□ 35	힘겹다	hard, difficult
□ 12	매듭	knot/tie	□ 24	윤리	ethics			

DAY 13

  are the words that appeared in the former tests, and you may get a higher grade if you study them together.

01 갈등

명 conflict

인간 관계에서 갈등이 생기면 대화를 통해서 푸는 것이 바람직하다.

When you have a conflict in relationships, it is best to resolve them through dialogue.

- 갈등 conflict
  - 세대 갈등 generation conflict
  - 노사 갈등 labor-management conflict, high-income conflict
  - 고부 갈등 conflict between mother in law and daughter in law
  - 지역 갈등 regional conflict

02 경기

명 economy

우리 나라의 경기가 회복되어 실업률이 감소하고 있다.

Our country's economy is recovering, so the unemployment rate is decreasing.

경기 침체 economic recession　불경기 recession
호황 economic boom　불황 recession/depression bust

03 공산주의

명 communism

대학 입학 후 공산주의에 대한 책을 읽게 되었다.

After entering college, I read a book about communism.

공산주의자 communist

04 과도하다

형 excessive

입시 위주의 교육에서는 학생들 사이의 과도한 경쟁이 문제가 된다.

In an education system focused on entrance exams, excessive competition among students is a problem.

05 급속

명 rapidity, swiftness, fast speed

상하기 쉬운 생선을 급속 냉동하면 맛이 변하지 않게 오래 보관할 수 있다.

Quick-freezing perishable fish can keep the taste unchanged for a long time.

급속하다 to be rapid/swift

06 냉담하다

형 to be cold

나를 향한 그 사람의 냉담한 태도에 상처를 받지 않을 수 없었다.

I couldn't help being hurt by that person's cold attitude toward me.

07 눈치를 보다

동 to be self-conscious, to read the room, to study other's reaction

졸업 후 1년이 넘도록 취직을 못해서 부모님 눈치를 보고 있다.

I am self-conscious around my parents because I have not been able to find work for more than a year since graduation.

08 대거

부 in a group, in great numbers

이번 사건을 해결하기 위해서 능력이 있는 검사를 대거 투입했다.

A large number of competent prosecutors were sent in to solve this case.

09 도

명 limit, degree, line

SNS를 사용하는 사람들의 악플이 도가 지나친 듯하다.

It seems that the malicious comments from people using SNS have crossed the line.

도를 넘어서다 go too far

10 동반

명 company, together

최근 집값과 전셋값이 동반 상승하였다.

Recently, house prices and lease prices have risen together.

부부 동반 go together as married couple

DAY 13 ★★

11 딱하다

형 pitiful, sad

지진으로 인해 피해를 입은 사람들의 딱한 사연이 소개되었다.

The pitiful stories of people affected by the earthquake were read.

12 매듭

명 knot/tie

내일까지 이번 프로젝트의 매듭을 지어야 한다.

I have to tie up this project by tomorrow.

매듭을 풀다 untie a knot

13 명심하다

동 keep in mind

창업을 하기 전에 명심해야 할 것은 현실을 직시하는 것이다.

Before you start a business, you have to keep in mind that you face reality.

14 물량

명 supply/volume

공장 직원들이 갑자기 퇴직하면서 주문 물량을 다 만들 수가 없다.

We cannot make all of the order volume since the factory workers suddently quit.

물량 확보 secure material

15 반목

명 hostility/feud/antagonism

그 가수는 소속사와의 반목으로 현재 모든 활동이 중지되었다.

The singer has now suspended all activities due to a feud with the agency.

반목하다 be hostile

16 벤처

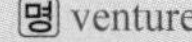

명 venture

유망한 벤처 기업에 투자할 기회를 얻었다.

I earned an opportunity to invest in a famous venture company.

17 성취하다

동 to achieve/accompany

그는 평생 노력하며 기도하더니 드디어 소원을 성취했다.

He worked hard all his life and prayed, and finally achieved his wish.

성취감 sense of achievement　　성취도 achievement level

18 얼떨떨하다

형 to be dazed/bewildered

그 아이돌 그룹은 음원 차트 1위에 오른 것이 아직 얼떨떨하다고 했다.

The idol group said that they were still dazed that they reached number one on the music charts.

DAY 13 ★★

19 예외

명 exception

법은 예외 없이 모든 사람에게 적용되어야 한다.

The law should apply to everyone without exception.

예외적 exceptional

20 우선순위

명 priority

일을 시작하기 전에 우선순위를 정하는 것이 효율적이다.

It is efficient to set priorities before starting work.

21 우여곡절

명 complications, twist and turns/ups and downs

이번 거래는 취소되는 듯 보였지만 우여곡절 끝에 우리 회사가 계약을 할 수 있었다.

This deal seemed to be canceled, but after many twists and turns, our company was able to sign the contract.

22 원자력

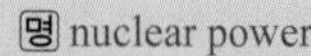

명 nuclear power

원자력 발전은 화석 에너지를 대체할 수 있지만 방사능 유출의 위험이 있다.

Nuclear power can replace fossil energy, but there is a risk of radiation leakage.

출제 경향 how this word appears in the test

에너지와 관련된 문제가 자주 출제되고 있습니다.
화석 에너지, 원자력 에너지, 신재생 에너지 등의 종류를 꼭 확인하세요.
Energy-related issues are frequently asked.
Be sure to check the types of fossil energy, nuclear energy, and renewable energy.

23 유권자

명 voters

서울 시장 후보들은 유권자들의 마음을 얻기 위해 여러 공약을 발표하였다.

Seoul mayoral candidates have made several promises to win voters' hearts.

24 윤리

명 ethics

인터넷 사용 윤리에 대한 교육이 필요하다

Education on Internet usage ethics is necessary.

윤리적 ethical

25 이성적

명 rational

감정적으로 반응하지 말고 이성적으로 생각해 보자.

Let's think rationally instead of reacting emotionally,

26 인권

명 human rights

유명 아동 보호 기관의 인권 탄압 실태가 밝혀져 충격을 주고 있다.

The revelation of human rights abuses by famous child protection agencies is shocking.

27 자립

명 self-reliance

그는 고등학교를 졸업하자마자 자립을 했다.

He became self-reliant as soon as he graduated from high school.

자립적 independent　자립하다 to become independent

28 재촉하다

동 to urge

은행으로부터 빌린 돈을 갚으라고 재촉하는 전화가 계속 와서 생활이 엉망이 되었다.

My life was ruined by constant calls from the bank urging me to pay back the money I borrowed.

재촉을 받다 to be rushed　재촉에 시달리다 to suffer under a rush

29 적정

명 optimum

여름철 실내 적정 온도는 26도라고 한다.

The optimum indoor temperature in summer is 26 degrees celcius.

적정하다 appropriate/fair/moderate

30 조정

명 adjustment

모두가 함께 만나기 위해서는 모임 시간 조정이 필요하다.

Meeting times need to be adjusted for everyone to meet together.

조정하다 to adjust　조정되다 to be adjusted

31 중소

명 small and medium

이 책에서는 한국에서 잘 알려지지 않은 유럽의 중소 도시를 소개하고 있다.

This book introduces small and medium-sized European cities that are not well known in Korea.

중소 기업 small/medium company

32 차분하다

형 to be calm

교통 사고가 났는데 박 선생님은 당황하지 않고 차분하게 문제를 해결했다.

Even though there was a car accident, Mr. Park calmly solved the problem without panicking.

33 투표권

명 right to vote

소중한 투표권을 행사하기 위해 투표소로 향하는 중이다.

They are heading to the polling place to exercise their precious voting rights.

34 허위

명 falsehood

의사는 그 가수의 부탁을 받고 허위로 진단서를 작성했다.

The doctor falsely filled out a medical certificate at the request of the singer.

허위 신고 false report

35 힘겹다

형 hard, difficult, tough, arduous

오랜만에 등산을 하는 김부장님은 산길을 힘겹게 걸어 올라갔다.

Senior Manager Kim, who has not hiked for a long time, struggled to climb the mountain path.

TOPIK에서 혼동하기 쉬운 단어

다의어 Polysemy

경기

❶ 경제 상황

예 우리 나라의 경기가 회복되어 실업률이 감소하고 있다.

Our country's economy is recovering, so the unemployment rate is decreasing.

❷ 운동 등의 대회

예 이번 월드컵 경기에서 우리나라가 이겼으면 좋겠다.

I hope Korea wins this World Cup match.

DAY 13 ★★

반의어 Antonym

이성적 rational ↔ **감정적** emotional

예 그는 언제나 냉철하게 생각하는 이성적인 사람이다.

He is a rational man who always thinks coldly.

예 감정적으로 반응하지 말고 차분하게 생각해야 한다.

Instead of thinking emotionally, you need to think calmly.

유의어 Synonym

성취하다 to achieve ≒ **이루다**

예 그는 평생 노력하며 기도하더니 드디어 소원을 성취했다.

그는 평생 노력하며 기도하더니 드디어 소원을 이루었다.

He worked hard all his life and prayed, and finally achieved his wish.

복습해 보세요

자연스러운 문장이 되도록 둘 중에서 알맞은 단어를 고르세요.

Try to complete the sentence in a natural way by selecting the correct word out of the two.

1. 인간 관계에서 (a. 갈등 / b. 경기)이/가 생기면 대화를 통해서 푸는 것이 바람직하다.

   When you have a conflict in relationships, it is best to resolve them through dialogue.

2. 공장 직원들이 갑자기 퇴직하면서 주문 (a. 동반 / b. 물량)을/를 다 만들 수가 없다.

   We cannot make all of the order volume since the factory workers suddently quit.

3. 법은 (a. 매듭 / b. 예외) 없이 모든 사람에게 적용되어야 한다.

   The law should apply to everyone without exception.

4. 인터넷 사용 (a. 윤리 / b. 반목)에 대한 교육이 필요하다.

   Education on Internet usage ethics is necessary.

5. 의사는 그 가수의 부탁을 받고 (a. 도 / b. 허위)(으)로 진단서를 작성했다.

   The doctor falsely filled out a medical certificate at the request of the singer.

서로 어울리는 단어를 찾아 연결해 보세요.

Find words that go with each other and connect them.

6. 경쟁 •	• a. 보다
7. 눈치 •	• b. 성취하다
8. 딱하다 •	• c. 과도하다
9. 소원 •	• d. 차분하다
10. 성격 •	• e. 사연

정답

1.a 2.b 3.b 4.a 5.b 6.c 7.a 8.e 9.b 10.d

DAY 14

확인해 보세요

빨간 시트지로 가리고 단어의 뜻을 알면, □에 ✓ 해 보세요.

After covering up the words with red cover, please check(✓) the box (□) when you know the meaning of the word.

□ 01	감당하다	to handle	□ 12	때우다	to fill/patch	□ 24	유기견	abandoned dogs
□ 02	경고하다	to warn	□ 13	매료시키다	to captivate	□ 25	융통성	flexibility
□ 03	공평하다	to be fair	□ 14	명예	reputation/ honor	□ 26	이열치열	fight fire with fire
□ 04	과소평가	underestimation	□ 15	물려받다	to inherit/ succeed	□ 27	인내심	patience
□ 05	과언	exaggeration	□ 16	반박하다	to refute	□ 28	자수성가	self-made
□ 06	냉혹하다	cold, harsh	□ 17	벼르다	to eagerly wait	□ 29	재충전하다	recharge
□ 07	뉘우치다	to be remorseful, to repent	□ 18	세균	bacteria	□ 30	적합하다	to be appropriate/ suitable for
□ 08	다그치다	to reprimand	□ 19	얼버무리다	to speak vaguely	□ 31	조치하다	to take measures/ actions
□ 09	대견하다	to be proud of	□ 20	여파	aftermath	□ 32	중시하다	to consider important
□ 10	도달	arrival, reaching	□ 21	예측하다	to predict	□ 33	차일피일	constantly procrastinate
□ 11	동병상련	You can have compassion/ understanding for another when you experience the same situation as them	□ 22	우열을 가리다	place above	□ 34	파격적	shocking, unconventional
			□ 23	운행	operation	□ 35	헌법	constitution

DAY 14

 are the words that appeared in the former tests, and you may get a higher grade if you study them together.

01 감당하다

동 to handle

이번 일을 감당할 수 있는 유능한 인재를 찾아야 한다.

We need to find a capable individual who can handle this job.

감당 handle, manage

02 경고하다

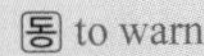

많은 경제학자들은 머지 않아 경제 위기가 올 수 있다고 경고하고 있다.

Many economists warn that economic depression might be just around the corner.

경고 warning

03 공평하다

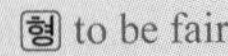

첫째 아이라고 해서 동생에게 모든 것을 양보해야 하는 것은 공평하지 않다.

It is unfair to demand that the firstborn yields everything to the younger sibling just because he is older.

반) 불공평하다 unfair

04 과소평가

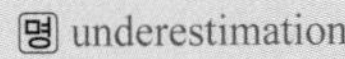

소극적인 사람들은 자기의 능력을 실제보다 과소평가하는 경향이 있다.

Shy people tend to underestimate their abilities than they really are.

과소평가를 하다 to underestimate

반) 과대평가 overestimation

05 과언

명 exaggeration

휴대폰은 일상생활에서 없어서는 안 되는 물건이라고 해도 과언이 아니다.

It is not an exaggeration to say that phones are a necessity to daily life.

이 단어는 보통 '-다고 해도 과언이 아니다'의 형태로 사용해요. 그리고 같이 사용하는 표현은 과장된 표현을 사용하는 것이 자연스러워요.
This word is usually used in the form of '–다고 해도 과언이 아니다'. And it is natural to use exaggerated expressions for expressions we use together.

착한 내 친구는 날개 없는 천사라고 해도 과언이 아니다.
It is no exaggeration to say that my friend who is so kind is an angel without wings.

06 냉혹하다

형 cold, harsh

능력 있는 사람만 살아 남을 수 있는 냉혹한 현실을 인정해야 한다.

We have to admit the harsh reality that only capable people can survive.

07 뉘우치다

동 to be remorseful, to repent

아이는 아버지에게 야단 맞았지만 잘못을 뉘우치는 기색이 없었다.

The child was scolded by his father, but there was no sign of remorse.

08 다그치다

동 to reprimand

아이의 잘못을 무조건 다그쳐서는 안 된다.

One shouldn't always reprimand a child.

09 대견하다

형 to be proud of

힘든 위기를 잘 이겨낸 선수들이 대견하다.

I am proud of the players to overcame this hard time.

DAY 14 ★★

10 도달

명 arrival, reaching

코로나 백신을 맞아도 당분간 집단 면역 도달은 어려울 것이라고 한다.

It is said that it will be hard to reach herd immunity even if covid vaccines are given out.

관련어 도달하다 to reach/arrive at

11 동병상련

명 You can have compassion/understanding for another when you experience the same situation as them

동병상련이라고 같은 처지에 처해 봐야 상대방을 이해할 수 있다.

Just as the saying goes, you can only understand the other person when you are in the same situation as them.

12 때우다

동 to fill/patch

매일 그렇게 대충 끼니를 때우다가는 건강에 문제가 생길 수도 있다.

If you fill up your meals roughly every day, you might have health problems.

13 매료시키다

동 to captivate

그 가수의 아름다운 목소리가 세계인을 매료시켰다.

The singer's beautiful voice captivated the world.

매료되다 to be captivated

14 명예

명 reputation/honor

다른 사람의 명예를 훼손하면 고소를 당할 수도 있다.

Defaming others' reputation may cause you to get sued.

15 물려받다

동 to inherit/succeed/take over (receive inheritance)

그는 할아버지로부터 유산을 물려받아 관리하고 있다.

He has been taking care of the inheritance that he received from his grandfather.

16 반박하다

㉬ to refute

이번 사고가 자동차 자체의 결함이 아니냐는 의문에 자동차 회사가 즉시 반박했다.

The automaker immediately refuted the question of whether the accident caused by a defect in the car itself.

반박 rebuttal　　반박문 refuting statement

반박 기사 refutation article

DAY 14 ★★

17 벼르다

㉬ to eagerly wait

그 식당이 맛집이라길래 벼르고 벼르다 다녀왔는데 그저 그랬어요.

I eagerly looked foward to that restaurant because it was famous for its taste but it turned out to be mediocre.

18 세균

㉭ bacteria

유통기한이 지난 재료에서 세균이 검출되었다.

Bateria was found in the expired ingredients.

19 얼버무리다

㉬ to speak vaguely

면접을 잘하려면 질문에 얼버무리지 말고 정확하게 대답해야 한다.

To do well in your interview, you have to answer clearly instead of speaking vaguely to the question.

20 여파

㉭ aftermath

태풍의 여파로 바다에는 아직 높은 파도가 일고 있다.

There are still high waves in the sea from the aftermath of the typhoon.

21 예측하다

㉬ to predict

경제학자들은 올해 우리나라의 경제 상황을 낙관적으로 예측했다.

Economists predicted optimistically about Korea's economic situation this year.

예측 prediction

22 우열을 가리다

동 place above

두 작품은 모두 우열을 가리기 힘들 정도로 뛰어나다.

The two works are both exceptional that it is hard to place one above the other.

23 운행

명 operation

연휴에는 지하철 운행 시간이 변경될 수 있다.

During the holidays, the subway's hours of operation can be changed.

운행하다 to operate 운행되다 to be operated

24 유기견

명 abandoned/homeless dogs

무리를 지어 길을 떠도는 유기견들이 사회적인 문제가 되고 있다.

Abandoned dogs wandering the streets in groups are becoming a social problem.

유기 동물 abandoned animal 유기하다 to abandon

25 융통성

명 flexibility

김 과장은 일은 잘하지만 너무 융통성이 없다.

Chief Kim is good at his job, but he is too inflexible.

융통성이 있다 to be flexible/adaptable

융통성이 없다 to be rigid/inflexible

26 이열치열

명 fight fire with fire

이열치열이라고 이렇게 더운 날은 뜨거운 삼계탕 어때요?

We should fight fire with fire and have Samgyetang (chicken soup) on a hot day like this.

27 인내심

명 patience

어린 아이를 돌볼 때 무엇보다 인내심이 필요하다.

Patience is most necessary when taking care of young children.

인내하다 to be patient, to endure

28 자수성가

명 self-made

가난한 집에서 태어나 자수성가한 그는 자신의 성공에 대한 자부심이 크다.

Being a self-made man who came from a poor family, he has great pride in his success.

DAY 14 ★★

29 재충전하다

동 recharge

이번 여행은 재충전을 할 수 있는 좋은 기회였다.

This trip was a good opportunity to recharge

30 적합하다

형 to be appropriate/suitable for

이 영화는 청소년들이 보기에 적합하지 않다는 판정을 받았다.

This movie has been deemed inappropriate for teenagers.

반) 부적합하다 to be inappropriate/unsuitable for

31 조치하다

동 to take measures/actions

응급대원들은 환자가 숨을 쉴 수 있도록 조치했다.

Emergency workers took measures to allow the patient to breathe.

조치 measures, actions

32 중시하다

동 to consider important

건강을 중시하는 사회적 분위기 속에서 흡연자의 설 자리가 점점 좁아지고 있다.

In the social atmosphere that values health, there is less space for smokers to stand on.

33 차일피일

부 put off/delay day by day, procrastinate

치과 치료를 받아야 하는데 가기 싫어서 차일피일 미루고 있다.

I need to go to the dentist but I've been procrasinating on it becuase I dont want to go.

34 파격적

명 shocking, unconventional, crazy, unprecedented

최근 젊은이들 사이에서 유행하는 패션을 파격적이라고 보는 시각도 있다.

There is also a view that the latest fashion among young people is unconventional.

파격 할인 crazy sale

35 헌법

명 constitution

헌법에 의하면 모든 국민이 행복을 추구할 권리가 있다.

According to the Constitution, every citizen has a right to pursue happiness.

헌법 개정 constitutional amendment

TOPIK에서 혼동하기 쉬운 단어

다의어 Polysemy

때우다

❶ 간단하게 식사를 해결하다

예 매일 그렇게 대충 끼니를 때우다가는 건강에 문제가 생길 수도 있다.

If you fill up your meals roughly every day, you might have health problems.

❷ 깨진 곳을 막다

예 자전거 바퀴에 난 구멍을 때우러 자전거 수리점에 가야 한다.

You have to go to a bicycle repair shop to fill up a hole in your bicycle wheel.

DAY 14 ★★

반의어 Antonym

공평하다 to be fair ↔ 불공평하다 unfair

예 첫째 아이라고 해서 동생에게 모든 것을 양보해야 하는 것은 공평하지 않다.

It is unfair to demand that the firstborn yields everything to the younger sibling just because he is older.

예 비슷한 상황인데 여자라고 배려해 주는 것은 불공평하다.

In a similar situation, it is unfair to be considerate to a person just because she is a woman.

유의어 Synonym

대견하다 to be proud of ≒ 기특하다

예 어린 나이지만 어려운 환경에서도 포기하지 않고 열심히 노력하는 그 학생이 정말 대견하다.

어린 나이지만 어려운 환경에서도 포기하지 않고 열심히 노력하는 그 학생이 정말 기특하다.

I am proud of the young student who did not give up and worked hard despite difficult circumstances.

복습해 보세요

자연스러운 문장이 되도록 완성해 보세요.
Try to complete the sentence in a natural way.

1. 소극적인 사람들은 자기의 능력을 실제보다 ㄱㅅㅍㄱ하는 경향이 있다.
   Shy people tend to underestimate their abilities than they really are.

2. 휴대폰은 일상생활에서 없어서는 안 되는 물건이라고 해도 ㄱㅇ이 아니다.
   It is not an exaggeration to say that phones are a necessity to daily life

3. 아이는 아버지에게 야단 맞았지만 잘못을 ㄴㅇㅊㄴ 기색이 없었다.
   The child was scolded by his father, but there was no sign of remorse.

4. 가난한 집에서 태어나 ㅈㅅㅅㄱ한 그는 자신의 성공에 대한 자부심이 크다.
   Being a self-made man who came from a poor family, he has great pride in his success.

5. 면접을 잘하려면 질문에 ㅇㅂㅁㄹㅈ 말고 정확하게 대답해야 한다.
   To do well in your interview, you have to answer clearly instead of speaking vaguely to the question.

다음 빈 칸에 알맞은 단어를 〈보기〉에서 골라 쓰세요.
Choose the appropriate word from <Example> to fill in the blanks below.

〈보기〉

a. 동병상련　b. 냉혹한　c. 적합하지 않다는　d. 인내심

6. 능력 있는 사람만 살아 남을 수 있는 (　　　　) 현실을 인정해야 한다.
   We have to admit the harsh reality that only capable people can survive.

7. (　　　　)(이)라고 같은 처지에 처해봐야 상대방을 이해할 수 있다.
   Just as the saying goes, you can only understand the other person when you are in the same situation as them.

8. 어린 아이를 돌볼 때 무엇보다 (　　　　)이/가 필요하다.
   Patience is most necessary when taking care of young children.

9. 이 영화는 청소년들이 보기에 (　　　　) 판정을 받았다.
   This movie has been deemed inappropriate for teenagers.

정답

1. 과소평가 2. 과언 3. 뉘우치는 4. 자수성가 5. 얼버무리지 6. b 7. a 8. d 9. c

DAY 15

확인해 보세요

빨간 시트지로 가리고 단어의 뜻을 알면, □에 ✓ 해 보세요.

After covering up the words with red cover, please check(✓) the box (□) when you know the meaning of the word.

- □ 01 감량 reduction, loss
- □ 02 겸하다 to engage in
- □ 03 과연 indeed, really
- □ 04 관세 duties, tariffs
- □ 05 급락 plummet, sudden drop
- □ 06 넘보다 to covet
- □ 07 느닷없이 abruptly, out of the blue
- □ 08 다다르다 to reach
- □ 09 대내적 internality
- □ 10 도덕 ethics, morals
- □ 11 동서고금 all times and places
- □ 12 떠밀리다 to be pushed into
- □ 13 매립 landfill
- □ 14 명확하다 clear
- □ 15 뭉클하다 to be touched/moved
- □ 16 반발심 resistance, rebellion
- □ 17 변덕 whim
- □ 18 소송 lawsuit
- □ 19 엄연하다 undeniable, clear
- □ 20 역부족 not enough
- □ 21 오류 error
- □ 22 우직하다 to be simple and honest
- □ 23 유기농 organic
- □ 24 융합하다 to combine
- □ 25 이외 besides, except
- □ 26 인상착의 description(look and dressing)
- □ 27 자숙하다 to self-reflect
- □ 28 재치 wit
- □ 29 전무후무 unprecedented
- □ 30 조합 combination
- □ 31 중점 a focus
- □ 32 차질 disruption
- □ 33 파업 strike
- □ 34 허탈하다 dejected, let-down
- □ 35 헐값 bargain price

DAY 15

  are the words that appeared in the former tests, and you may get a higher grade if you study them together.

01 감량

명 reduction, loss

쓰레기 감량을 위해 분리 수거를 실시하고 있다.

Recycling is being done to reduce the amount of trash.

체중 감량 weight loss 감량하다 to lose/reduce

02 겸하다

동 to engage in

공무원은 다른 직업을 겸하는 것이 금지되어 있다.

Civil servants are prohibited from engaging in other jobs.

겸직 concurrent job

03 과연

부 indeed, really

두 사람의 주장이 다른데 과연 누구의 말이 맞는 것일까?

The two have different claims, but really who is right?

04 관세

명 duties, tariffs

수입 물품에는 보통 관세를 붙인다.

Imported goods are usually subject to tariffs.

관세를 물다 to impose a tariff/customs duties

05 급락

명 plummet, sudden drop

환율 급락으로 해외여행자가 증가하고 있다.

There is an increase in tourists after a plummet in currency exchange rates.

급락하다 to plummet

반) 급등 skyrocket

06 넘보다

동 to covet

열심히 노력하지는 않고 다른 사람이 가진 것을 넘보는 사람들을 보면 한심하다는 생각이 든다.

I think that people who covet what others have without working hard are pathetic.

07 느닷없이

부 abruptly, out of the blue

잘 놀던 아기가 느닷없이 울기 시작했다.

The baby who had been playing well abruptly started crying.

08 다다르다

동 to reach

모두 한계에 다다른 듯하므로 더 이상 진행하는 것은 무리입니다.

Just as everything reaches a limit, it is impossible to proceed any further.

09 대내적

명 internal

지난해 우리 경제는 극심한 대내적 변화를 겪었다.

Last year, our economy underwent severe internal changes.

10 도덕

명 ethics, morals

기업인에게 가장 필요한 것은 정직과 도덕이다.

Honesty and ethics are the most needed traits of a businessman.

도덕성 morality, ethicality　　도덕적 moral, ethical

11 동서고금

명 all times and places

동서고금을 막론하고 사랑은 문학에서 보편적으로 다루는 주제다.

No matter the time or place, love is a common topic discussed in literature.

DAY 15 ★★

12 떠밀리다

동 to be pushed into

나는 정말 하기 싫었지만 친구들에게 떠밀리다시피 해서 회장 선거에 나갔다.

Though I really hated it, I was pushed into running for president by my friends.

13 매립

명 landfill

공항 부근에서 진행되던 바다 매립 공사가 중단되었다.

The sea reclamation work near the airport was put on hold.

14 명확하다

형 clear

창업을 하려면 구체적이고 명확한 목표를 세워야 한다.

In order to start a business, you need to set specific and clear goals.

15 뭉클하다

형 to be touched/moved

아이들이 써 준 편지를 보고 나는 마음이 뭉클해졌다.

My heart was moved when I saw the letter that the children wrote for me.

16 반발심

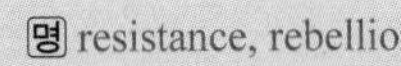
명 resistance, rebellion

학생들의 복장에 대한 지나친 간섭은 오히려 반발심만 유발할 수 있다.

Excessive interference with students' desscode can only cause resistance.

반발 resistance/opposition　　반발하다 to resist/oppose

17 변덕

명 whim

그 친구는 변덕이 심해서 툭하면 마음을 바꾸기에 같이 일을 하기 힘들다.

That friend changes his mind on a whim, making it difficult to work with him.

변덕스럽다 to be fickle/unpredictable

변덕을 부리다 behave erratically, act on a whim

18 소송

명 lawsuit

그는 회사에서 부당 해고를 당하자 소송을 걸었다.

He sued the company when he was fired unjustly.

소송을 제기하다 to file a lawsuit　　소송을 하다 to sue

19 엄연하다

형 undeniable, clear

인간이 사회를 떠나서 혼자 살 수 없다는 것은 엄연한 사실이다.

It is an undeniable fact that human beings cannot live alone apart from society.

DAY 15 ★★

20 역부족

명 not enough

모든 사원들이 회사를 살리기 위해 최선을 다했지만 역부족이었다.

All the employees did their best to save the company, but it was not enough.

21 오류

명 error

책을 읽다 보면 문법적인 오류가 발견되는 경우가 종종 있다.

Grammatical errors are often found while reading a book.

22 우직하다

형 to be simple and honest

그는 묵묵히 자신이 맡은 일을 우직하게 해냈다.

He silently did his job with honesty.

'우직하다'는 어떤 단어와 같이 사용할까요?
What words do you use with '우직하다'?

성품 personality
심성 heart
행동 behavior
성격 personality
\+ 우직하다

23 유기농

명 organic

조금 비싸더라도 농약을 쓰지 않은 유기농 과일을 사서 먹고 있다.

Even if it is a little expensive, I buy and eat organic fruits that do not use pesticides.

24 융합하다

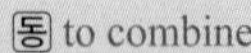

최근에는 여러 분야를 융합하여 연구하는 학문이 각광을 받고 있다.

Recently, studies that combine various fields have been receiving the spotlight.

융합 반응 fusion reaction　　융합 실험 fusion experiments
융합되다 to be integrated/fused/combined

25 이외

명 besides, except, in addition to

이 카페에는 한국 사람 이외에도 여러 나라의 외국인들이 자주 찾아온다.

This cafe has many foreigners who visit in addition to korean customers.

26 인상착의

명 description (look and dressing)

CCTV를 통해서 이번 사건 범인의 인상착의를 확인했다.

We identified the look and dress of the perpetrator through the CCTV.

27 자숙하다

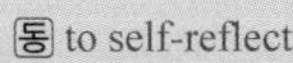

음주운전으로 처벌을 받은 그 연예인은 한동안 자숙하기로 했다.

The celebrity who was indicted for drunk driving decided to self-reflect for a while.

자숙 self-reflection

28 재치

그 여배우는 기자의 다소 당황스러운 질문에도 재치 있게 대답했다.

The actress also wittily answered the reporter's somewhat embarrassing questions.

29 전무후무

명 unprecedented

그는 전무후무한 기록을 가진 세계 최고의 선수이다.

He is the world's best player with an unprecedented record.

30 조합

명 combination

숫자와 영어의 조합으로 만들어진 비밀번호를 설정해야 한다.

You must set a password made up of a combination of numbers and English.

조합하다 to combine　　조합되다 to be made up with

31 중점

명 a focus

이 수업에서는 영어 말하기와 듣기를 중점적으로 가르치고 있다.

This class focuses on teaching English speaking and listening.

중점을 두다 to put emphasis on

DAY 15 ★★

32 차질

명 disruption

원재료의 공급이 늦어지면서 생산에 차질을 빚고 있다.

There was a disruption in production due to a delay in the supply of raw materials.

33 파업

명 strike

지하철 민영화에 반대하기 위해 파업을 하기로 결정했다.

They decied to go on strike in order to oppose the privatization of the subway.

파업에 들어가다 to enter into a strike

34 허탈하다

형 dejected, let-down

축구 경기에서 열심히 싸운 선수들은 패배라는 결과에 허탈해했다.

The players who fought hard in the soccer match were let-down with the result of defeat.

35 헐값

명 bargain price

자전거를 사 놓고 사용하지 않다가 결국 헐값에 팔아 버렸다.

I bought a bike, didn't use it, and eventually sold it at a bargain price.

TOPIK에서 혼동하기 쉬운 단어

다의어 Polysemy

과연

❶ 결과에서도 진짜로

예 두 사람의 주장이 다른데 과연 누구의 말이 맞는 것일까?

The two have different claims, but really who is right?

❷ 생각과 실제가 같을 때 정말로

예 이 학생은 과연 똑똑한 학생이구나.

This student is truly a very smart student.

반의어 Antonym

급락 plummet ↔ 급등 skyrocket

예 환율 급락으로 해외여행자가 증가하고 있다.

There is an increase in tourists after a plummet in currency exchange rates.

예 태풍으로 인한 농작물 피해가 극심하여 농산물 가격이 급등하고 있다.

Due to the typhoon severely damaging the crops, the prices of agricultural products are sky rocketing.

유의어 Synonym

다다르다 to reach ≒ 이르다

예 모두 한계에 다다른 듯하므로 더 이상 진행하는 것은 무리입니다.

모두 한계에 이른 듯하므로 더 이상 진행하는 것은 무리입니다.

Just as everything reaches a limit, it is impossible to proceed any further.

복습해 보세요

서로 어울리는 단어를 찾아 연결해 보세요.

Find words that go with each other and connect them.

1. 직업	a. 물다
2. 관세	b. 급락
3. 주가	c. 다다르다
4. 한계	d. 들어가다
5. 파업	e. 겸하다

DAY 15 ★★

자연스러운 문장이 되도록 완성해 보세요.

Try to complete the sentence in a natural way.

6. 두 사람의 주장이 다른데 ㄱㅇ 누구의 말이 맞는 것일까?
   The two have different claims, but really who is right?

7. ㄷㅅㄱㄱ을 막론하고 사랑은 문학에서 보편적으로 다루는 주제다.
   No matter the time or place, love is a common topic discussed in literature.

8. 그는 묵묵히 자신이 맡은 일을 ㅇㅈㅎㄱ 해냈다.
   He silently did his job with honesty.

9. 음주운전으로 처벌을 받은 그 연예인은 한동안 ㅈㅅㅎㄱㄹ 했다.
   The celebrity who was indicted for drunk driving decided to self-reflect for a while.

10. 학생들의 복장에 대한 지나친 간섭은 오히려 ㅂㅂㅅ만 유발할 수 있다.
    Excessive interference with students' desscode can only cause resistance.

정답

1. e 2. a 3. b 4. c 5. d 6. 과연 7. 동서고금 8. 우직하게 9. 자숙하기로 10. 반발심

❶ 불(不) non

불합리하다 be unreasonable
불평등하다 be unequal
불건전하다 unwholesome
불공정하다 unfair
불규칙적 irregular
불만족스럽다 dissatisfied

❷ 비(非) non-

비정상적 abnormal
비공개 nondisclosure
비공식 unofficial
비효율적 inefficient
비상식적 unusual

▲불평등하다 be unequal

주간 복습 day 11 - day 15

아래 단어를 보고 빈 칸에 뜻을 적어 보세요. 그리고 점선대로 접어서 적은 뜻이 맞는지 확인해 보세요. (만일 틀렸다면 뒷면의 단어 앞 □에 ✓ 하세요.)

Write down the meaning of the given word in the blank. Also, fold the page along a dotted line and check whether you got it right or wrong. (If you got it wrong tick the box in front of the word in next page.)

▼접는선

단어	뜻
과감하다	
눈을 붙이다	
연료	
조작하다	
희생하다	
과대평가	
내쫓다	
당선	
이상 기후	
차단하다	
냉담하다	
동반	
얼떨떨하다	
조정	
투표권	
경고하다	
다그치다	
반박하다	
운행	
적합하다	
감량	
느닷없이	
엄연하다	
융합하다	
차질	

※접어서 뜻이 맞는지 확인해보세요.

주간 복습 day 11 - day 15

빈 칸에 한국어 단어를 3번 적고 다시 외워 봅시다.

Write down the Korean word 3 times in the blank and try to memorize it again.

◀접는선

뜻	단어		
☐ to be daring/ decisive	과감하다		
☐ get some sleep, take a little nap	눈을 붙이다		
☐ fuel	연료		
☐ to operate/create	조작하다		
☐ to sacrifice	희생하다		
☐ overestimation	과대평가		
☐ kick out	내쫓다		
☐ election	당선		
☐ abnormal climates	이상 기후		
☐ to block	차단하다		
☐ to be cold	냉담하다		
☐ company, together	동반		
☐ to be dazed/ bewildered	얼떨떨하다		
☐ adjustment	조정		
☐ right to vote	투표권		
☐ to warn	경고하다		
☐ to reprimand	다그치다		
☐ to refute	반박하다		
☐ operation	운행		
☐ to be appropriate/ suitable for	적합하다		
☐ reduction, loss	감량		
☐ abruptly, out of the blue	느닷없이		
☐ undeniable, clear	엄연하다		
☐ to combine	융합하다		
☐ disruption	차질		

DAY 16

확인해 보세요

빨간 시트지로 가리고 단어의 뜻을 알면, □에 ✓ 해 보세요.

After covering up the words with red cover, please check(✓) the box (□) when you know the meaning of the word.

□ 01	감명	inspiration	□ 13	매매	sales, trading	□ 25	응모	application
□ 02	경로	route	□ 14	모방하다	to mimic/ copy	□ 26	이의	objection
□ 03	관습	custom/ practice	□ 15	미달	insufficiency, shortfall	□ 27	인색하다	to be stingy/ sparing
□ 04	권위	authority, prestige	□ 16	반전	twist, reversal	□ 28	자아실현	self-acutalization
□ 05	급증하다	to increase rapidly	□ 17	변수	variable	□ 29	재택	be (at) home
□ 06	노골적	obvious/open	□ 18	손실	loss	□ 30	전성기	prime, best days
□ 07	능동적	active	□ 19	업적	achievement	□ 31	조화	harmony
□ 08	다수결	majority	□ 20	역설적	irony	□ 32	증가하다	to increase/ rise
□ 09	대대적	large- scale, extensive	□ 21	오름세	upward trend	□ 33	참고하다	to refer to
□ 10	도도하다	haughty, arrogant, proud	□ 22	우스꽝스럽다	ridiculous	□ 34	판단하다	to judge/ consider
□ 11	동식물	animals and plants	□ 23	우호적	friendly	□ 35	헛디디다	to miss one's step
□ 12	떳떳하다	to have a clear conscience	□ 24	유난히	especially/ particularly			

DAY 16

  are the words that appeared in the former tests, and you may get a higher grade if you study them together.

01 감명

명 inspiration

다리가 불편하지만 마라톤에서 끝까지 달린 선수의 이야기가 많은 사람들에게 깊은 감명을 주고 있다.

Although his legs are uncomfortable, the story of a runner who ran to the end of the marathon is deeply impressive to many people.

 감명을 받다 to be inspired/impressed

02 경로

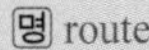
명 route

앱을 통해서 행선지의 경로를 미리 알 수 있다.

Through the app, you can know the route to the destination in advance.

03 관습

명 custom/practice/tradition

나라나 지역마다 다양한 관습이 있는데 그 나라에 가면 그 나라의 관습을 따르는 것이 옳다.

Each country or region has its various customs, and it is right to follow the country's customs when you are there.

04 권위

명 authority, prestige

요즘 학교에서 선생님들의 권위가 없어졌다는 우려의 목소리가 나오고 있다.

Nowadays, there are voices of concern that teachers' authority in school has been erased.

권위적 authoritative　　　　권위가 있다 to have authority

'권위적이다'와 '권위가 있다'는 다른 뜻이에요.
'권위적이다'는 권위만 중요하게 생각하는 상황에서 보통 부정적으로 사용해요.
The meanings of '권위적이다' and '권위가 있다' are different.
'권위적이다' is usually used negatively in situations where only authority is important.

예 우리 사장님은 너무 권위적이라서 자신의 생각만 맞다고 여기면서 다른 직원의 말은 무시할 때가 많다.

Our boss is so authoritative that he often thinks only his own thoughts are right and ignores the opinions of other employees.

05 급증하다

동 to increase rapidly

해외 이민을 고려하고 있는 사람들이 급증하고 있다.

The number of people considering immigration is increasing rapidly

반) 급감하다 to decline sharphy

06 노골적

명 obvious/open/direct

그 사람은 나에 대한 불만을 노골적으로 드러냈다.

The person openly expressed his dissatisfaction with me.

07 능동적

명 active

힘들다고 피해 가지 말고 능동적으로 해결해야 한다.

You have to solve problems actively instead of avoiding it because it's hard.

반) 수동적 passive

08 다수결

명 majority

민주주의 국가에서는 다수결의 원칙에 의해서 의사를 결정한다.

In a democratice state, decisions are made based on the majority-rule.

09 대대적

명 large- scale, extensive

그 회사는 신제품에 대한 대대적인 홍보를 시작했다.

The company started a large-scale promotion for its new product.

10 도도하다

형 haughty, arrogant, proud, conceited

그녀는 보기에는 도도해 보여도 실제 성격은 소탈한 편이다.

Although she seems haughty, in reality, she has an easygoing personality.

11 동식물

명 animals and plants

환경오염이 동식물의 생태계를 파괴하고 있다.

Environmental pollution is destroying the ecosystem of plants and animals.

12 떳떳하다

형 to have a clear conscience, to have dignity

스스로가 떳떳하다면 조사에 응해야 한다.

If you have a clear conscience, you should respond to the investigation.

13 매매

명 sales, trading

부동산 매매 계약서를 잘 보관해야 한다.

Real estate sales contracts should be stored safely.

매매하다 to trade/sell　　매매되다 be sold/traded

14 모방하다

동 to mimic/copy/imitate

인공지능의 핵심은 인간의 뇌를 모방한 것이다.

The key to artificial intelligence is to imitate the human brain.

모방 범죄 copycat crime

15 미달

명 insufficiency, shortfall, below the standard

지방에 있는 대학이 정원 미달로 어려움을 겪고 있다고 한다.

Colleges in the provinces are facing troubles due to insufficient enrollment.

미달되다 to become insufficient

DAY 16 ★★

16 반전

명 twist, reversal

영화 후반부에 그런 반전이 있을 줄은 정말 몰랐다.

I really did not know about the twist at the latter half of the movie.

17 변수

명 variable

미국 증시가 국내에도 큰 변수로 작용하였다.

The US stock market also acted as a major variable in Korea.

변수가 되다 to become a variable

18 손실

명 loss

그는 투자 실패로 막대한 경제적 손실을 입었다.

He suffered tremendous financial loss due to a failed investment.

손실을 입히다 to cause loss   손실을 가져오다 to bring loss

19 업적

명 achievement

그는 연구 업적을 인정 받아 노벨상 후보에 올랐다.

His research achievement was recognized, earning him a Noble prize nomination.

20 역설적

명 irony

최근 결혼 인구가 감소함에 따라 역설적으로 결혼의 중요성이 강조되고 있다.

As the married population decrease in recent years, the importance of marriage is ironically being more emphasized.

21 오름세

명 upward trend

경기가 회복됨에 따라 주가의 오름세가 계속되고 있다.

As the economy recovers, the upward trend of stocks is continuing.

반) 내림세 downward trend

22 우스꽝스럽다

형 ridiculous

과장된 그의 행동이 우스꽝스러워 보였다.

His exaggerated actions looked ridiculous.

23 우호적

명 friendly

우호적이었던 두 국가의 관계가 이번 사건으로 어긋나기 시작했다.

The friendly relationship of the two countries began to deteriorate due to this event.

우호 관계 friendly relations　　우호 증진 promotion of friendship
우호 협력 friendly cooperation　　우호를 다지다 to build friendship

24 유난히

부 especially/particularly

우리 아버지는 유난히 보수적인 편이시다.

My father is particularly conservative.

유난스럽다 unusual

25 응모

명 application

아이디어 공모전의 응모 기간이 다음주까지다.

The application deadline for the Idea Contest is next week.

응모하다 to apply　　응모 기간 application deadline

26 이의

명 objection

이 안건에 대해 이의가 없으시면 다음 안건으로 넘어가도록 하겠습니다.

If there are no objections to this topic, we will move on to the next matter.

이의를 제기하다 to raise an objection

DAY 16 ★★

27 인색하다

형 to be stingy/sparing

칭찬에 인색한 교수님의 칭찬에 학생의 표정이 밝아졌다.

The student's face brightened up with the praise of a professor who usually compliments very sparingly.

인색 stinginess

28 자아실현

명 self-acutalization

사람은 누구나 자아실현의 욕구가 있다.

Everyone has a desire for self-actualization.

29 재택

명 be (at) home

신종 코로나 바이러스의 대유행으로 재택 근무를 하는 사람이 급증했다.

Due to the novel coronavirus pandemic, the number of people working from home has increased dramatically.

30 전성기

명 prime, best days, golden age

오늘은 르네상스에 전성기를 누리던 화가들에 대해 공부했다.

Today we learned about the artists during the golden age of the Renaissance.

31 조화

명 harmony

건물이 주변 환경과 조화를 이루는 것이 중요하다.

It is important for the building to be in harmony with the surrounding environment.

조화롭다 to be harmonious

32 증가하다

동 to increase/rise/grow

한국 사회는 다문화 가정이 증가하는 추세이다.

There is a growing trend of multicultural families in Korean society.

반) 감소하다 to decrease

출제 경향 how this word appears in the test

증가하다, 감소하다, 늘다, 줄다, 급증하다, 급감하다 등의 단어는 자주 출제됩니다. 꼭 기억해 두세요!

Words such as 증가하다(increase), 감소하다(decrease), 늘다(gain), 줄다(lose), 급증하다(increase rapidly), and 급감하다(decrease rapidly) are frequently asked. Be sure to remember.

33 참고하다

동 to refer to

지속 가능한 개발과 관련해서는 이 책들을 참고하면 도움이 될 거예요.

On sustainable development, these books will be helpful to refer to.

34 판단하다

동 to judge/believe/consider

저희는 지금을 주식 투자의 적기로 판단하고 있습니다.

We believe that right now is the best time to invest.

35 헛디디다

동 to miss one's step

계단에서 발을 헛디뎌서 넘어졌다.

I missed my step on the stairs and fell.

TOPIK에서 혼동하기 쉬운 단어

다의어 Polysemy

경로

❶ 일이 진행되는 방법이나 순서

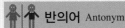

예 경찰은 인체에 해로운 냉동 식품이 유통된 경로를 추적하고 있다.

Police are tracking the distribution route of frozen food that is harmful to the human body.

❷ 지나는 길

예 네비게이션으로 목적지까지 가는 최단 경로를 알아보았다.

I checked the shortest route to the destination by navigation.

반의어 Antonym

능동적 active ↔ 수동적 passive

예 힘들다고 피해 가지 말고 능동적으로 해결해야 한다.

You have to solve problems actively instead of avoiding it because it's hard.

예 수동적인 자세로 말하기 수업에 참가하면 실력이 늘기 힘들다.

If you participate in a speaking class with a passive attitude, it is difficult to improve your skills.

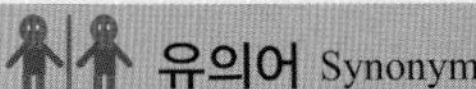

유의어 Synonym

손실 loss ≒ 손해

예 주식 투자 실패로 큰 경제적 손실을 입었다.

주식 투자 실패로 큰 경제적 손해를 입었다.

He suffered huge economic losses due to his failure to invest in stocks.

복습해 보세요

자연스러운 문장이 되도록 완성해 보세요.
Try to complete the sentence in a natural way.

1. 혼자 사는 1인 가구가 ㅈㄱㅎㄴ 추세이다.
   The number of single-person households living alone is on the rise.

2. ㄱㅇㅈㅇ 상사에 대해 반감을 가지는 젊은이들이 많다.
   There are many young people who have antagonism towards their authoritative bosses.

3. 이번 수업 리포트를 작성할 때 이 책을 ㅊㄱㅎ 주시기 바랍니다.
   When writing this class report, please reference this book.

4. 아이를 키울 때 칭찬에 ㅇㅅㅎㄷ 게 후회가 돼요.
   I regret that I was stingy with compliments when raising my child.

5. 작가님이 쓰신 소설을 읽고 큰 ㄱㅁㅇ 받았어요.
   I read the novel written by the author and received a big inspiration.

자연스러운 문장이 되도록 둘 중에서 알맞은 단어를 고르세요.
Try to complete the sentence in a natural way by choosing the correct word.

6. 선거가 2주 뒤로 다가오면서 각 정당들은 (a. 대대적인 / b. 역설적인) 선거 운동을 펼치고 있다.
   As the election approaches two weeks later, each party is campaigning extensively.

7. 부동산에 투자했다가 큰 (a. 반전 / b. 손실)을/를 입었다.
   I invested in real estate and suffered a huge loss.

8. 두 나라는 (a. 우호적인 / b. 노골적인) 관계를 유지하기 위해 여러 방면에서 노력해 왔다.
   The two countries have made efforts in various ways to maintain friendly relations.

9. 학교 캐릭터 이름 짓기 (a. 응모 / b. 업적) 기간은 다음 주 월요일까지이다.
   The application period for naming the school character ends next Monday.

10. 부모로서 바르게 행동하지 않으면 아이 앞에서 (a. 도도할 / b. 떳떳할) 수 없다.
    If you don't act right as a parent, you can't have a clear conscienc in front of your child.

정답

1. 증가하는 2. 권위적인 3. 참고해 4. 인색했던 5. 감명을 6. a 7. b 8. a 9. a 10. b

DAY 16

Memo

DAY 17

확인해 보세요

빨간 시트지로 가리고 단어의 뜻을 알면, □에 ✓ 해 보세요.

After covering up the words with red cover, please check(✓) the box (□) when you know the meaning of the word.

	No.	Word	Meaning		No.	Word	Meaning		No.	Word	Meaning
□	01	가공	process, manufacture	□	13	뜸하다	to be infrequent to lose touch (for)	□	25	의기소침하다	dispirited, down
□	02	감염	infection	□	14	매섭다	to be fierce/harsh	□	26	이익	profit/interest
□	03	경유	stopover	□	15	모범	model	□	27	인신공격하다	to make a personal attack
□	04	광범위하다	to be extensive/broad	□	16	미덕	virtue	□	28	자외선	UV-light
□	05	극복하다	to overcome	□	17	반항	rebellion	□	29	재활	rehabilitation
□	06	기부금	donation	□	18	변천	change	□	30	전염되다	to spread a contagious disease
□	07	노령	old age	□	19	수용	accomodation, acceptance	□	31	종사자	worker
□	08	능률	efficiency	□	20	연연하다	to cling/stick to	□	32	증상	symptom
□	09	다스리다	to manage/rule	□	21	온대	temperate (climates)	□	33	채용하다	to hire
□	10	대두되다	to come up, to be on the rise	□	22	올바르다	correct, right	□	34	팽팽하다	to be tense/strained
□	11	도래하다	to come/arrive	□	23	우후죽순	spring up everywhere	□	35	헛수고	vain attempt/effort
□	12	동요하다	to disturb/waver	□	24	유대감	bond				

DAY 17

 are the words that appeared in the former tests, and you may get a higher grade if you study them together.

01 가공

명 process, manufacture

가공 식품을 자주 섭취하면 건강에 안 좋은 결과를 초래할 수 있다는 우려의 목소리가 높다.

There are voices of concern that the frequent consumption of processed foods can have adverse health consequences.

가공 과정 processing process　　식품 가공 food processing

02 감염

명 infection

면역력이 약한 사람들의 바이러스 감염을 막기 위해 예방접종을 실시하고 있다.

Vaccination is being conducted to prevent viral infections in people with weak immune systems.

바이러스 감염 viral infection　　세균 감염 bacterial infection
감염자 infected patient　　감염되다 to be infected
감염시키다 to infect

03 경유

명 stopover

다음달부터 서울 시내 버스의 경유 노선이 변경될 예정이다.

Starting next month, the stopover route of buses for downtown Seoul will be changed.

경유하다 via to transit/stopover

04 광범위하다

형 to be extensive/broad/widespread

요즘 청소년들 사이에서 유행어나 줄임말을 사용하는 언어 습관이 광범위하게 나타나고 있다.

The habit of using trendy words or abbreviations among teenagers is becoming widespread.

'광범위하다'는 어떤 단어와 같이 사용할까요?

What words do you use with '광범위하다'?

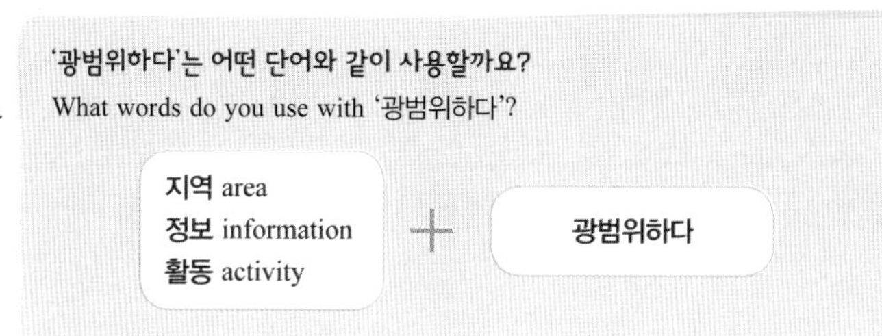

지역 area
정보 information
활동 activity
+
광범위하다

DAY 17 ★★

05 극복하다

동 to overcome

정말 힘든 시간이었지만 친구의 도움으로 어려움을 극복할 수 있었다.

It was a very difficult period but I could overcome it with the help of my friend.

이 단어는 '어려움, 고난, 단점, 위기, 장애, 시련'과 같이 부정적인 단어들과 주로 사용해요.

This word is often used with negative words such as '어려움(difficulty), 고난(hardship), 단점(shortcomings), 위기(crisis), 장애(disability), 시련(ordeal)'.

장애를 극복하고 올림픽에서 금메달을 따 낸 선수의 기사를 읽고 큰 감동을 받았다.

I was very moved by reading the article about an athlete who over came obstacles and won a gold medal at the Olympics

06 기부금

명 donation

불우 이웃을 돕기 위한 기부금을 모금하고 있다.

Donations are being raised to help our neighbors in need.

07 노령

명 old age

우리 할아버지는 80세가 넘는 노령에도 불구하고 아주 건강하시다.

My grandfather is very healthy despite his old age of being over 80.

노령 연금 old age pension　　노령 인구 elderly population

08 능률

명 efficiency

공부를 할 때 음악을 들으면서 하면 능률이 오른다.

If you listen to music while studying, you are more efficient.

능률적 efficient

09 다스리다

동 to manage/rule

자신의 마음을 잘 다스리고 컨트롤할 수 있는 사람이 성공한다.

A person who can manage and control one's heart well will succeed.

'다스리다'는 어떤 단어와 같이 사용할까요?

What word do you use with word '다스리다'?

건강 health
나라 country
마음 mind

\+ 다스리다

10 대두되다

동 to come up, to be on the rise

코로나 위기로 심각한 경제 문제가 대두되었다.

The corona crisis has caused serious economic problems to come up.

11 도래하다

동 to come/arrive

신종 바이러스로 인해 새로운 정보화 시대가 도래했다.

A new information age has arrived due to a new virus.

12 동요하다

동 to disturb/waver

그는 냉정한 성격이라서 어떤 상황에서도 감정이 동요하지 않는다.

He has a cold personality, so his emotions never waver under any the circumstances.

동요되다 to be disturbed

13 뜸하다

형 to be infrequent/rare, to lose touch (for)

자주 연락하던 친구가 요즘 연락이 뜸해졌다.

A friend who used to contact me often has lost touch these days.

14 매섭다

형 to be fierce/harsh

경기 전 상대방을 쳐다보는 선수의 눈초리가 매서웠다.

The eyes of the player looking at the opponent before the match were harsh.

15 모범

명 model

이 식당은 청결하고 직원이 친절하여 모범 음식점으로 선정되었다.

This restaurant was selected as a model restaurant for its cleanliness and friendly staff.

모범생 model student　　모범적 model exemplary

16 미덕

명 virtue

예전에는 겸손이 미덕이라고 생각했지만 지금은 그렇지 않다.

I considered humility as a virtue before, I do not now.

17 반항

명 rebellion

나는 폭력적인 아버지에 대한 반항으로 집을 나왔다.

I left home in rebellion against my abusive father.

반항심 rebellious spirit　　반항적 rebellious

반항하다 to rebel

18 변천

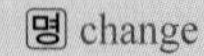

이번 전시회에서 한복의 변천사를 한 눈에 알 수 있었다.

I saw the changing history of Hanbok in one glance from this exhibition.

시대의 변천 change of the times
변천하다 to change
변천되다 to be changed

19 수용

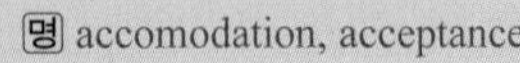

이 행사장의 수용 인원은 많아야 300명 정도이다.

The accomodation for this venue is 300 people at most.

수용자 consumer/user
수용하다 to accept/accomodate

20 연연하다

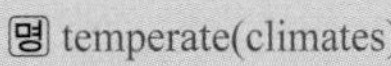

과거에만 연연하다 보면 더 나은 삶을 살 수 없다.

If you cling on the past, you can't live a better life.

21 온대

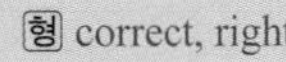

벼는 온대 기후에서 잘 자라는 작물이다.

Rice is a crop that thrives in temperate climates.

기후를 나타내는 표현들은 다음과 같아요.
The expressions for the climate are: '건조 기후(dry climate), 열대 기후(tropical climate), 냉대 기후(cold climate)'

22 올바르다

형 correct, right

항상 일을 할 때는 결과만 생각할 것이 아니라 올바른 방법을 선택해야 한다.

When you do your work, you should always choose the right method, instead of just focusing on the results.

23 우후죽순

명 spring up everywhere

우리 가게가 맛집으로 TV에 나온 후 근처에 비슷한 가게들이 우후죽순처럼 생겨났다.

Similar shops sprung up everywhere in the neighborhood after our restaurant appeared on TV as a delious must-visit restaurant.

24 유대감

명 bond

오랫동안 회사 생활을 하면서 동료들과 깊은 유대감이 생겼다.

Through my long career in the company, I developed a deep bond with my colleagues.

25 의기소침하다

형 dispirited, down

늘 자신있던 그녀의 의기소침한 모습이 낯설었다.

It was unfamiliar to see her so dispirited when she is usually always confident.

26 이익

명 profit/interest

자기 이익을 잘 챙기는 게 꼭 나쁜 건 아니지만, 가끔 안 좋아 보일 때도 있다.

It isn't necessarily a bad thing to look after one's own interest, but it does sometimes look bad on you.

관련어 이익을 보다 to make profit　　이익을 달성하다 to achieve a profit

27 인신공격하다

동 to make a personal attack

자신과 생각이 다르다고 상대를 인신공격하면 안 된다.

You shouldn't make personal attacks on others just because they think differently.

28 자외선

명 UV-light

자외선이 강한 날에는 모자를 쓰는 것이 좋다.

It is good to wear a hat on days where the UV-light is strong.

29 재활

명 rehabilitation

경기에서 큰 부상을 입은 선수들은 병원 치료 후에 재활 치료를 받게 된다.

Players who suffered from severe injuries during a game recieves rehabilitation treatment after their hospital care.

재활 운동 rehabilitation exercise

30 전염되다

동 to spread a contagious disease

마스크를 하면 공기를 통해 전염되는 병을 예방하는 데 도움이 된다.

Wearing masks helps prevent the spread of diseases contagious through the air.

전염병 contagious disease　　전염력 contagious level

31 종사자

명 worker

고객을 많이 만나는 서비스업 종사자들이 우울감을 호소하는 경우가 많다고 한다.

It is said that service workers who meet many customers often complain of depression.

종사하다 work in/at

32 증상

명 symptom

췌장암은 초기에는 증상이 나타나지 않는 경우가 많다.

Pancreatic cancer often does not develop symptoms in the early stages.

33 채용하다

동 to hire

우리 학교에서는 음악을 담당할 선생님을 한 분 채용할 예정입니다.

Our school is planning to hire a teacher to be in charge of the music program.

채용되다 to be hired　　채용 hire

34 팽팽하다

형 to be tense/strained/tight

양쪽의 의견이 팽팽해서 오늘 결론이 나오기 힘들 것 같다.

It seems hard to reach a conclusion by today because each side's opinions are tense.

DAY 17 ★★

35 헛수고

명 vain attempt/effor

기자님, 여기서 계속 기다려 봤자 안 오니까 헛수고하지 말고 돌아가세요.

Reporter, your efforts will be in vain even if you keep waiting here so go back.

헛수고로 끝나다 end in vain

TOPIK에서 혼동하기 쉬운 단어

다의어 Polysemy

다스리다

❶ (마음이나 감정을) 노력해서 바로잡다

예 사회 생활에서는 자신의 감정을 다스리지 못하면 곤란한 상황이 생길 수 있다.

In social life, you can get in trouble if you can't control your emotions.

❷ (국가나 사회, 단체, 집안의 일을) 보살펴 관리하고 통제하다

예 자신의 가정도 잘 다스리지 못하는 사람이 어떻게 나라 일을 할 수 있겠어요?

How can a person who can't manage his own family do work for the nation?

반의어 Antonym

이익 profit ↔ 손해 loss

예 주식 투자에 성공해서 큰 이익을 봤어요.

I made a huge profit by successfully investing in stocks.

예 주식 투자에 실패해서 큰 손해를 봤어요.

I had a huge loss of money because my stock investment failed.

유의어 Synonym

증상 symptom ≒ 증세

예 췌장암은 초기에는 증상이 나타나지 않는 경우가 많다.

췌장암은 초기에는 증세가 나타나지 않는 경우가 많다.

Pancreatic cancer often does not develop symptoms in the early stages.

복습해 보세요

다음 빈 칸에 알맞은 단어를 〈보기〉에서 골라 쓰세요.

Choose the appropriate word from <Example> to fill in the blanks below.

〈보기〉

a. 광범위하게 b. 의기소침한 c. 인신공격성 d. 종사해 e. 올바른

1. 말을 짧게 줄인 표현이 젊은 사람들 사이에서 (   ) 사용되고 있다.
Shortened expressions are being used extensively among young people.

2. 인터넷 상에서 다른 사람의 글에 (   ) 댓글을 다는 사람들이 문제가 되고 있다.
On the internet, people who comment personal attacks on other's posts are becoming a problem.

3. 그는 15년 이상 금융투자 분야에 (   ) 온 경험을 살려서 책을 출판했다.
He published a book based on his experience of working more than 15 years in financial investment.

4. 교사는 학생들이 (   ) 방향으로 성장해 갈 수 있도록 지도해야 한다.
Teachers should guide their students to develop in the right direction.

5. 아이는 부모님에게 크게 혼나서 (   ) 상태이다.
The child is in a dispirited state because he was greatly scolded by his parents.

서로 어울리는 단어를 찾아 연결해 보세요.

Find words that go with each other and connect them.

6. 어려움 •	• **a.** 도래하다
7. 시대 •	• **b.** 채용하다
8. 직원 •	• **c.** 극복하다
9. 이익 •	• **d.** 뜸하다
10. 연락 •	• **e.** 내다

DAY 17 ★★

정답

1.a 2.c 3.d 4.e 5.b 6.c 7.a 8.b 9.e 10.d

Memo

DAY 18

확인해 보세요

빨간 시트지로 가리고 단어의 뜻을 알면, □에 ✓ 해 보세요.

After covering up the words with red cover, please check(✓) the box (□) when you know the meaning of the word.

□ 01	각광	spotlight	□ 13	마니아	mania, enthusiast	□ 25	이타주의	altruism
□ 02	감탄하다	to admire/ wonder	□ 14	매입하다	to purchase, to buy	□ 26	인위적	unnatural (something)
□ 03	계기	chance, opportunity	□ 15	모색하다	seek, find	□ 27	작동하다	to work/ function
□ 04	괘씸하다	disgusting/ disgraceful	□ 16	미묘하다	subtle	□ 28	저가	low-cost
□ 05	금융업	financial business	□ 17	발각되다	to be discover	□ 29	전형적	typical
□ 06	기압	atmospheric pressure	□ 18	변형되다	to be modified	□ 30	좌절	setback, frustration
□ 07	노릇	role	□ 19	수익	profit	□ 31	지독하다	awful, terrible
□ 08	능숙하다	to be skilled/ proficient at	□ 20	염증	infection, inflammation	□ 32	책정하다	to set
□ 09	다지다	to brace oneself	□ 21	옹호하다	to protect, to support	□ 33	편견	prejudice
□ 10	대들다	to challenge/ defy	□ 22	운송	transportation	□ 34	허전하다	empty
□ 11	도리	duty, right	□ 23	유도하다	to inducc/ guide	□ 35	혁신	revolution
□ 12	동원하다	mobilize, gather	□ 24	의례적	formal			

DAY 18

 are the words that appeared in the former tests, and you may get a higher grade if you study them together.

01 각광

명 spotlight

최근 새롭게 개발된 자동차의 뛰어난 기술이 각광을 받고 있다.

The newly created car's outstanding technology are bieng put in the spotlight.

02 감탄하다

동 to admire/wonder, to be amazed/awed

피겨 스케이트 선수의 뛰어난 연기에 사람들이 감탄했다.

People were amazed by the figure skater's outstanding performance.

감탄 admiration　　감탄사 exclamation

03 계기

명 chance, opportunity

여행 중 한국인 친구를 만난 것을 계기로 한국어 공부를 시작하게 되었다.

I started studying Korean through the chance of befriending a Korean while traveling.

04 괘씸하다

형 disgusting/disgraceful/detestable

믿었던 친구가 나에게 거짓말을 하다니 정말 괘씸하다는 생각이 들었다.

I thought it was disgusting that a friend I trusted lied to me.

05 금융업

명 financial business

취업 준비생들 사이에서 금융업이 인기가 많았던 시대가 있었다.

There was an era when the financial business was popular among job seekers.

'금융업'처럼 'N업' 형태의 단어는 '종사하다'와 같이 사용해요.

Like '금융업 (financial business)', a word in the form of 'N업 (something business)' is used with '종사하다 (work in/at)'.

제조업에 종사하는 사람들을 대상으로 설문 조사를 실시하였다.
A survey was conducted with people who work in the manufactur ing industry.

DAY 18 ★★

06 기압

명 atmospheric pressure

바람은 기압의 차이로 생기는 것이다.

Winds are created due to the differences in air pressure.

고기압 high atmospheric pressure
저기압 low atmospheric pressure

07 노릇

명 role

소년소녀 가장은 어린 동생들에게 부모 노릇까지 대신하는 경우가 많다.

In many cases, the child breadwinner takes on the role of parent to the younger siblings.

08 능숙하다

형 to be skilled/proficient at

그 사람은 컴퓨터 전공이라 컴퓨터를 능숙하게 사용할 수 있다.

He is a computer major, so he can use computers proficiently.

09 다지다

동 to brace oneself, determine to keep

새해가 되면 한 해의 계획을 세우고 매번 각오를 다지지만 뜻대로 잘 안 된다.

When the new year comes, I make plans for the year and determine to keep the resolutions every time, but it doesn't go my way.

'다지다'는 어떤 단어와 같이 사용할까요?
What word would you use with the word '다지다'?

각오 resolve
기초 foundation
땅 land
\+ 다지다

10 대들다

동 to challenge/defy

한국에서는 어른에게 대들면 예의가 없다고 한다.

In Korea, you are considered to have no manners if challenge an adult.

11 도리

명 duty, right, moral

그런 행동은 인간으로서의 도리에 어긋난다.

Such behavior is contrary to the moral duty of a human being.

12 동원하다

동 mobilize, gather, draw

이사회에서는 다양한 방법을 동원해서 문제를 해결하고자 하였다.

The board of directors tried to solve the problem by mobilizing various methods.

동원 mobilization

13 마니아

명 mania, enthusiast

골프 마니아층을 겨냥한 여행 상품을 출시했다.

It launched a travel product aimed at golf enthusiasts.

영화 마니아 movie mania

14 매입하다

동 to purchase, to buy

시세보다 비싸게 부동산을 매입한 듯하다.

It looks like you bought the property at a higher price than the market price.

매입 purchase 매입되다 to be bought

15 모색하다

동 seek, find

모두가 안전하게 살아갈 수 있는 방법을 모색해야 한다.

We need to find a way for everyone to live safely.

DAY 18 ★★

16 미묘하다

형 subtle

그는 내 미묘한 감정 변화도 바로 알아챌 정도로 예민한 사람이다.

He is sensitive enough to notice even subtle changes in my emotions.

17 발각되다

동 to be discover

거짓말한 것이 발각되었지만 그는 끝까지 자신의 말이 사실이라고 우겼다.

It was discovered that he lied, but he insisted that what he said was true until the end.

18 변형되다

동 to be modified

이 유모차는 자동차 안전 시트로 변형될 수 있다.

This stroller can be transformed into a car safety seat.

변형하다 to modify

변형시키다 to transform

19 수익

명 profit

수익이 보장된 사업이라고 해서 함부로 손을 대서는 안 된다.

Just because it's a guaranteed profit business, you shouldn't touch it recklessly.

수익성이 좋다 to have good profit

20 염증

명 infection, inflammation

상처가 났을 때 빨리 치료하지 않으면 다친 부위에 염증이 생길 수 있다.

If the wound is not treated promptly, there can be an infection of the injured area.

21 옹호하다

동 to protect, to look out for, to support

어느 사회에나 자신의 이익만을 옹호하는 사람들이 있기 마련이다.

In any society, there are bound to be people who only look out for their own interests.

22 운송

명 transportation

기름 값이 오르자 운송 업체들이 큰 피해를 입을 수밖에 없었다.

Transportation companies suffered massive losses when the gas prices rose.

운송하다 to transport　　운송되다 to be transported/carried

23 유도하다

동 to induce/guide

콘서트에서 그 가수는 관객들의 참여를 유도하기 위해 노력했다.

At the concert, the singer tried to induce audience engagement.

유도 inducement

24 의례적

명 formal

그 직원은 손님들에게 의례적인 웃음을 보였다.

The staff gave guests a formal smile.

의례적 행사 formal event　　의례적 인사 formal greeting

25 이타주의

명 altruism

어떻게 하면 이기주의를 지양하고 이타주의를 추구하며 살도록 가르칠 수 있을까?

How can we teach people to avoid selfishness and to live in pursuit of altruism?

26 인위적

명 unnatural (something)

그 배우는 인위적인 표정 연기로 비난을 받고 있다.

The actor is under fire for his unnatural facial expression.

반) 자연적 natural (something)

27 작동하다

동 to work/function

냉장고가 작동하지 않아서 음식물이 다 상했다.

The refrigerator was not functioning so all the food went bad.

작동 operation
작동되다 to be operated
작동시키다 to activate
오작동 malfunction

28 저가

명 low-cost

이번에 저가 항공을 이용했는데 식사는커녕 주스도 한 잔 안 주더라고요.

This time I was on a low-cost airline, and they didn't even give me a glass of juice, let alone a meal.

29 전형적

명 typical

이 범죄는 전형적인 보이스피싱 수법을 사용한 것이다.

This crime uses typical voice phishing techniques.

30 좌절

명 setback, frustration, disappointment, failure

수많은 좌절을 겪었지만 절대 포기하지 않고 끝까지 도전했다.

Despite many setbacks, I never gave up and continued to try.

좌절하다 despair

DAY 18 ★★

31 지독하다

형 awful, terrible

쓰레기 냄새가 너무 지독해서 토할 것 같았다.

The smell of trash was so terrible that I felt like throwing up.

32 책정하다

동 to set

이번에 개발된 신상품은 가격 책정하는 것만 남겨 두고 있어요.

The new product developed this time is only left is to set the price.

책정되다 to be set

33 편견

명 prejudice

우리 사회에 존재하는 장애인에 대한 차별과 편견에 맞서 싸우고 싶다.

I want to fight against discrimination and prejudice against people with disabilities that exist in our society.

34 허전하다

형 empty

아이가 독립해서 나가자 집이 텅 빈 것 같고 너무 허전하다.

After my child became independent, the house and my heart feel so empty.

출제 경향 how this word appears in the test

읽기에서는 글을 쓴 저자나 글의 주인공의 심정을 묻는 문제가 항상 출제되고 있어요.

In reading, questions are always asked about the feelings of the author or the main character of the article.

심정을 묻는 다음 단어들을 같이 공부하세요.

Study the following words that express feelings.

'억울하다(feel victimized)', '서운하다(disappointed)', '흡족하다(satisfied)', '난처하다(awkward)', '담담하다(calm)', '의심스럽다(doubtful)', '혼란스럽다(confused)', etc.

35 혁신

명 revolution

기술 혁신을 통해 생산성이 높아졌다.

Productivity has gone up due to the the technological revolution.

혁신적 revolutionary

DAY 18 ★★

TOPIK에서 혼동하기 쉬운 단어

다의어 Polysemy

다지다

❶ (흙이나 땅을) 밟아서 단단하게 하다

예 먼저 땅을 다진 후에 도로를 만드는 작업을 시작할 겁니다.

First, we'll trample the ground and then start building roads.

❷ (힘이나 실력을) 더 강하거나 뛰어나게 하다

예 영어 실력을 다지기 위해 매일 1시간씩 공부하고 있다.

I am studying for an hour every day to strengthen my English skills.

❸ (마음이나 뜻을) 굳게 가지다

예 새해가 되면 한 해의 계획을 세우고 매번 각오를 다지지만 뜻대로 잘 안 된다.

Every new year, I set plans for the year and make resolutions every time, but it doesn't go as I planned.

반의어 Antonym

저가 low-cost ↔ 고가 high-priced

예 요즘은 저가의 물건이라고 꼭 품질이 나쁜 것도 아니다.

These days, just because it's a low-cost item doesn't mean it's bad quality.

예 학생들 사이에 고가의 패딩이 유행하고 있다.

High-priced padding is trending amoung the students.

유의어 Synonym

노릇 role ≒ 역할

예 소년소녀 가장은 어린 동생들에게 부모 노릇까지 대신하는 경우가 많다.

소년소녀 가장은 어린 동생들에게 부모 역할까지 대신하는 경우가 많다.

In many cases, the child breadwinner takes on the role of parent to the younger siblings.

복습해 보세요

서로 어울리는 단어를 찾아 연결해 보세요.
Find words that go with each other and connect them.

1. 금융업 • • a. 발각되다
2. 도리 • • b. 작동하다
3. 각오 • • c. 다지다
4. 컴퓨터 • • d. 어긋나다
5. 거짓말 • • e. 종사하다

DAY 18 ★★

자연스러운 문장이 되도록 완성해 보세요.
Try to complete the sentence in a natural way.

6. 어떤 ㄱㄱㄹ 한국어 공부를 시작했어요?
Through what chance did you start studying Korean?

7. 10년 정도 미국에 살았더니 이제는 ㄴㅅㅎㄱ 영어로 이야기할 수 있게 됐다.
After living in the United States for about ten years, I can speak English proficiently

8. 이제는 두 나라가 평화롭게 지내기 위한 방법을 ㅁㅅㅎㅇ 할 때이다.
Now, it is time to seek a way for both countries to live peacefully.

9. 지하철 옆 자리에 앉은 사람의 향수 냄새가 너무 ㅈㄷㅎㅅ 머리가 아프다.
My head hurts because the perfume smell from the person sitting next to me on the subway was awful.

10. 키우던 강아지가 죽은 후에 한동안 너무 ㅎㅈㅎㅅ 견딜 수가 없었다.
After my puppy died, I felt so empty that I couldn't stand it for a while.

정답

1. e 2. d 3. c 4. b 5. a 6. 계기로 7. 능숙하게 8. 모색해야 9. 지독해서 10. 허전해서

Memo

DAY 19

확인해 보세요

빨간 시트지로 가리고 단어의 뜻을 알면, □에 ✓ 해 보세요.

After covering up the words with red cover, please check(✓) the box (□) when you know the meaning of the word.

□ 01	갑작스럽다	sudden	□ 13	마다하다	resist	□ 25	의식적	conscious
□ 02	거치다	go through	□ 14	맥	pulse, energy	□ 26	이해관계	interest
□ 03	고갈	depletion	□ 15	모순	inconsistency	□ 27	인재	talented person
□ 04	교대하다	to change shift	□ 16	미생물	microbe	□ 28	작용하다	apply, action
□ 05	급여	wages	□ 17	발굴되다	to be excavated	□ 29	저물다	get dark
□ 06	기여하다	contribute	□ 18	병행하다	combine, do	□ 30	전환	transformation
□ 07	노사	labor and management	□ 19	습득	acquisition	□ 31	죄책감	guilt
□ 08	능통하다	fluent in/at	□ 20	열풍	fever, craze	□ 32	지방자치단체	local government
□ 09	다채롭다	to be colorful/ diverse	□ 21	영리	profit	□ 33	처벌	punishment
□ 10	대등하다	equal	□ 22	완곡하다	euphemistic	□ 34	편파적	partial
□ 11	도모	to promote/ plan	□ 23	웃돌나	exceed	□ 35	현저하다	marked, noticeable
□ 12	동일하다	same	□ 24	유독	especially			

DAY 19

 are the words that appeared in the former tests, and you may get a higher grade if you study them together.

01 갑작스럽다

유명 배우의 갑작스러운 은퇴 발표에 팬들이 당황해하고 있다.

Fans are bewildered by the sudden announcement of the famous actor's retirement.

02 거치다

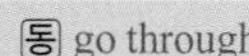

사춘기는 누구나 거쳐야 하는 자연스러운 과정이다.

Adolescence is a natural process that everyone goes through.

03 고갈되다

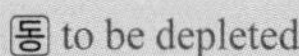

사람들의 무분별한 사용으로 지하 자원이 빠르게 고갈되고 있다.

Underground resources are rapidly depleting due to people's reckless use.

04 교대하다

동 to change, shift

간호사들은 일정한 시간마다 근무를 교대한다.

Nurses shift work at regular intervals.

교대 rotate/shift/take turn

05 급여

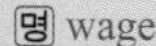

회사 상황이 안 좋아지면서 급여가 미지급되고 있는 상황이다.

As the company's situation worsens, wages are not being paid.

'급여'와 관련된 단어는 뭐가 있을까요?

What are the words related to "급여"?

Make sure you know words such as 시급(hourly wage), 일당(daily wage), 월급(salary), 연봉(annual salary), 특별수당(special allowance), and 상여금 (bonus).

06 기여하다

동 contribute

회사 발전에 기여한 정도에 따라 연말에 상여금을 지급한다.

Bonuses are paid at the end of the year according to the degree of contribution to the development of the company.

기여 contribution

07 노사

명 labor and management

어느 회사나 노사 간의 갈등이 없는 회사는 없다.

There is no company without conflict between labor and management.

노사 교섭 labor negotiations
노사 문제 labor and management problems
노사 합의 labor and management settlement

DAY 19 ★★

08 능통하다

형 fluent in/at

해외 영업 부서에서는 외국어에 능통한 사람이 필요하다.

Overseas operation departments need people who are fluent in foreign languages.

09 다채롭다

형 to be colorful/diverse

매년 지역마다 다채로운 행사가 열리는 덕분에 지역 경제가 활성화되고 있다.

Thanks to diverse events held every year in each region, the local economy is revitalizing.

10 대등하다

형 equal

나라와 나라 간의 관계가 늘 대등한 것은 아니다.

Relations between countries are not always equal.

11 도모

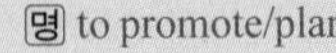
명 to promote/plan

회원 간의 친목 도모를 위해서 한 달에 한 번 식사 모임을 가지려고 한다.

We try to have a meal together once a month to promote friendship among the members.

도모하다 to promote/plan

12 동일하다

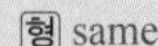
형 same

동일한 사건에 대해서 언론사마다 관점이 다르다.

Different media outlets have different views on the same event.

동일인 same person

13 마다하다

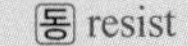
동 resist

선배의 동아리 가입 권유를 마다하지 못하고 결국 가입했다.

I couldn't resist the suggestion of my senior to join the club, and I finally joined.

14 맥

명 pulse, energy

그에게 실망한 나머지 맥이 빠져서 아무것도 하고 싶지 않았다.

I lost all of my energy from being so disappointed in him that I didn't want to do anything.

15 모순

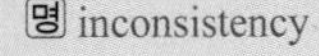
명 inconsistency

건강보험의 구조적인 모순을 바로잡아야 한다.

Structural inconsistencies in health insurance must be corrected.

16 미생물

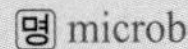
명 microbe

눈에 보이지 않는 미생물을 관찰하기 위해 현미경을 이용한다.

Microscopes are used to observe microbes invisible to the naked eye.

17 발굴되다

동 to be excavated

아파트 건설 현장에서 유적이 발굴되어 공사가 중단되었다.

The construction was halted because ruins were excavated at the apartment construction site.

발굴 excavation discovery 유적 발굴 excavation ruins
인재 발굴 discover talent/people 발굴하다 to discover/excavate

18 병행하다

동 combine, do/run both

요즘에는 두 가지 일을 병행하는 사람들이 늘고 있다.

These days, there are an increasing amount of people who do both jobs at the same time.

병행 going side by side, run together, parallelism

19 습득

명 acquisition, learning

제2언어 습득에는 개인차가 있다.

There are individual differences in second language acquisition.

습득하다 to aquire/learn 습득되다 to be aquired

20 열풍

명 fever, craze, frenzy

몇 년 전부터 우리나라에서는 조기교육 열풍이 불고 있다.

Early education craze has been blowing in Korea for several years.

'열풍'은 뜨거운 바람이라는 뜻이지만 보통 '사람들 사이에서 관심이나 인기가 많은 일'을 나타낼 때 사용해요.
'열풍' means hot winds but it is usually used to indicate 'something that is of great interest or popularity among people'.

건강에 대한 사람들의 관심이 높아지면서 자전거로 출퇴근하기 열풍이 불고 있다.
As people's interest in health increases, a craze for commuting by bicycle is blowing.

21 영리

명 profit

기업은 영리 추구를 목적으로 한다.

Companies aim to earn profits.

22 완곡하다

형 euphemistic

그 친구는 나의 부탁을 완곡하게 거절했다.

The friend euphemistically declined my request.

23 웃돌다

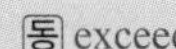

동 exceed

올해 집값 상승률이 지난해의 수준을 크게 웃돌고 있다.

The rate of increase in house prices this year significantly exceeds the level of last year.

24 유독

부 especially

올해 겨울은 유독 춥게 느껴진다.

This winter feels especially cold.

25 의식적

명 conscious

잘못된 자세를 교정하기 위해 의식적으로 어깨를 펴고 반듯하게 앉았다.

To correct the wrong posture, I consciously spread my shoulders and sat up straight.

관련어

의식하다 be conscious of, be aware

반) 무의식적 unconscious, involuntary

26 이해관계

명 interest

이 문제는 각 집단의 이해관계가 얽혀 있기 때문에 해결하기 어렵다.

This problem is difficult to solve because the interests of each group are intertwined.

이해관계가 얽히다 interests are entangled
이해관계를 떠나다 leave interests

27 인재

명 talented person

기업들은 좋은 인재를 찾기 위한 많은 시스템을 갖추고 있다.

Companies have many systems to find good talent.

28 작용하다

동 apply, action

그의 증언은 나에게 불리하게 작용했다.

His testimony was applied negatively against me.

작용 application, action　　작용되다 function, work
반작용 reaction

29 저물다

동 get dark, grow dark

겨울 산에서는 해가 빨리 저문다.

In the winter mountains, the sky grows dark quickly.

30 전환

명 transformation, change

우울했는데 운동을 했더니 기분 전환이 되었다.

I was depressed, but after exercising, my mood transformed.

전환기 turning point　전환하다 to transition/change
전환되다 be changed

31 죄책감

명 guilt

그는 거짓말을 하면서 전혀 죄책감을 느끼지 않는다.

He doesn't feel guilty at all while lying.

DAY 19 ★★

32 지방자치단체

명 local government

지방자치단체 중 재정 자립도가 가장 높은 곳은 서울특별시이다.

Among local governments, Seoul Metropolitan Government has the highest level of financial independence.

33 처벌

명 punishment

과대 광고는 처벌의 대상이 될 수 있다.

Overexaggerated advertisements can be subject to punishment.

처벌하다 to punish 처벌되다 to be punished

34 편파적

명 partial

이 기사는 한쪽 입장만 듣고 편파적으로 쓰여졌다.

This article was written with partiality in listening to one side of the story.

35 현저하다

형 marked, noticeable

두 아이의 태권도 실력은 현저하게 차이가 났다.

The two children's Taekwondo skills were noticeably different.

TOPIK에서 혼동하기 쉬운 단어

다의어 Polysemy

열풍

❶ 많은 사람들 사이에서 유행처럼 번지는 기세

예 건강에 대한 사람들의 관심이 높아지면서 자전거로 출퇴근하기 열풍이 불고 있다.

As people's interest in health increases, a craze for commuting to work by bicycle is blow ing.

❷ 뜨거운 바람

예 의류 건조기는 열풍으로 옷을 말린다.

A clothes dryer dries clothes with hot air.

반의어 Antonym

웃돌다 exceed ↔ 밑돌다 to be slightly lower than

예 6월인데 벌써 30도를 웃도는 날씨가 계속되고 있다.

It's only June, but the weather already exceeds 30 degrees.

예 국회의원 선거 투표율이 60퍼센트를 밑돌고 있다.

Voter turnout in the National Assembly elections is sightly less than 60 percent.

유의어 Synonym

저물다 get dark ≒ 지다

예 겨울 산에서는 해가 빨리 저문다.

겨울 산에서는 해가 빨리 진다.

In the winter mountains, the sky get dark quickly.

복습해 보세요

서로 어울리는 단어를 찾아 연결해 보세요.
Find words that go with each other and connect them.

1. 근무 •	• a. 지급되다
2. 급여 •	• b. 교대하다
3. 관계 •	• c. 발굴되다
4. 유적 •	• d. 대등하다
5. 해 •	• e. 저물다

자연스러운 문장이 되도록 둘 중에서 알맞은 단어를 고르세요.
Try to complete the sentence in a natural way by selecting the correct word out of the two.

6. 그 작가는 기자의 인터뷰 요청에 (a. 현저하게 / b. 완곡하게) 거절을 뜻을 표현했다.
   The writer euphemistically refused the reporter's request for an interview.

7. 아르바이트하면서 대학 공부를 (a. 병행하는 / b. 작용하는) 것은 쉬운 일이 아니었다.
   It was not easy to work part-time and study at the same time.

8. 우리 회사는 중국어에 (a. 다채로운 / b. 능통한) 인재를 구하고 있습니다.
   Our company is looking for talented people who are fluent in Chinese.

9. 같은 잘못을 해도 (a. 미생물 / b. 죄책감)을/를 크게 느끼는 사람이 있다.
   There are people who feel a lot more guilt even if they make the same mistake.

10. (a. 편파적인 / b. 의식적인) 보도가 되지 않도록 양쪽 주장을 균형있게 방송해야 한다.
    Both claims should be broadcast in a balanced way to avoid biased reporting.

정답

1.b 2.a 3.d 4.c 5.e 6.b 7.a 8.b 9.b 10.a

DAY 20

확인해 보세요

빨간 시트지로 가리고 단어의 뜻을 알면, □에 ✓ 해 보세요.

After covering up the words with red cover, please check(✓) the box (□) when you know the meaning of the word.

- □ 01 강력하다 strong, powerful
- □ 02 고령화 aging
- □ 03 구독 subscription
- □ 04 기막히다 unbelievable
- □ 05 기상 weather
- □ 06 기증 donation
- □ 07 노숙자 homeless
- □ 08 다국적 multinational
- □ 09 단가 unit price
- □ 10 대략적 general/ outline
- □ 11 노약하다 jump, leap
- □ 12 동정하다 to have pity
- □ 13 마일리지 mileage
- □ 14 맥락 context
- □ 15 모욕적 insult
- □ 16 미세 micro, fine
- □ 17 발급 issue, get
- □ 18 보건 health
- □ 19 시행착오 trials and errors
- □ 20 여간 ordinarily, normally
- □ 21 완료하다 to complete
- □ 22 요양하다 to recuperate, nurse
- □ 23 웅장하다 grand, magnificent
- □ 24 유동적 flexible
- □ 25 의식주 basic necessities of life; food, clothing, shelter
- □ 26 인상적 memorable, impressive
- □ 27 인종 race
- □ 28 잔인하다 cruel, merciless
- □ 29 저서 books
- □ 30 장담 guarantee, assure
- □ 31 주거 living, residence
- □ 32 지배적 majority, dominance
- □ 33 철저히 thoroughly, strictly
- □ 34 폐지되다 to be abolished
- □ 35 혐오 hatred

DAY 20

 are the words that appeared in the former tests, and you may get a higher grade if you study them together.

01 강력하다

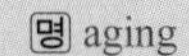 strong, powerful

여당이 제안한 정책에 대해 야당은 강력하게 반대하고 있다.

The opposition party is strongly opposing the policy proposed by the ruling party.

02 고령화

명 aging

급격한 출산율 저하와 평균 수명의 연장이 고령화 사회의 원인으로 꼽힌다.

The rapid decline in the birth rate and the extension of the average life expectancy are cited as the causes of an aging society.

출제 경향 how this word appears in the test

한국 사회는 급격하게 고령화가 진행되고 있기 때문에, '고령화 사회'라는 주제는 토픽에서도 자주 다루어지고 있어요.
Since Korean society is rapidly aging, the topic of 'aging society' is frequently discussed in Topik.
Study words such as 평균 수명(life expectancy), 노령화 사회(aging society), 저출산 사회(low fertility society), and 인구 고령화(aging population).

03 구독

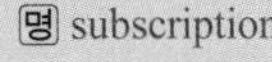

요즘은 신문을 보는 사람이 감소하면서 신문 구독을 신청하는 사람도 줄고 있다.

As the number of newspaper readers decline, people who apply for newspaper subscriptions are declining.

구독하다 to subscribe

04 기막히다

형 unbelievable, in disbelief

이 식당은 음식 맛이 기막혀서 단골 손님이 많다.

This restaurant has unbelievably good food, so it has many regular customers.

이 단어는 긍정적인 뜻으로도 부정적인 뜻으로도 사용할 수 있어요.
This word can be used both positively and negatively.

이 곳은 경치가 기막힌 것으로 이름난 관광지다. (긍정적인 뜻)
This place is famous for its unbelievably amazing view. (Positive)
늦게 온 친구가 나한테 사과를 하기는커녕 오히려 화를 내서 기막혔다. (부정적인 뜻)
I was in disbelief that my friend who was late got angry at me rather than apologizing.(Negative)

DAY 20 ★★

05 기상

명 weather

기상이 악화되어 비행기 출발 시간이 지연되고 있다.

The flight departure time is delayed because the weather got worse.

06 기증

명 donation

이 미술관은 김 선생님이 기증한 그림을 전시하는 곳이다.

This art museum is a place to display the artworks that Teacher Kim (Mr. Kim) donated.

장기 기증 organ donation

07 노숙자

명 homeless

이곳은 노숙자들을 위한 무료 급식을 제공하고 있다.

This place provides free meals to the homeless.

08 다국적

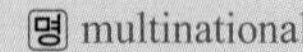

multinational

많은 다국적 기업들이 한국에 대한 투자를 늘리고 있다.

Many multinational companies are increasing investments into Korea.

09 단가

명 unit price

신제품 단가를 대폭 낮추어 타 회사와의 경쟁력을 갖추게 되었다.

We became competitive with the other companies by significantly lowering the unit cost of new products.

10 대략적

명 general/rough, outline

지금까지 문학의 개념에 대해 대략적으로 알아보았습니다.

Up till now, we have looked at the general concept of literature.

11 도약하다

동 jump, leap

우리 야구 팀은 이번에 처음으로 전국 대회에 참가하면서 한 단계 도약할 수 있었습니다.

Our baseball team was able to take a leap forward by participating in the national competition for the first time.

12 동정하다

동 to have pity/sympathy (for)

그렇게 동정하는 눈으로 쳐다보지 마세요.

Don't look with those pitying eyes.

동정 pity/sympathy

13 마일리지

명 mileage, (card) rewards

그동안 적립한 마일리지로 선물을 샀다.

I bought a gift using the mileage I saved up.

마일리지가 쌓이다 accumulate mileage/rewards

14 맥락

명 context

글의 앞뒤 맥락을 모르면 이 부분의 내용을 정확히 이해할 수 없다.

If you don't know the context behind the text, you can't really understand the content of this part.

맥락이 통하다 be on the same page, understand the same context

15 모욕적

명 insulting

채팅에서 모욕적인 말을 했다면 모욕죄 성립이 가능하다.

If you insulting comments while texting, it may be applicable for defamation.

모욕 insult

16 미세

명 micro, fine, tiny, minute

최근 며칠 동안 미세 먼지가 많아서 환기를 못 하고 있다.

There has been a lot of fine dust in recent days, so I can't ventilate.

미세하다 minutely

17 발급

명 issue, get

비자 발급 신청을 하고 시간이 많이 지났지만 아직 연락이 없다.

It's been a long time since I applied to get a visa, but I haven't heard back yet.

발급하다 to issue　　발급되다 to be issued

18 보건

명 health

보건 당국은 코로나 백신 접종을 무료로 실시하겠다고 밝혔다.

Health authorities said they would provide free coronavirus vaccinations.

관련어

보건 시설 health facilities　　보건소 public health center

19 시행착오

명 trials and errors

여러 번의 시행착오 끝에 신제품을 개발하였다.

After many trials and errors, we developed a new product.

20 여간

부 ordinarily, normally, commonly

그 일을 혼자서 다 해낸다는 것은 여간 어려운 일이 아니다.

It is not a ordinary thing to complete all that work by yourself.

이 단어는 주로 부정문의 형태로 사용해요.
This word is usually used in a negative sentences.

이 아이는 여간 영리한 아이가 아니다.
This child is an exceptionally bright child.

21 완료하다

동 to complete

이 작업을 이번주까지 완료해야 한다.

I need to finish the work by this week.

완료되다 to be finished   완료 finish

22 요양하다

동 to recuperate, nurse, care for health

그 작가는 건강이 안 좋아져서 조용한 시골로 가서 요양하고 있다.

The author is recuperating in the countryside because his health deteriorated.

요양 시설 nursing facility   요양원 care center, nursing home

요양사 nursing care worker

23 웅장하다

형 grand, magnificent

입구에 들어서자 웅장한 건물이 가장 먼저 눈에 띄었다.

Upon entering the entrance, the magnificent building was the first thing that caught my eye.

24 유동적

명 flexible

아르바이트라서 임금이 유동적이다.

The wages are flexible since it is a part-time job.

반) 고정적 set, permanent

25 의식주

명 basic necessities of life; food, clothing, shelter

난민들은 의식주 문제를 해결하기 위해 애를 쓰고 있다.

Refugees are struggling to solve the problem of meeting basic necessities.

26 인상적

명 memorable, impressive, striking

그 영화는 시작이 굉장히 인상적이라서 아직도 기억에 생생하다.

I still vividly remember that movie because it's beginning was so memorable.

27 인종

명 race

시대가 많이 바뀌었음에도 불구하고 여전히 인종 차별이 문제가 되고 있다.

Although times have change a lot, racial discrimination is still a problem.

28 잔인하다

형 cruel, merciless

길고양이를 잔인하게 해친 사건이 연달아 일어났다.

관련어

There was a series of incidents where stray cats were cruelly harmed.

잔인 cruel　　잔인성 cruelty

29 저서

명 books

그 교수님이 쓴 저서만 해도 100권이 넘는다.

There are more than 100 books written by that professor alone.

30 장담

명 guarantee, assure

이번에 합격할 수 있을지 장담을 못하겠다.

I can't guarantee if I'll be able to pass this time.

장담하다 guarantee

31 주거

명 living, residence

주거 환경이 삶의 질을 결정하는 경우가 많다.

Living environment often determines the quality of life.

주거 공간 residential space　　주거비 housing cost

32 지배적

명 majority, dominance, ruling, prevailing

3년 사이에 집값이 급격히 오르자 집값을 안정화시켜야 한다는 여론이 지배적이다.

As house prices have risen sharply in three years, the prevailing public opinion is that house prices should be stabilized.

지배 dominance, rule　　지배하다 to be ruling, dominant

33 철저히

부 thoroughly, strictly

사고 예방을 위해 안전 기준은 철저히 지켜 주시기 바랍니다.

Please strictly observe safety standards to prevent accidents.

철저하다 to be strict/thorough

34 폐지되다

동 to be abolished

2015년에 배우자가 불륜을 저지를 경우 처벌하는 간통법이 폐지되었다.

In 2015, the adultery law, which punishes spouses if they commit an affair, was abolished.

폐지하다 to abolish

35 혐오

명 hatred

인터넷 댓글을 보면 외국인에 대한 혐오를 가진 사람이 생각보다 많다.

If you look at comments on the internet, more people than expected have hatred towards foreigners.

혐오 시설 unpleasant/hated facilities

DAY 20 ★★

TOPIK에서 혼동하기 쉬운 단어

다의어 Polysemy

기막히다

❶ 너무 놀랍거나 기분이 나빠서 할 말이 없다

예 약속 시간에 1시간이나 늦다니 정말 기막혔다.

It was unbelievable that you are an hour late for an appointment.

❷ 뭐라고 말할 수 없을만큼 대단하다

예 이 집 잔치국수는 정말 기막힌 맛이에요.

This home-made noodle soup is truly amazing.

반의어 Antonym

유동적 flexible ↔ **고정적** set, permanent

예 아르바이트라서 임금이 유동적이다.

The wages are flexible since it is a part-time job.

예 월급은 고정적인데 지출이 점점 늘고 있어서 큰일이다.

The fact that expenses are increasing while salaries are set is a big problem.

유의어 Synonym

잔인하다 cruel ≒ **무참하다**

예 길고양이를 잔인하게 해친 사건이 연달아 일어났다.

길고양이를 무참하게 해친 사건이 연달아 일어났다.

There was a series of incidents where stray cats were cruelly harmed.

복습해 보세요

다음 빈 칸에 알맞은 단어를 〈보기〉에서 골라 쓰세요.
Choose the appropriate word from <Example> to fill in the blanks below.

〈보기〉
a. 도약할 b. 잔인하게 c. 웅장한 d. 완료해야 e. 기막혀서

1. 이 식당은 음식 맛이 (   ) 단골 손님이 많다.
This restaurant has unbelievably good food, so it has many regular customers.

2. 이 작업을 이번주까지 (   ) 한다.
I need to finish the work by this week

3. 입구에 들어서자 (   ) 건물이 가장 먼저 눈에 띄었다.
Upon entering the entrance, the magnificent building was the first thing that caught my eye.

4. 길고양이를 (   ) 해친 사건이 연달아 일어났다.
There was a series of incidents where stray cats were cruelly harmed.

5. 우리 야구 팀은 이번에 처음으로 전국 대회에 참가하면서 한 단계 (   ) 수 있었습니다.
Our baseball team was able to take a leap forward by participating in the national competition for the first time.

DAY 20 ★★

자연스러운 문장이 되도록 둘 중에서 알맞은 단어를 고르세요.
Try to complete the sentence in a natural way by choosing the correct word.

6. 이 미술관은 김 선생님이 (a. 기증 / b. 기상)한 그림을 전시하는 곳이다.
This art museum is a place to display the artworks that Teacher Kim (Mr. Kim) donated.

7. 신제품 (a. 단가 / b. 맥락)을/를 대폭 낮추어 타 회사와의 경쟁력을 갖추게 되었다.
We became competitive with the other companies by significantly lowering the unit cost of new productc.

8. 최근 며칠 동안 (a. 보건 / b. 미세) 먼지가 많아서 환기를 못 하고 있다.
There has been a lot of fine dust in recent days, so I can't ventilate.

9. 사고 예방을 위해 안전 기준은 (a. 철저히 / b. 여간) 지켜 주시기 바랍니다.
Please strictly observe safety standards to prevent accidents.

정답

1.e 2.d 3.c 4.b 5.a 6.a 7.a 8.b 9.a

❶ 대(大) big

대규모 large scale
대도시 a big city
대량 mass
최대 maximum
대기업 a big company
대가족 a large family

❷ 소(小) small

소규모 small scale
소도시 a small town
소량 small amount
소극장 a small theater

❸ 급(急) rapid

급변하다 change rapidly
급증하다 increase rapidly
급감하다 drop sharply
급등하다 soar
급락하다 drop sharply
급경사 steep slope
급정거 sudden stop

▲ 소극장 a small theater

주간 복습 day 16 – day 20

아래 단어를 보고 빈 칸에 뜻을 적어 보세요. 그리고 점선대로 접어서 적은 뜻이 맞는지 확인해 보세요. (만일 틀렸다면 뒷면의 단어 앞 □에 ✓ 하세요.)

Write down the meaning of the given word in the blank. Also, fold the page along a dotted line and check whether you got it right or wrong. (If you got it wrong tick the box in front of the word in next page.)

▼접는선

단어	뜻
급증하다	
능동적	
손실	
증가하다	
판단하다	
극복하다	
모범	
올바르다	
종사자	
채용하다	
계기	
능숙하다	
수익	
전형적	
편견	
기여하다	
능통하다	
동일하다	
습득	
편파적	
고령화	
시행착오	
의식주	
폐지되다	
혐오	

※접어서 뜻이 맞는지 확인해보세요.

주간 복습 day 16 – day 20

빈 칸에 한국어 단어를 3번 적고 다시 외워 봅시다.

Write down the Korean word 3 times in the blank and try to memorize it again.

◀ 접는선

뜻	단어		
☐ to increase rapidly	급증하다		
☐ active	능동적		
☐ loss	손실		
☐ to increase/rise	증가하다		
☐ to judge/believe	판단하다		
☐ to overcome	극복하다		
☐ model	모범		
☐ correct, right	올바르다		
☐ worker	종사자		
☐ to hire	채용하다		
☐ chance, opportunity	계기		
☐ to be skilled/ proficient at	능숙하다		
☐ profit	수익		
☐ typical	전형적		
☐ prejudice	편견		
☐ contribute	기여하다		
☐ fluent	능통하다		
☐ same	동일하다		
☐ acquisition, learning	습득		
☐ partial	편파적		
☐ aging	고령화		
☐ trials and errors	시행착오		
☐ basic necessities of life; food, clothing, shelter	의식주		
☐ to be abolished	폐지되다		
☐ hatred	혐오		

DAY 21

확인해 보세요

빨간 시트지로 가리고 단어의 뜻을 알면, □에 ✓ 해 보세요.

After covering up the words with red cover, please check(✓) the box (□) when you know the meaning of the word.

□ 01	강렬하다	strong, intense	□ 13	맥박	pulse	□ 25	인성	character, personality
□ 02	고르다	even, fair	□ 14	모질다	harsh, heartless	□ 26	인증하다	to certify
□ 03	구성하다	to form/build	□ 15	미숙하다	inexperienced	□ 27	잡음	static noise
□ 04	기한	deadline	□ 16	발령	appointment, assignment	□ 28	저소득	low-income
□ 05	끔찍하다	terrible, grusome	□ 17	보편적	common, universal	□ 29	절차	procedure
□ 06	내실	interior	□ 18	실업	unemployment	□ 30	주관하다	to be in charge of
□ 07	노출	exposure	□ 19	여건	condition	□ 31	지불	payment
□ 08	단결	unity, solidarity	□ 20	완만하다	gentle, gradual	□ 32	첨부	attachment
□ 09	대립되다	be opposed to, competing	□ 21	우선시하다	to prioritize	□ 33	촉구하다	to call for, to demand
□ 10	도입하다	to implement/ introduce	□ 22	워낙	such	□ 34	표절	plagiarism
□ 11	동조하다	to agree	□ 23	유래	origin	□ 35	형편없다	poor, terrible
□ 12	마케팅	marketing	□ 24	의외로	unexpectedly, surprisingly			

DAY 21

 are the words that appeared in the former tests, and you may get a higher grade if you study them together.

01 강렬하다

형 strong, intense

나를 바라보는 그 사람의 강렬한 눈빛이 너무 부담스러웠다.

The intense eyes of the person looking at me was so uncomfortable.

02 고르다

형 even, fair, regular

그 학생은 읽기, 듣기, 쓰기, 말하기 성적이 고른 편이다.

The student has even grades in reading, listening, writing and speaking.

03 구성하다

동 to form/build/establish

이번 사고에 대해 철저하게 조사하기 위해 조사단을 구성했다.

An investigation team was formed to thoroughly investigate this incident.

구성되다 be formed 구성원 member

04 기한

명 deadline

신청서 제출 기한은 다음주 금요일까지입니다.

The deadline to submit the application is by next Friday.

기한을 지키다 to meet the deadline 유통기한 expiration date

05 끔찍하다

형 terrible, grusome, horrible, awful

얼마 전 옆동네에서 끔찍한 살인 사건이 일어났다.

Not long ago, there was a terrible murder in the neighborhood.

'끔찍하다'는 부정적인 의미의 단어이지만 긍정적인 상황에서도 사용할 수 있는 표현도 있어요. '끔찍하게 아끼다'라는 표현은 어떤 것을 매우 아낀다는 것을 강조할 때 사용해요.

'끔찍하다' is a negative word, but there are also expressions that can be used in positive situations. The expression '끔찍하게 아끼다' is used to emphasize how much you care for something.

내 친구는 자기 가족을 끔찍하게 아낀다.
My friend cherishes his family terribly.

06 내실

명 interior, internal stability

새로운 제품을 개발할 때 화려한 겉모습보다는 내실을 기하는 데에 힘써야 한다.

When developing a new product, it is necessary to focus on the interior rather than flashy appearances.

DAY 21 ★★

07 노출

명 exposure

유명 연예인들은 사생활 노출을 무척 꺼린다.

Famous celebrities are strongly unwilling to expose their private life.

정보 노출 exposure of information
노출이 심하다 too much exposure, too revealing
노출하다 to expose　　노출되다 to be exposed

08 단결

명 unity, solidarity

온 국민의 단결로 IMF의 어려움을 극복했다.

The hardships of the IMF were overcome through national unity.

단결하다 to unify　　단결되다 to be unified
단결시키다 to bring together

09 대립되다

동 be opposed to, competing

양측은 줄곧 대립된 입장을 견지하는 듯했다.

The two sides seemed to always take opposing positions.

대립하다 to oppose

10 도입하다

동 to implement/introduce

기존 시험의 문제점을 해결하기 위해 새로운 시험 제도를 도입했다.

We have introduced a new test system to solve the problems of existing tests.

도입 implementation/introduction

도입되다 to be implemented/introduced

11 동조하다

동 to agree

아무리 친해도 그의 극단적인 의견에는 동조할 수 없다.

No matter how close we are, I cannot agree to his extreme oppinions.

12 마케팅

명 marketing

SNS로 소비자에게 다가가는 마케팅 전략을 모색 중이다.

We are searching for a marketing tactic that approaches consumers via social media.

13 맥박

명 pulse

맥박의 세기로 심장의 상태를 알 수 있다.

The strength of the pulse can be used to figure out the healthiness of the heart.

14 모질다

형 harsh, heartless, severe

정부의 모진 탄압에도 굴복하지 않고 민주주의를 이뤄냈다.

Democracy was achieved without succumbing to harsh government oppression.

성격이 모질다 have a bad temper

15 미숙하다

형 inexperienced

나는 아직 운전이 미숙해 장거리 운전은 하지 않는다.

I am still inexperienced in driving so I don't drive long-distance.

미숙 inexperience, premature

16 발령

명 appointment, assignment

해외 지사 발령을 희망했지만 내가 아닌 동료가 가게 되었다.

I was hoping to be assigned an overseas branch, but a colleague went instead of me.

발령하다 to issue 발령되다 to be assigned

17 보편적

명 common, universal

앱보다는 카드나 현금으로 결재하는 것이 보편적이다.

It is more common to pay by card or cash than by app.

보편화 generalization 보편성 universal general

18 실업

명 unemployment

정부는 다양한 방법으로 실업 문제를 해결하고 있다.

The government is solving the problem of unemploymen in various ways.

실업률 unemployment rate 실업자 unemployed person

19 여건

명 condition

경제적인 여건만 허락된다면 계속 연구를 진행하고 싶다.

If financial conditions allow, I would like to continue the research.

20 완만하다

형 gentle, gradual, slow

이 산은 완만한 편이라 처음 등산하는 사람도 어렵지 않게 올라갈 수 있다.

This mountain has a gentle slope, so even first-time hikers can climb it easily.

DAY 21 ★★

21 우선시하다

동 to prioritize

우리 회사는 신입사원을 뽑을 때 학벌보다 능력을 우선시한다.

Our company prioritizes skill over educational background when picking a new employee.

22 워낙

부 such

그는 워낙 내성적인 성격이라 다른 사람들 앞에 나서는 것을 극도로 꺼린다.

He is such an introvert that he is extremely reluctant to stand in front of others.

23 유래

명 origin

이 축제는 유래가 깊은 지역 행사이다.

This festival is a local event of deep origin.

유래하다 to originate/derive 유래되다 to originate from

24 의외로

부 unexpectedly, surprisingly

성인이 되었지만 독립하지 못하는 자녀들이 의외로 많다.

Surprisingly, there are many children who have become adults but cannot become independent.

의외의 대답 unexpected answer 의외의 결과 unexpected result

25 인성

명 character, personality

학교 공부보다 인성 교육이 더 중요하다는 것은 두말할 필요가 없다.

It goes without saying that teaching about good character is more important than schoolwork.

26 인증하다

동 to certify

국가가 인증한 자격증을 가지고 있으면 취업에 도움이 되겠지요.

It would be helpful to get a job if you have a certificate certified by the state.

인증 certification authorization 인증되다 be certified

인증서 certification

27 잡음

명 static noise

자동차 라디오에서 잡음이 난다.

There is static noises coming from the car radio.

28 저소득

명 low-income

정부는 저소득층을 위한 지원을 강화하겠다고 밝혔다.

The government has announced that it will strengthen assistance for the low-income class.

반) 고소득 high-income

DAY 21 ★★

29 절차

명 procedure

모든 일은 절차대로 진행해야 추후에 문제가 발생하지 않는다.

Everything needs to be done according to the procedure so that there is no problem in the future.

30 주관하다

동 to be in charge of, to oversee/organize

정부에서 주관하는 이번 행사에 많은 시민들이 참여하였다.

Many citizens participated in this government-organized event.

주관 supervision, oversee 주관처 host organizer

31 지불

명 payment

저희 가게에서는 현금 지불만 가능합니다.

Our shop only accepts cash payments.

지불하다 to pay 지불되다 to be paid

32 첨부

명 attachment

첨부 파일을 보내 드리오니 확인해 주시기 바랍니다.

I will send you an attached file, so please check it.

33 촉구하다

동 to call for, to press/demand

공사 현장 노동자의 사망이 어어지자 대책 마련을 촉구하는 목소리가 높아지고 있다.

As the death of construction site workers continues, voices calling for countermeasures are growing.

출제 경향 how this word appears in the test

읽기에서는 필자의 태도를 묻는 문제가 매번 출제되고 있어요. 필자의 태도를 나타내는 어휘로 '촉구하다', '우려하다', '평가하다', '비판하다', '강조하다', '예상하다', '옹호하다', '요구하다' 등의 단어가 출제된 적이 있으니까 기억해 두세요.

In reading, there are always questions that ask about the author's attitude. Remember words that express the author's attitude such as 촉구하다(demand), 우려하다(worry), 평가하다(evaluate), 비판하다(criticize), 강조하다(emphasize), 예상하다(anticipate), 옹호하다(support), and 요구하다(demand) because they have been used before.

34 표절

명 plagiarism

인기 작가의 소설에 대해 표절 의혹이 일고 있다.

There are suspicions of plagiarism against a novel by a popular author.

표절 시비 plagiarism dispute

35 형편없다

형 poor, terrible, awful, lousy

이번 달 영업 실적이 형편없어서 스트레스를 받고 있다.

I'm stressed out because of this month's poor sales performance.

TOPIK에서 혼동하기 쉬운 단어

동음이의어 Homonym

고르다

❶ 크기, 양 등의 차이 없이 같다 (형용사)

예 그 학생은 읽기, 듣기, 쓰기, 말하기 성적이 고른 편이다.

The student has even grades in reading, listening, writing and speaking.

❷ 여러 가지 중에서 선택하다 (동사)

예 내가 신발 고르는 것 좀 도와줄래?

Can you help me choose some shoes?

반의어 Antonym

저소득 low-income ↔ **고소득** high-income

예 정부는 저소득층을 위한 지원을 강화하겠다고 밝혔다.

The government has announced that it will strengthen assistance for the low-income class.

예 정부에서는 고소득자에 대한 세금을 인상하는 방안을 검토 중이다.

The government is considering raising taxes on high-income earners.

유의어 Synonym

보편적 common ≒ **일반적**

예 앱보다는 카드나 현금으로 결제하는 것이 보편적이다.

앱보다는 카드나 현금으로 결제하는 것이 일반적이다.

It is more common to pay by card or cash than by app.

DAY 21 ★★

복습해 보세요

서로 어울리는 단어를 찾아 연결해 보세요.
Find words that go with each other and connect them.

1. 제도	a. 동조하다
2. 의견	b. 도입하다
3. 경사	c. 주관하다
4. 행사	d. 완만하다
5. 대책 마련	e. 촉구하다

다음 빈 칸에 알맞은 단어를 〈보기〉에서 골라 쓰세요.
Choose the appropriate word from <Example> to fill in the blanks below.

〈보기〉
a. 강렬해서 b. 우선시하는 c. 형편없어서 d. 고르게 e. 미숙해서

6. 그 사람은 이가 (   ) 난 편이다.
That person has pretty even teeth.

7. 햇빛이 너무 (   ) 양산을 쓰고 다녔다.
The sunlight was too intense, so I carried around a parasol.

8. 아직 요리가 (   ) 요리를 완성하는 데에 시간이 많이 걸리는 편이다.
I am still inexperienced at cooking, so it still takes a lot of time to finish a dish.

9. 신입사원을 뽑을 때 학벌보다 능력을 (   ) 회사가 조금씩 늘고 있다.
There is a gradual increase of companies that prioritize skill over educational background when picking new employees.

10. 이번 시험 성적이 (   ) 스트레스를 받고 있다.
I'm stressed because this test score is terrible.

정답

1.b 2.a 3.d 4.c 5.e 6.d 7.a 8.e 9.b 10.c

DAY 22

확인해 보세요

빨간 시트지로 가리고 단어의 뜻을 알면, □에 ✓ 해 보세요.

After covering up the words with red cover, please check(✓) the box (□) when you know the meaning of the word.

□ 01	가늠	estimate	□ 13	맵시	appearance, style	□ 25	유행가	pop songs
□ 02	강제적	forced	□ 14	모형	model	□ 26	의욕	will
□ 03	고립	isolation	□ 15	미약하다	weak, slight	□ 27	인종	race
□ 04	구직	job hunting	□ 16	발신자	sender	□ 28	인지	cognition, recognition
□ 05	기호	symbol, sign	□ 17	벅차다	overwhelming, difficult	□ 29	절감	reduction
□ 06	낙관적	optimistic	□ 18	보수적	conservative	□ 30	저조	low, poor
□ 07	노폐물	waste	□ 19	실용	utility, practicality	□ 31	점검하다	to inspect
□ 08	단계적	in stages/ step-by-step	□ 20	여론	public opinion	□ 32	지속	continuance
□ 09	대변하다	to talk on behalf of	□ 21	여지	room, margin	□ 33	체감	sense, feel
□ 10	도처	everywhere	□ 22	완치	full recovery	□ 34	필수품	necessity
□ 11	동종업계	same field/ industry	□ 23	원격	remote	□ 35	혜택	benefit
□ 12	마취	anesthesia	□ 24	유력하다	strong, dominant			

DAY 22

 are the words that appeared in the former tests, and you may get a higher grade if you study them together.

01 가늠

명 estimate

바닷물의 깊이가 가늠이 안 된다.

I cannot estimate the depth of the seawater.

가늠하다 to estimate

02 강제적

명 forced

아이에게 강제적으로 책을 읽히면 오히려 독서를 싫어하게 될 수 있다.

If you force your children to read books, they might actually end up disliking reading.

반강제적 half-forced

03 고립

명 isolation

홍수로 우리 마을이 고립 상태에 놓였다.

The flood left our village in isolation.

고립되다 to be isolated

04 구직

명 job hunting

최근 불황으로 인해 구직을 포기하는 졸업생들이 늘고 있다.

There is an increase of graduates who give up job hunting due to the recent recession.

관련어

구직난 difficulty in finding a job, lack of employment

구직자 job-seeker

05 기호

명 symbol, sign

영어 발음 기호를 보면 모르는 영어 단어도 쉽게 읽을 수 있다.

If you look at the English pronunciation signs, you can easily read English words that you don't know.

06 낙관적

명 optimistic

경제학자들은 올해 국내 경제 상황을 낙관적으로 보고 있다.

Economists are optimistic about the domestic economic situation this year.

낙관하다 to be optimistic

반) 비관적 pessimistic

'낙관적'과 '낙천적'은 뭐가 다를까요?
'낙관적'은 보통 미래에 대한 전망을 이야기할 때 사용해요.

What is the difference between '낙관적' and '낙천적'?
'낙관적' is usually used to talk about the future.

김 후보는 이번 선거 결과를 낙관적으로 보고 있다.
Candidate Kim is optimistic about the results of this election.

DAY 22 ★★

07 노폐물

명 waste

잘못된 식습관으로 혈관에 노폐물이 쌓이면 성인병을 유발할 수 있다.

Stacking up waste in blood vessels due to poor eating habits can cause adult diseases.

08 단계적

명 in stages/phases, step by step

3개월동안 단계적 절차를 거쳐서 결혼 비자를 받았다.

I got a marriage visa after going through a step-by-step process for 3 months.

09 대변하다

동 to talk on behalf of

회장이 전체 학생들의 입장을 대변해서 말했다.

The class president spoke on behalf of all students.

대변인 spokesman

10 도처

명 everywhere

아직도 위험이 도처에 널려 있으므로 조심하십시오.

Danger is still everywhere, so be careful.

11 동종업계

명 same field/industry

우리 회사는 지속적인 연구개발로 동종업계에서 우위를 차지하고 있다.

Our company has the upper hand in the our industry because of our continuous research and development.

12 마취

명 anesthesia

수술할 때 전신 마취를 해야 한다고 해서 걱정이다.

I'm worried that I have to get general anesthesia during surgery.

마취하다 to anesthetize

13 맵시

명 appearance, style

헤어스타일을 맵시 있게 연출하는 법을 알려 드립니다.

Here's how to make your hairstyle look stylish.

맵시가 나다 to be stylish

14 모형

명 model

실제로 지어진 건물이 건축 전에 제작한 건물 모형과 달라서 실망했다.

I was disappointed that the actual building was different from the model that was made before construction.

15 미약하다

형 weak, slight

어젯밤에 느꼈던 미약한 진동이 지진 때문이라는 것을 알게 되었다.

I found out that the slight vibration I felt last night was due to the earthquake.

16 발신자

명 sender

누가 우편으로 선물을 보냈는지 확인하려고 했지만 발신자 정보가 없었다.

I tried to check who sent the gift by mail, but there was no sender information.

관련어

반) 수신자 recipient

17 벅차다

형 overwhelming, difficult

이 월급으로는 서울에서 생활하기 벅차다.

It is difficult to live in Seoul with this salary.

DAY 22 ★★

18 보수적

명 conservative

보수적인 사람들은 기존 질서를 지키려는 경향이 강하다.

Conservative people have a strong tendency to uphold the existing order.

관련어

반) 진보적 progressive

19 실용

명 utility, practicality

가까운 시일 내에 전기자동차가 실용화 될 것이다.

Electric vehicles will be put to practical use in the near future.

관련어

실용성 practical use/value　　실용적 practical/useful

실용 학문 practical study

20 여론

명 public opinion

정부가 발표한 새로운 정책에 대해 부정적인 여론이 형성되고 있다.

Negative public opinion is forming on the new policy announced by the government.

관련어

여론 조사 public opinion poll

21 여지

명 room, margin

두 회사 중에서 고민할 여지 없이 당연히 더 유명한 A 회사에 입사하기로 결정했다.

Without room for hesitation, I decided to join the more famous company A.

22 완치

명 full recovery

그는 그녀의 완치를 기대하고 있다.

He expects her to make a full recovery.

완치하다 to fully heal
완치되다 to be fully recovered

23 원격

명 remote

인터넷 상황이 좋지 않아서 원격 수업을 듣는 데 어려움이 있다.

I had difficulty in taking remote classes due to poor internet conditions.

원격 강의 remote lecture
원격 장치 remote device
원격 조종 remote control

24 유력하다

형 strong, dominant, potential

유력한 용의자가 나타났지만 범인이라는 증거가 부족하다.

A strong suspect has emerged, but there is insufficient evidence that he is the culprit.

유력 influence, leading, strong

25 유행가

명 pop songs

나는 노래방에 가면 보통 최신 유행가를 부르는 편이다.

When I go to karaoke, I usually sing the latest pop songs.

26 의욕

명 will

그는 모든 일에 의욕이 없다.

He is unwilling to do everything.

의욕적 motivated

27 인종

명 race

인종 차별은 세계 곳곳에서 다양한 형태로 나타나고 있다.

Racism takes many forms around the world.

소수 인종 racial minority

28 인지

명 cognition, recognition, perception

나이가 들수록 인지 능력이 떨어진다는 연구 결과가 나왔다.

Studies show that cognitive ability decreases with age.

인지하다 recognize, perceive

DAY 22 ★★

29 절감

명 reduction

에너지 절감을 위해 가급적 에어컨 사용을 하지 않으려고 한다.

I try not to use air conditioners as much as possible to reduce energy usage.

절감하다 to reduce cut   절감되다 to be reduced/cut

30 저조

명 low, poor

지방 의회 의원 선거의 투표율 저조는 어제오늘의 문제가 아니다.

Low turnout in local council elections is not a new problem.

실적 저조 poor performance   참여율 저조 low participation

31 점검하다

동 to inspect

콘서트 전 무대 시설을 꼼꼼하게 점검했다.

Before the concert, the stage facilities were thoroughly inspected.

점검 inspection

32 지속

명 continuance, sustenance

지속 가능한 개발의 일환으로 전세계적으로 온실 가스를 줄이려고 노력하고 있다.

As part of sustainable development, efforts are being made to reduce greenhouse gases worldwide.

지속하다 to persist/sustain 지속되다 to last/continue

33 체감

명 sense, feel

오늘 기온은 높은 편인데 바람이 불어서 체감 온도는 훨씬 낮다.

Today's temperature is high, but the temperature feels much lower because of the blowing wind.

34 필수품

명 necessity, essential goods

신종 코로나 바이러스의 유행으로 마스크가 외출 필수품이 되었다.

Masks have become a necessity due to new covid pandemic.

생활 필수품 bare/life necessities

35 혜택

명 benefit

종교 단체가 세금 면제 혜택을 받는 것에 대해 불만의 목소리가 크다.

There is loud voices of dissatisfaction with religious groups getting tax exemption benefits.

의료보험 혜택 Healthcare benefits　　　할인 혜택 discount benefits

TOPIK에서 혼동하기 쉬운 단어

다의어 Polysemy

벅차다

❶ 어떤 일을 해 내기 어렵다

예 이 월급으로는 서울에서 생활하기 벅차다.

It is difficult to live in Seoul with this salary.

❷ 감격, 기쁨, 희망 등이 넘칠 정도로 가득하다

예 회사의 최종 면접에 합격했다는 소식에 가슴이 벅찼다.

I was overwhelmed by the news that I passed the company's final interview.

반의어 Antonym

낙관적 optimistic ↔ **비관적** pessimistic

예 경제학자들은 올해 국내 경제 상황을 낙관적으로 보고 있다.

Economists are optimistic about the domestic economic situation this year.

예 비관적으로 생각하는 사람은 우울한 감정을 느끼기 쉽다.

It is easier for people who think pessimistically to feel depressed.

유의어 Synonym

절감 reduction ≒ **절약**

예 에너지 절감을 위해 가급적 에어컨 사용을 하지 않으려고 한다.

에너지 절약을 위해 가급적 에어컨 사용을 하지 않으려고 한다.

I try not to use air conditioners as much as possible to reduce energy usage.

DAY 22 ★★

복습해 보세요

서로 어울리는 단어를 찾아 연결해 보세요.
Find words that go with each other and connect them.

1. 전신	a. 조사
2. 여론	b. 저조
3. 체감	c. 마취
4. 할인	d. 온도
5. 투표율	e. 혜택

자연스러운 문장이 되도록 둘 중에서 알맞은 단어를 고르세요.
Try to complete the sentence in a natural way by choosing the correct word.

6. 경제학자들은 올해 하반기 국내 경제 상황을 (a. 낙관적으로 / b. 강제적으로) 예상하고 있다.
   Economists are optimistic about the domestic economic situation this year.

7. (a. 단계적인 / b. 보수적인) 사람들은 기존 질서를 지키려는 경향이 강하다.
   Conservative people have a strong tendency to uphold the existing order.

8. 잘못된 식습관으로 혈관에 (a. 필수품 / b. 노폐물)이/가 쌓이면 성인병을 유발할 수 있다.
   Stacking up waste in blood vessels due to poor eating habits can cause adult diseases.

9. 조카는 대학 졸업을 앞두고 (a. 구직 / b. 고립) 활동을 하느라 정신이 없는 상태이다.
   My nephew is busy looking for a job before graduating from college.

10. 아르바이트와 학업을 병행하기가 (a. 벅차서 / b. 미약해서) 아르바이트를 줄이려고요.
    I'm trying to reduce my part-time work because it's overwhelming to work part-time and study at the same time.

정답

1.c 2.a 3.d 4.e 5.b 6.a 7.b 8.b 9.a 10.a

DAY 23

확인해 보세요

빨간 시트지로 가리고 단어의 뜻을 알면, □에 ✓ 해 보세요.

After covering up the words with red cover, please check(✓) the box (□) when you know the meaning of the word.

□ 01	가속	acceleration	□ 13	맹렬하다	fierce	□ 25	육류	meat
□ 02	강조하다	to emphasize	□ 14	모호하다	ambiguous	□ 26	의존도	dependency
□ 03	고소	sue	□ 15	미정	undefined	□ 27	인파	crowd
□ 04	구체화	materialization, specification	□ 16	민낯	true/naked face	□ 28	일거양득	killing two birds with one stone
□ 05	기호	taste, preference	□ 17	발휘하다	demonstrate, show	□ 29	잦다	frequent
□ 06	내딛다	to set foot on (to start/begin)	□ 18	복원	restoration	□ 30	저하	decline, deterioration
□ 07	노화	aging	□ 19	실행	implementation, execute	□ 31	접종	vaccination
□ 08	단념하다	give up	□ 20	여전하다	still	□ 32	지수	index, quotient
□ 09	대북	(towards) North Korea	□ 21	연일	day after day, everyday	□ 33	체결하다	to sign/enter into
□ 10	도태되다	to die out, to be selected out	□ 22	왜곡	distortion, twist	□ 34	하락	fall, decline
□ 11	동질성	homogeneity	□ 23	원동력	driving force	□ 35	혹평	criticism
□ 12	막다르다	dead end	□ 24	유망	promising, bright			

DAY 23

 are the words that appeared in the former tests, and you may get a higher grade if you study them together.

01 가속

명 acceleration

여러 단체의 투자를 받으면서 이번 연구에 가속이 붙기 시작했다.

This research began to accelerate as it received investments from various organizations.

가속화 accelerating

02 강조하다

동 to emphasize

요즘에는 개성을 강조하는 옷차림이 눈길을 끌고 있다.

Attire that emphasizes individuality is attracting attention these days.

출제 경향 how this word appears in the test

읽기에서는 글을 쓴 목적을 묻는 문제가 매번 출제되고 있어요. 그때, 사지선다 문항에 자주 등장하는 단어가 '강조하다', '경고하다', '지적하다', '설명하다', '분석하다', '제기하다', '제시하다' 예요. 함께 기억해 두세요.

In reading, the question of the purpose of writing is always asked. At that time, the words that frequently appear in the choice question are '강조하다(emphasize)', '경고하다(warning)', '지적하다(point out)', '설명하다(explain)', '분석하다(analyze)', '제기하다(propose)', and '제시하다 (present)'. Remember it together.

'강조하다'는 어떤 단어와 같이 사용할까요?
What words do you use with '강조하다'?

의의 significance
중요성 importance
필요성 necessity
\+ 강조하다

03 고소

명 sue

나는 그 사람에 대한 고소를 취하하기로 했다.

I decided to cancel the sue against him.

고소하다 to sue

04 구체화

명 materialization, actualization, specification

정책의 구체화를 위해 전문가들이 모여서 논의하고 있다.

Experts have gathered to discuss the specifics of the policy.

구체적 being specific/detailed/concrete

05 기호

명 taste, preference

소비자의 기호에 맞는 제품을 개발하기 위해 밤낮으로 연구하고 있다.

I'm working day and night to develop products that suit consumers' tastes.

기호식품 preferred food　　기호품 item of personal preference

06 내딛다

동 to set foot on, to take a step (to start/begin)

갑자기 들려온 소리에 내딛던 걸음을 멈추고 주위를 둘러봤다.

I stopped in my steps at a sudden sound and looked around.

이 단어는 '발을 이동하다'라는 원래 뜻보다 '어떤 일을 시작하다'의 뜻으로 더 많이 사용돼요.

This word is used more often to mean 'to start something' than to mean 'to move one's feet'.

대학 졸업 후 사회에 첫걸음을 내딛었다.

After graduating from college, I took the first step into society.

DAY 23 ★★

07 노화

명 aging

많은 사람들이 노화 방지를 위해 여러가지 건강에 좋은 음식이나 영양제를 섭취하고 있다.

Many people are taking a variety of healthy foods and nutritional supplements to prevent aging.

08 단념하다

동 give up

그 일을 끝까지 해 보지도 않고 단념했다.

I gave up without even trying to finish it.

단념 abandonment, giving up

09 대북

명 (towards) North Korea

대북 정책에 대한 국민적 합의가 마련되어야 한다.

A national consensus on North Korea policy must be established.

대북 사업 business with North Korea

10 도태되다

동 to die out, to be selected out

부실한 기업은 경쟁에서 도태되기 쉽다.

Poor businesses are likely to be eliminated from competition.

11 동질성

명 homogeneity

두 나라 사이에는 문화적 동질성이 엿보인다.

Cultural homogeneity is evident between the two countries.

12 막다르다

형 dead end

경제가 어려워지자 청년들이 막다른 길로 내몰리고 있다.

As the economy worsens, young people are being pushed to a dead end.

13 맹렬하다

형 fierce

태풍이 맹렬한 기세로 다가오고 있다.

A typhoon is approaching fiercely.

14 모호하다

혱 ambiguous

교수님의 설명이 모호해서 이해하기 힘들었다.

The professor's explanation was difficult to understand because it was ambiguous.

15 미정

명 undefined

약속 시간은 말씀 드린 대로 다음 주 수요일입니다만, 아직 장소는 미정입니다.

The appointment time is next Wednesday as mentioned, but the location is still undefined.

16 민낯

명 true/naked face

이번 조사를 통해 직원들의 인권을 무시해 온 기업의 민낯이 드러났다.

This investigation revealed the true face of a company that has been ignoring the human rights of its employees.

민낯은 원래 '화장하지 않은 얼굴'이라는 뜻이지만, 뉴스나 기사에서 '숨기고 있던 사실'이라는 의미로 사용돼요.
'민낯' originally means 'a face without makeup', but it is used in news and articles to mean 'hidden fact'.

17 발휘하다

동 demonstrate, display, show

교사는 아이들이 자신의 실력을 마음껏 발휘할 수 있도록 격려해 주어야 한다.

Teachers should encourage children to show their abilities to the fullest.

발휘 display

DAY 23 ★★

18 복원

명 restoration

이 그림은 심하게 변색되어 복원이 어렵다고 한다.

The restoration of this painting is said to have be difficult because it is severely discolored.

문화재 복원 cultural assets restoration　　복원하다 to restore
복원되다 to be restored

19 실행

명 implementation, execute

계획을 실행에 옮기는 것이 중요하다.

It is important to execute the plan.

실행하다 to execute/implement　실행되다 to be executed/implemented

20 여전하다

형 still

낯선 사람을 만나면 부끄러워하는 그의 성격은 지금도 여전하다.

His personality of being shy when meeting strangers is still there.

21 연일

부 day after day, for days on end, everyday

연일 계속되는 폭염으로 인해 농작물의 피해가 극심하다.

The damage to crops is severe due to the heat wave that continues day after day.

22 왜곡

명 distortion, twist

세상의 신화와 전설은 약간의 과장이나 왜곡이 있기 마련이다.

The myths and legends of the world are bound to have some exaggeration or distortion.

왜곡하다 to distort/twist　　왜곡되다 to be distorted/twisted

23 원동력

명 driving force

시민들의 강한 의지가 빠른 경제 성장의 원동력이라고 할 수 있다.

The strong will of citizens is the driving force for rapid economic growth.

24 유망

명 promising, bright

과거의 유망 직종과 지금의 유망 직종은 차이가 크다.

There is a big difference between promising jobs in the past and promising jobs now.

관련어 유망하다 show promise

25 육류

명 meat

붉은 육류를 너무 많이 섭취하면 건강에 좋지 않다.

Eating too much red meat is bad for your health.

26 의존도

명 dependency

한국은 수출 의존도가 높은 나라에 속한다.

Korea is a country with a high dependence on exports.

의존하다 to depend on

27 인파

명 crowd

휴일에 놀이공원처럼 인파가 몰리는 곳에는 가고 싶지 않다.

I don't want to go to crowded places like amusement parks on holidays.

28 일거양득

명 killing two birds with one stone

이 사업은 노인들에게는 일자리가 생겨서 좋고, 시 입장에서는 길거리가 깨끗해져서 좋고, 일거양득이다.

This project kills two birds with one stone because it creates jobs for the elderly and keeps the streets clean for the city.

29 잦다

형 frequent

이 노트북은 고장이 잦아서 새 노트북을 사려고 해요.

This laptop breaks down frequently, so I'm looking to buy a new one.

30 저하

명 decline, deterioration

70대에 들어서면서 체력 저하를 온 몸으로 느끼고 있다.

As he enters his 70s, he is feeling a decline in physical strength.

시력 저하 deteriorating vision

31 접종

명 vaccination

다음주부터 보건소에서 독감 예방 접종을 시작한다고 한다.

From next week, public health centers are said to start flu vaccinations.

접종하다 to vaccinate

32 지수

명 index, quotient

아이들의 감성 지수를 키워주는 장난감들이 인기를 끌고 있다.

Toys that increase the emotional index of children are gaining popularity.

물가 지수 price index　　불쾌지수 the discomfort index

33 체결하다

동 to sign/enter into

그 아이돌은 기존의 소속사와 결별하고 새로운 소속사와 전속 계약을 체결했다.

The idol broke up with his existing agency and signed an exclusive contract with his new agency.

관련어

조약을 체결하다 to sign/enter into a treaty

34 하락

명 fall, decline

주식 시장의 급격한 하락으로 시장은 충격에 빠졌다.

The market was shocked by a sharp fall in the stock market.

하락하다 to fall/decline

35 혹평

명 criticism

이 영화는 대중들한테는 인기가 있지만 평론가들한테는 혹평을 받고 있다.

The film is popular with the public, but it is criticized by critics.

TOPIK에서 혼동하기 쉬운 단어

다의어 Polysemy

내딛다

❶ 발을 옮겨 이동하다

예 갑자기 들려온 소리에 내딛던 걸음을 멈추고 주위를 둘러봤다.

I stopped in my steps at a sudden sound and looked around.

❷ 시작하거나 처음 들어서다

예 대학 졸업 후 사회에 첫걸음을 내딛었다.

I took my first step in society after graduating from college.

반의어 Antonym

하락 fall, decline ↔ 상승 rise

예 주식 시장의 급격한 하락으로 시장은 충격에 빠졌다.

The market was shocked by a sharp fall in the stock market.

예 최근 주가 상승이 계속되자 주식 투자를 문의하는 사람들이 많아졌다.

As the stock price continues to rise in recent years, more and more people are inquiring about stock investment.

유의어 Synonym

발휘하다 show ≒ 펼치다

예 교사는 아이들이 자신의 실력을 마음껏 발휘할 수 있도록 격려해 주어야 한다.

교사는 아이들이 자신의 실력을 마음껏 펼칠 수 있도록 격려해 주어야 한다.

Teachers should encourage children to show their abilities to the fullest.

복습해 보세요

다음 빈 칸에 알맞은 단어를 〈보기〉에서 골라 쓰세요.
Choose the appropriate word from <Example> to fill in the blanks below.

〈보기〉
a. 막다른 b. 맹렬한 c. 잦아서 d. 체결했다 e. 도태되기

1. 부실한 기업은 경쟁에서 (   ) 쉽다.
   Poor businesses are likely to be eliminated from competition.

2. 경제가 어려워지자 청년들이 (   ) 길로 내몰리고 있다.
   As the economy worsens, young people are being pushed to a dead end.

3. 태풍이 (   ) 기세로 다가오고 있다.
   A typhoon is approaching fiercely.

4. 이 노트북은 고장이 (   ) 새 노트북을 사려고 해요.
   This laptop breaks down frequently, so I'm looking to buy a new one.

5. 그 아이돌은 기존의 소속사와 결별하고 새로운 소속사와 전속 계약을 (   ).
   The idol broke up with his existing agency and signed an exclusive contract with his new agency.

자연스러운 문장이 되도록 완성해 보세요.
Try to complete the sentence in a natural way.

6. 이번 조사를 통해 직원들의 인권을 무시해 온 기업의 ㅁㄴㅇ 드러났다.
   This investigation revealed the true face of a company that has been ignoring the human rights of its employees.

7. 나는 그 사람에 대한 ㄱㅅㄹ 취하하기로 했다.
   I decided to cancel the sue against him.

8. 낯선 사람을 만나면 부끄러워하는 그의 성격은 지금도 ㅇㅈㅎㄷ.
   His personality of being shy when meeting strangers is still there.

9. 다음주부터 보건소에서 독감 예방 ㅈㅈㅇ 시작한다고 한다.
   From next week, public health centers are said to start flu vaccinations.

10. 이 영화는 대중들한테는 인기가 있지만 평론가들한테는 ㅎㅍㅇ 받고 있다.
    The film is popular with the public, but it is criticized by critics.

정답

1. e 2. a 3. b 4. c 5. d 6. 민낯이 7. 고소를 8. 여전하다 9. 접종을 10. 혹평을

DAY 24

확인해 보세요

빨간 시트지로 가리고 단어의 뜻을 알면, □에 ✓ 해 보세요.

After covering up the words with red cover, please check(✓) the box (□) when you know the meaning of the word.

□ 01	가라앉다	to settle/ subside	□ 13	무력	armed/ military force	□ 25	이산가족	separated families
□ 02	가열하다	to heat	□ 14	무분별하다	thoughtless, indiscriminate	□ 26	임기	term, tenure
□ 03	거세다	strong, harsh	□ 15	무인	self service, unmanned	□ 27	자영업	self-employment
□ 04	공공시설	public facilities	□ 16	밀어붙이다	push (ahead)	□ 28	정체성	identity
□ 05	권유하다	to recommend, suggest	□ 17	배설물	waste, excretion	□ 29	제기하다	to raise/ bring up
□ 06	난처하다	in a dilemma, awkward	□ 18	분담	division of labor	□ 30	조퇴	early leave
□ 07	논하다	to discuss	□ 19	불경기	recession	□ 31	직위	position
□ 08	단합하다	to unify	□ 20	연령	age	□ 32	취지	purpose
□ 09	달성하다	to reach/ achieve	□ 21	우려하다	to worry	□ 33	한창	the height, full bloom
□ 10	독점하다	to have a monopoly	□ 22	위독하다	critical	□ 34	효력	effect, power
□ 11	뒤풀이	afterparty	□ 23	유언비어	wild/groundless rumor			
□ 12	만료되다	to be expired	□ 24	응하다	respond to, accept			

DAY 24

 are the words that appeared in the former tests, and you may get a higher grade if you study them together.

01 가라앉다

동 to settle/sink/subside

이번 사태에 대해 대통령이 직접 사과를 하면서 국민들의 분노가 가라앉고 있다.

The public's anger is subsiding as the President personally apologized for this incident.

가라앉히다 to calm/sink/cool down

02 가열하다

동 to heat

채소나 과일을 가열하면 영양소가 파괴될 수 있다.

Heating vegetables or fruits can destroy nutrients.

가열되다 to be heated

실제로 온도가 뜨겁지 않아도 뜨거운 분위기를 나타낼 때도 자주 사용하는 단어예요.

It is a word that is often used to express a heated up atmosphere even when the temperature is not really hot.

콘서트장의 분위기가 한창 가열되고 있다.
The atmosphere in the concert hall is heating up.

03 거세다

형 strong, harsh

제주도는 바람이 거세기로 유명한 곳이다.

Jeju Island is famous for its strong winds.

04 공공시설

명 public facilities

공공시설은 개인 소유가 아니므로 더 아껴서 사용해야 한다.

Public facilities are not privately owned and should be used with greater care.

05 권유하다

동 to recommend, suggest, ask

고등학교 때 선생님이 가수를 해 보라고 권유하신 것을 계기로 가수의 꿈을 갖게 되었다.

When I was in high school, my teacher recommended me to become a singer, so I had a dream of becoming a singer.

권유 recommendation, offer

06 난처하다

형 in a dilemma, awkward

나와 친한 두 친구가 서로 싸웠는데 둘 중 어느 쪽 편도 들 수 없고 내 입장이 난처해졌다.

I was in an awkward position because two close friends of mine fought with each other and I couldn't take either side.

07 논하다

동 to discuss

오랜만에 만난 동창들과 술잔을 기울이며 인생을 논했다.

I had a drink with my classmates who I haven't seen in a while and discussed life.

08 단합하다

동 to unify

우리 당이 단합해야만 국민들께 신뢰를 줄 수 있다.

Only when our party is united can we give the people confidence.

단합되다 to be unified　　단합시키다 to bring together

단합 unity

09 달성하다

동 to reach/achieve

올해 목표를 100% 달성해 성과급을 받았다.

He achieved 100% of this year's goal and received bonus.

DAY 24 ★★

10 독점하다

동 to have a monopoly, to be exculsive

큰 손자가 할머니의 사랑을 독점하였다.

The eldest grandchild held a monopoly on the grandmother's love.

독점 광고 exclusive advertising 독점 판매 exclusive sales

11 뒤풀이

명 afterparty

행사가 끝나면 공지해 드린 뒤풀이 장소로 오십시오.

After the event, please come to the afterparty venue that was announced.

12 만료되다

동 to be expired

차일피일 미루다 보니 입학 서류 접수 기한이 만료되었다.

After delaying day after day, the application deadline for admission has expired.

만료하다 to expire 만료 expiration

13 무력

명 armed/military force

국경 지역에서 무력 충돌이 발생해 긴장감이 고조되고 있다.

Tensions are rising due to armed clashes in the border area.

무력 감축 reduce armed force 무력 싸움 armed struggle

14 무분별하다

형 thoughtless, indiscriminate

무분별한 처방이 심각한 수준에 이르고 있다.

Indiscriminate prescriptions are coming to a serious level.

15 무인

명 self service, unmanned

나는 이 가게가 무인 판매점이라는 것을 모르고 계산하려고 기다리고 있었다.

I didn't know this store was an self-service shop and was waiting to check out.

무인도 deserted island

16 밀어붙이다

동 push (ahead)

모두 이사에 반대했지만 어머니는 이사 계획을 그대로 밀어붙였다.

Everyone opposed the move, but my mother pushed ahead with the move.

17 배설물

명 waste, excretion

비둘기 배설물로 인한 시설물 부식이 문제가 되고 있다.

Corrosion of facilities caused by pigeon waste is becoming a problem.

배설 excretion　　배설 기관 excretory organs
배설하다 to excrete

18 분담

명 division of labor

팀플을 할 때는 역할 분담이 잘 이루어져야 한다.

When playing a team project, the division of roles must be created well.

분담하다 to divide　　분담되다 to be divided
분담시키다 assign a part of

DAY 24 ★★

19 불경기

명 recession

극심한 불경기로 인해 회사의 구조 조정이 불가피하다.

Due to the severe recession, restructuring of the company is inevitable.

20 연령

명 age

연령에 따라서 다른 방식의 조사를 실시해야 한다.

Different methods of investigation must be conducted depending on age.

연령대 age group　　연령층 age bracket

21 우려하다

동 to worry

의료 관계자들은 이번 전염병에 대해 심각하게 우려할 필요가 없다고 말한다.

Medical officials say there is no need to worry seriously about the epidemic.

우려되다 be worried/concerned　우려 worry

22 위독하다

형 critical

산에서 조난을 당해 생명이 위독한 환자를 헬기로 이송하였다.

A patient in critical condition was transported by helicopter after suffering a distress on the mountain.

위독 a critical[serious] condition of illness

23 유언비어

명 wild/groundless rumor

유언비어를 유포하는 사람들을 처벌하는 법이 강화되어야 한다.

Laws should be strengthened to punish those who spread groundless rumors.

24 응하다

동 answer, respond to, accept

바쁘신 중에 인터뷰에 응해 주셔서 정말 감사합니다.

Thank you so much for accepting the interview even though you are busy.

'응하다'는 어떤 단어와 같이 사용할까요?
What words do you use with '응하다'?

요청 request
질문 question
협상 negotiation
\+ 응하다

25 이산가족

명 separated families

전쟁 때문에 가족과 헤어진 후 만나지 못하고 살아온 이산가족들이 이번 남북회담에 큰 관심을 보이고 있다.

The separated families who haven't seen each other due to the Korean war showed great interest in the Korean peace talks.

이산가족 상봉 separated family reunion

26 임기

명 term, tenure

한국 대통령의 임기는 5년이다.

The term of office of the Korean president is five years.

임기를 채우다 complete one's term   임기 만료 expiration of term
임기말 end of term

27 자영업

명 self-employment

한국은 자영업에 종사하는 사람들의 비율이 다른 OECD 국가보다 높다고 한다.

It is said that the proportion of people who are self-employed in Korea is higher than in other OECD countries.

자영업에 종사하다 engage in self-employment
자영업자 self-employer

28 정체성

명 identity

재외 교포들 중에는 자신의 정체성에 혼란을 느끼는 경우가 많다.

Many Korean immigrants often feel confused about their identity.

정체성을 찾다 to find one's identity

29 제기하다

동 to raise/bring up

그는 이번 연구 결과에 의문을 제기했다.

He raised doubts about the findings of the study.

제기 raise, bring up   제기되다 be raised, be made

DAY 24 ★★

30 조퇴

명 early leave

나는 오늘 일찍 조퇴를 하고 집에서 푹 쉬었다.

I left early today and rested well at home.

조퇴하다 to leave early

학교나 회사에서 모두 '조퇴'라는 단어를 쓸 수 있어요. 그렇지만 학교에 가지 않는 것은 결석, 회사에 가지 않는 것은 결근으로 구별해서 사용해야 해요.
You can use the word '조퇴 (early leave)' both at school and at work. However, not going to school is 결석 (absence from school), and not going to work is 결근 (absence from work).

31 직위

명 position

일부 IT 회사에서는 직위에 상관없이 서로를 별명으로 부른다고 한다.

It is said that some IT companies call each other by nicknames regardless of their position.

32 취지

명 purpose

유기 동물을 보호하자는 취지로 이번 행사를 준비하게 되었습니다.

The purpose of this event is to protect abandoned animals.

취지에 맞다 fit/align with the purpose

33 한창

명 the height, full bloom, the peak, the climax

오랜만에 찾은 경주는 벚꽃이 한창이다.

Cherry blossoms are in full bloom in Gyeongju, which I visited after a long time.

34 효력

명 effect, power, validity

공증을 받지 않은 구두 합의는 법적 효력이 없다.

Unnotarized verbal agreements have no legal effect.

효력을 가지다 to have power/effect
효력을 발휘하다 prove effective, to take effect

TOPIK에서 혼동하기 쉬운 단어

다의어 Polysemy

독점하다

❶ 혼자서 사랑을 모두 차지하다

예 큰 손자가 할머니의 사랑을 독점하였다.
The eldest grandchild held a monopoly on the grandmother's love.

❷ 개인이나 단체가 생산과 시장을 혼자 차지하다

예 기업이 시장을 독점해서 물건의 가격이 올랐다.
The price of goods rises because firms monopolize the market.

반의어 Antonym

거세다 strong, harsh ↔ **부드럽다** gentle, soft

예 제주도는 바람이 거세기로 유명한 곳이다.
Jeju Island is famous for its strong winds.

예 바닷가로 나가니 부드러운 바람이 불어왔다.
As we went out to the beach, a gentle breeze blew.

유의어 Synonym

우려하다 to worry ≒ **걱정하다**

예 아버님이 우려하시는 일은 일어나지 않을 것입니다.
아버님이 걱정하시는 일은 일어나지 않을 것입니다.
What your father is worried about will not happen.

복습해 보세요

자연스러운 문장이 되도록 완성해 보세요.
Try to complete the sentence in a natural way.

1. 근거 없는 ㅇㅇㅂㅇ가 사람들의 불안감을 키우고 있다.
   Groundless rumors are fueling people's anxiety.

2. 이 회사는 모든 광고를 ㄷㅈㅎㅇ 이익을 내고 있다.
   This company is making a profit by having a monopoly on all commercials.

3. 목표량을 ㄷㅅㅎㄱ 위해 24시간 공장을 가동하고 있다.
   The factory is operating 24 hours a day to achieve the target amount.

4. 참다 못한 학생들이 문제를 ㅈㄱㅎㅈ 학교 측에서 해명에 나섰다.
   When the students who couldn't wait further brought up the problem, the school tried to give an explantion.

자연스러운 문장이 되도록 둘 중에서 알맞은 단어를 고르세요.
Try to complete the sentence in a natural way by choosing the correct word.

5. 이 전시회는 (a. 연령 / b. 임기)에 따라 입장료에 차이가 있다.
   Admission fees vary according to age for this exhibition.

6. 사춘기는 자신의 (a. 정체성 / b. 불경기)을/를 찾아가는 시기이다.
   Adolescence is a time of finding one's identity.

7. 이번 정책이 일부 국민들에게 피해를 가져올까봐 (a. 만료된다 / b. 우려된다)
   I am concerned that this policy will harm some citizens.

8. 부모님의 의견이 달라 누구의 의견을 따라야 할지 (a. 권유하다 / b. 난처하다)
   My parents have different opinions, so it is difficult to decide whose suggestion to follow.

정답

1. 유언비어 2. 독점하여 3. 달성하기 4. 제기하자 5. a 6. a 7. b 8. b

DAY 25

확인해 보세요

빨간 시트지로 가리고 단어의 뜻을 알면, □에 ✓ 해 보세요.

After covering up the words with red cover, please check(✓) the box (□) when you know the meaning of the word.

□ 01	가려내다	to distinguish/ determine	□ 13	무례	disrespect, rudeness	□ 25	이색적	unusual, unique
□ 02	가파르다	steep	□ 14	무상	free	□ 26	임대하다	to rent (out)
□ 03	건의	suggestion/ proposal	□ 15	무작정	blindly, recklessly	□ 27	자존심	pride, self-respect
□ 04	공교육	public education	□ 16	밀어주다	to support, to back (up)	□ 28	재테크	investment techniques
□ 05	귀하다	rare, precious	□ 17	배열	arrangement	□ 29	적도	equator
□ 06	남녀평등	gender equality	□ 18	분배	distribution, division	□ 30	제공하다	to provide
□ 07	농경	agriculture, farming	□ 19	불과하다	just, only	□ 31	제대하다	to be discharged from the military
□ 08	단호하다	stern, firm	□ 20	열광하다	to go wild, to get excited	□ 32	진단하다	to diagnose
□ 09	달아오르다	to heat up, to blush	□ 21	우수성	superiority, excellence	□ 33	치안	public security
□ 10	독창성	uniqueness, originality	□ 22	위력	power	□ 34	합리적	logical
□ 11	뒷받침	backing, support	□ 23	유용하다	useful	□ 35	후유증	aftermath
□ 12	만만하다	easygoing, insignificant	□ 24	의도	motive/ intention			

DAY 25

  are the words that appeared in the former tests, and you may get a higher grade if you study them together.

01 가려내다

동 to distinguish/identitfy/determine

첫인상만 보고 좋은 사람인지 나쁜 사람인지 가려내는 것은 불가능하다고 본다.

It seems impossible to determine if a person is good or bad depending on first impressions.

관련어 잘잘못을 가려내다 distinguish right and wrong

02 가파르다

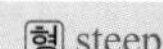

그 산은 가파르기 때문에 등산할 때 등산화를 준비하는 것이 안전하다.

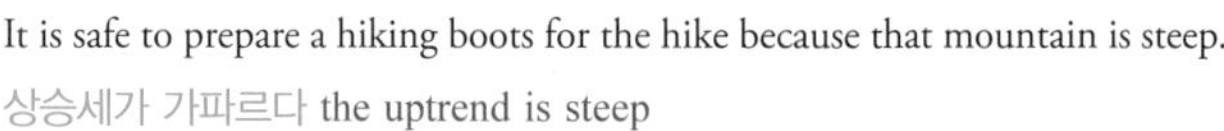

It is safe to prepare a hiking boots for the hike because that mountain is steep.

상승세가 가파르다 the uptrend is steep

이 단어는 산이나 언덕의 경사도가 크다는 것을 의미하지만 '상승세'나 '하락세'와도 자주 같이 사용해요. 상승하거나 하락하는 정도가 매우 빠르거나 크다는 것을 나타내요.

This word means that the slope of a mountain or hill is steep, but it is also often used with '상승세(uptrend)' or '하락세(downtrend)'.

 한국 전자 주식의 하락세가 매우 가팔라서 투자자들의 우려가 커지고 있다.
The decline in Korean electronics stocks is very steep, raising concerns among investors.

03 건의

명 suggestion/proposal

회사 내에 휴게실을 만들자는 나의 건의는 받아들여지지 않았다.

My proposal to make a lounge in the company was rejected.

건의 사항 suggestion/proposal 건의하다 to suggest/ propose

04 공교육

명 public education

교사의 권위가 없어지면서 공교육이 붕괴되고 있다는 비판이 있다.

There is criticism that public education is collapsing as teachers' authority disappears.

반) 사교육 private education

05 귀하다

형 rare, precious

귀한 자식일수록 더 엄격하게 키워야 한다.

The more precious the child, the stricter you have be with him.

06 남녀평등

명 gender equality

많은 사람들이 지금은 남녀평등 시대라고 하지만 여전히 남녀차별이 존재하고 있다.

Many people say we live in a gender equal world, but sexism still exists.

반) 남녀차별 sexism

출제 경향 how this word appears in the test

평등한 사회와 관련된 문제가 출제됩니다.
양성평등, 남녀고용평등, 육아휴직 등의 관련 단어도 확인해 보세요.

Issues related to an egalitarian society will be asked.
Also check related words such as 양성평등(gender equality), 남녀고용평등(gender equality in employment), and 육아휴직(parental leave).

DAY 25 ★★

07 농경

명 agriculture, farming

옛날부터 큰 강 유역을 중심으로 농경이 발달하였다.

Since ancient times, agriculture has developed mainly in the basins of large rivers.

농경 생활 agrarian life　　농경 사회 agrarian society

08 단호하다

형 stern, firm, resolute

악의적인 댓글에는 단호한 대처가 필요하다.

Malicious comments need a stern response.

09 달아오르다

동 to become/turn hot/red, to heat up, to blush

직사광선 때문에 얼굴이 벌겋게 달아올랐다.

My face turned red because of direct sunlight.

'달아오르다'는 어떤 단어와 같이 사용할까요?

What words do you use with '달아오르다'?

냄비 pot
분위기 atmosphere
\+ **달아오르다**

10 독창성

명 uniqueness, originality

이 작품은 작가의 예술적 독창성이 뛰어난 작품이다.

This work is a work of outstanding artistic originality by the creator.

11 뒷받침

명 backing, support

부모의 뒷받침이 없었더라면 지금의 나는 존재하지 않았을 것이다.

Without the support of my parents, the me I am today would not exist.

12 만만하다

형 easygoing, insignificant, easy to deal with

회사 생활을 만만하게 생각했던 것 같아 후회가 된다.

I regret thinking that corporate life was easy to deal with.

13 무례

명 disrespect, rudeness

공식적인 자리인만큼 무례를 범하지 않도록 조심하십시오.

Please be careful not to be rude as it is an official occasion.

무례하다 to be disrespectful/rude

14 무상

명 free

1년 안에 상품에 문제가 생길 경우 무상 교환을 해 드립니다.

If there is a problem with the product within a year, we will exchange it for free.

15 무작정

부 blindly, recklessly

다음 직장을 구하지 않고 무작정 회사를 그만두는 것은 무모한 일이다.

It is foolish to blindly quit the company without finding the next job.

DAY 25 ★★

16 밀어주다

동 to support, to back (up)

그 감독이 특정 여배우를 밀어준다는 소문이 돌고 있다.

Rumors are circulating that the directors is backing a certain actress.

17 배열

명 arrangement

예상보다 강의를 들으러 온 사람들이 많아서 의자 배열을 다시 했다.

More people came to listen to the lecture than expected, so the chairs were rearranged.

배열하다 to arrange 배열되다 to be arranged

18 분배

명 distribution, division

모든 국민을 위한 소득 분배 정책이 필요하다.

We need an income distribution policy that covers every citizen.

분배하다 to distribute/divide 분배되다 to be distributed/divided
분배시키다 to distribute/divide

19 불과하다

형 just, only, simply

회의에 참석한 인원이 절반에 불과하다.

Only half of the people attended the meeting.

20 열광하다

동 to go wild, to get excited/enthusiatic

경기에서 골을 넣자 관중들은 모두 일어나서 열광했다.

The crowd all stood up and went wild when they scored a goal in the game

열광의 도가니 a frenzy of enthusiasm 열광적 enthusiastic, wild

21 우수성

명 superiority, excellence

이번 박람회를 통해 우리 회사 제품의 우수성을 전세계에 알릴 수 있었다.

Through this fair, we were able to promote the excellence of our products to the world.

우수하다 to be excellent

22 위력

명 power

이 상품이 텔레비전 광고가 나간 후 다음 날 모두 팔린 걸 보면 정말 광고의 위력이 대단하다.

Seeing that this product was sold out the next day after the TV commercial was released, the power of advertising is really great.

23 유용하다

형 useful

그가 알려준 정보는 면접 준비하는 데 아주 유용하였다.

The information he gave was very useful in preparing for the interview.

반) 무용하다 useless

24 의도

명 motive/intention

그림을 볼 때 화가가 어떤 의도로 그렸는지 생각해 본다.

When I look at pictures, I think about what the artist intended when drawing.

25 이색적

명 unusual, unique

이 빵집은 이색적인 빵이 많기로 유명한 곳이에요.

This bakery is famous for having many unusual breads.

26 임대하다

동 to rent (out)

여행객들에게 집을 단기 임대하는 사람들이 늘고 있다.

More and more people are renting short-term homes to travelers.

관련어
임대료 rent fee　　임대 아파트 rent apartment
임대되다 to be rented out

DAY 25 ★★

27 자존심

명 pride, self-respect, self-esteem

배달 아르바이트를 하다가 예전 직장 동료를 만나서 자존심이 상했다.

My pride was hurt when I met my former co-worker while working part-time in delivery.

관련어
자존심을 지키다 keep one's pride/self-respect

28 재테크

명 investment techniques

주식으로 재테크를 해 자산이 늘어났다.

I increased my assests using stocks with investment techniques.

재테크하다 to invest

29 적도

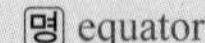
명 equator

적도에서 발생하는 이상기후 현상이 남극의 생명체에게 영향을 미친다는 연구 결과가 발표되었다.

Research results have been published that abnormal climate events occurring at the equator affect life in Antarctica.

출제 경향 how this word appears in the test

지구의 기후변화와 관련한 단어들을 기억하세요.
Remember the words related to global climate change:
극지방(polar regions), 적도(equator), 지구온난화(global warming), 이상기후(abnormal climate), 해수면(sea level), 지표면(earth's surface)

30 제공하다

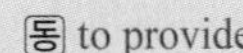
동 to provide

행사에 참가한 사람들에게 점심 도시락을 제공하기로 했다.

It was decided to provide a packed lunch to those who participated in the event.

제공되다 to be provided

31 제대하다

동 to be discharged from the military

군대를 제대한 후 바로 학교에 복학했다.

I returned to school immediately after being discharged from the military.

제대 discharge
반) 입대 enter the military

32 진단하다

동 to diagnose

의사는 아버지를 위암으로 진단했다.

Doctors diagnosed my father with stomach cancer.

진단되다 to be diagnosed

33 치안

명 public security

치안이 좋지 않은 나라를 여행할 때는 많은 주의가 필요하다.

You need to have much caution when traveling to a country with poor public security.

치안 유지 maintenance of public security

34 합리적

명 logical

그 방법이 가장 합리적인 것 같으니까 그렇게 하죠.

Let's do it that way because I think it is the most logical.

반) 비합리적 illogical

35 후유증

명 aftermath

친구는 교통 사고 후유증으로 고생하고 있다.

My friend is suffering from the aftermath of a car accident.

DAY 25 ★★

TOPIK에서 혼동하기 쉬운 단어

다의어 Polysemy

밀어주다

❶ 특정한 지위를 차지하도록 지지하다

예 이번 선거에서 많은 사람들이 나를 밀어준 덕분에 당선되었다.

I was elected thanks to a lot of people supporting me in this election.

❷ 뒤에서 앞으로 나가도록 힘을 주다

예 나는 우는 동생을 그네에 태워 밀어주었다.

I put my crying younger sibling on a swing and pushed her.

반의어 Antonym

제대하다 to be discharged from the military ↔ **입대하다** enlist, enter the military

예 군대를 제대한 후 바로 학교에 복학했다.

I returned to school immediately after being discharged from the military.

예 그는 입대한 후에 처음으로 휴가를 나왔다.

He went on vacation for the first time after enlisting.

유의어 Synonym

귀하다 precious ≒ **소중하다**

예 할머니는 항상 나를 귀하게 여기셨다.

할머니는 항상 나를 소중하게 여기셨다.

My grandmother always treaed me preciously.

복습해 보세요

서로 어울리는 단어를 찾아 연결해 보세요.

Find words that go with each other and connect them.

1. 자존심이	a. 제공하다
2. 무상으로	b. 제대하다
3. 군대를	c. 상하다
4. 시작에	d. 진단하다
5. 폐암으로	e. 불과하다

다음 빈 칸에 알맞은 단어를 〈보기〉에서 골라 쓰세요.

Choose the appropriate word from <Example> to fill in the blanks below.

〈보기〉

a. 유용한 b. 밀어주어 c. 만만한지 d. 단호하게

6. 친구는 나의 부탁을 ( ) 거절하였다.
   My friend firmly refused my request.

7. 친구가 보내준 ( ) 정보 덕분에 면접에 합격할 수 있었다.
   Thanks to the useful information my friend sent me, I was able to pass the interview.

8. 친구들이 적극적으로 ( ) 회장에 당선되었다.
   I was elected president with my friends' active support.

9. 엄마는 내가 ( ) 나에게만 야단을 치셨다.
   My mom only scolded me as if I was easy to deal with.

정답

1.c 2.a 3.b 4.e 5.d 6.d 7.a 8.b 9.c

❶ 무(無) nonexistence

무료 no charge

무해하다 harmless

무식하다 ignorant

무능력 incompetence

무선 wireless

무명 nameless

무급휴가 unpaid leave

무형문화재 intangible culturalasset[property]

❷ 유(有) existence

유료 charged

유해하다 harmful

유식하다 knowledgeable, educated

유급휴가 paid leave

유형문화재 tangible cultural asset[property]

유선 cable, wire

유명 famous (for)

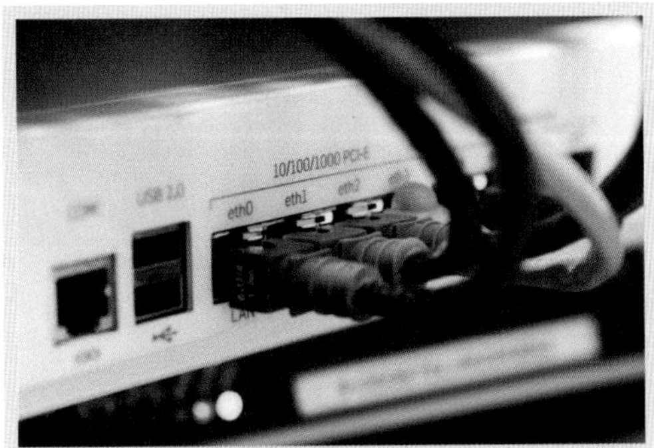

▲유선 cable, wire

주간 복습 day 21 – day 25

아래 단어를 보고 빈 칸에 뜻을 적어 보세요. 그리고 점선대로 접어서 적은 뜻이 맞는지 확인해 보세요. (만일 틀렸다면 뒷면의 단어 앞 □에 ✓ 하세요.)

Write down the meaning of the given word in the blank. Also, fold the page along a dotted line and check whether you got it right or wrong. (If you got it wrong tick the box in front of the word in next page.)

▼접는선

단어	뜻
구성하다	
대립되다	
미숙하다	
실업	
절차	
강제적	
구직	
낙관적	
보수적	
유력하다	
강조하다	
구체화	
여전하다	
지수	
하락	
공공시설	
무분별하다	
불경기	
우려하다	
효력	
공교육	
독창성	
분배	
유용하다	

※접어서 뜻이 맞는지 확인해보세요.

주간 복습 day 21 – day 25

빈 칸에 한국어 단어를 3번 적고 다시 외워 봅시다.

Write down the Korean word 3 times in the blank and try to memorize it again.

◀접는선

뜻	단어		
☐ to form/build/establish	구성하다		
☐ be opposed to, competing	대립되다		
☐ inexperienced	미숙하다		
☐ unemployment	실업		
☐ procedure	절차		
☐ forced	강제적		
☐ job hunting	구직		
☐ optimistic	낙관적		
☐ conservative	보수적		
☐ strong, dominant, potential	유력하다		
☐ to emphasize	강조하다		
☐ materialization, actualization, specification	구체화		
☐ still	여전하다		
☐ index, quotient	지수		
☐ fall, decline	하락		
☐ public facilities	공공시설		
☐ thoughtless, indiscriminate	무분별하다		
☐ recession	불경기		
☐ to worry	우려하다		
☐ effect, power, validity	효력		
☐ public education	공교육		
☐ uniqueness, originality	독창성		
☐ districution, division	분배		
☐ useful	유용하다		

DAY 26

확인해 보세요

빨간 시트지로 가리고 단어의 뜻을 알면, □에 ✓ 해 보세요.

After covering up the words with red cover, please check(✓) the box (□) when you know the meaning of the word.

□ 01	고위	high-ranking	□ 13	몰두하다	be absorbed/ engrossed	□ 25	음원	song, track
□ 02	국제적	international	□ 14	미각	taste	□ 26	이끌다	to lead
□ 03	끝맺다	to end/finish	□ 15	민망하다	embarrased, awkward	□ 27	일리	point
□ 04	난폭하다	violent, reckless	□ 16	방사능	radioactivity	□ 28	입장	position, stance
□ 05	녹초	utterly exhausted	□ 17	방지	prevention	□ 29	재난	(natural) disaster
□ 06	누리다	to enjoy	□ 18	복합	complex, compound	□ 30	전화위복	blessing in disguise
□ 07	단속	crackdown, enforcement	□ 19	안쓰럽다	pity, sorry	□ 31	정서	emotion
□ 08	대안	alternative	□ 20	역효과	adverse effect, backfire	□ 32	지적하다	to point out
□ 09	독립적	the elderly independent	□ 21	요소	factor, element	□ 33	추구하다	to strive for, to pursue
□ 10	독거노인	the elderly people living alone	□ 22	용의자	suspect	□ 34	학대	abuse
□ 11	막막하다	at a loss	□ 23	원본	original (text/ document)	□ 35	환기하다	to ventilate
□ 12	면역력	immunity	□ 24	유비무환	Better safe than sorry			

DAY 26

 are the words that appeared in the former tests, and you may get a higher grade if you study them together.

01 고위

명 high-ranking

고위 관리라고 법을 지키지 않고 마음대로 행동해서는 안 된다.

A high-ranking official should not act as he pleases without obeying the law.

고위 공무원 high-ranking government official

고위직 high-ranking position

02 국제적

명 international

이제는 자기 나라에서만 활동하는 사람이 아니라 국제적인 전문가가 되는 것이 중요하다.

It is now important to become an international expert, instead of working solely in your own country

03 끝맺다

동 to end/finish

일을 시작하는 것도 중요하지만 잘 끝맺는 것도 중요하다.

It's important to start a job, but it's also important to finish it well.

04 난폭하다

형 violent, reckless

도로에서 난폭하게 운전을 하는 사람들에 대한 강력한 규제가 필요하다.

Strong regulations are needed against those who drive recklessly on the road.

난폭 violent, reckless

05 녹초

명 utterly exhausted

하루종일 농사일을 한 탓에 녹초가 되어 집으로 돌아왔다.

I was utterly exhausted from farming all day and came back home.

06 누리다

동 to enjoy

전쟁이 끝나고 사람들은 평화로운 생활을 누리게 되었다.

After the war, people were able to enjoy a peaceful life.

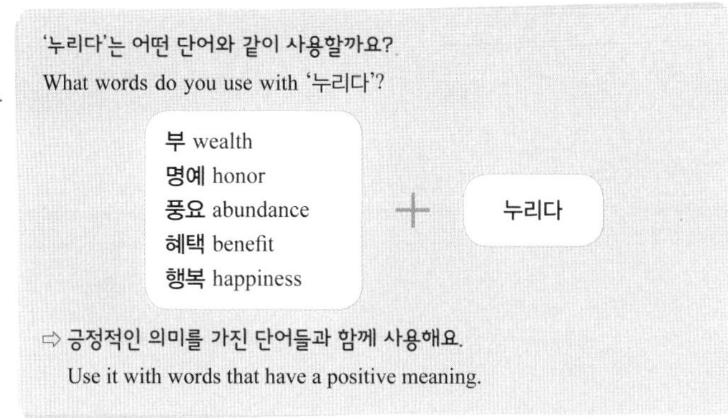

'누리다'는 어떤 단어와 같이 사용할까요?
What words do you use with '누리다'?
부 wealth
명예 honor
풍요 abundance
혜택 benefit
행복 happiness
+
누리다
⇨ 긍정적인 의미를 가진 단어들과 함께 사용해요.
Use it with words that have a positive meaning.

DAY 26 ★★

07 단속

명 crackdown, enforcement, regulation

다음달부터 음주 운전에 대한 특별 단속이 시작된다고 한다.

It is said that special crackdowns on drunk driving will start from next month.

단속하다 to crackdown on, to regulate 단속 기간 enforcement period
음주 단속 drunk driving enforcement

08 대안

명 alternative

실업 문제에 대한 현실성 있는 대안을 세워야 한다.

A realistic alternative to the unemployment problem must be established.

대안 학교 alternative school

09 독립적

명 independent

독립적인 아이가 사회성도 뛰어나다고 한다.

Independent children are said to have excellent social skills.

10 독거노인

명 the elderly people living alone

매년 독거노인이 증가하여 사회적 문제가 되고 있다.

The number of the elderly people living alone has increased every year, becoming a social problem.

출제 경향 how this word appears in the test

토픽에서 인구의 변화나 가족의 형태가 달라지는 사회적 이슈가 출제되는 경향이 있습니다. 다양한 가족 형태에 대해 같이 공부해 보세요.
Topik tend to be about social issues that change population or the shape of the family. Study various types of families together:
한부모 가족(single-parent families), 입양 가족(adoptive families), 동성 결혼 가족(same-sex married families), 독신 가족(single families), 재혼 가족(remarried families), 다문화 가족(multicultural families)

11 막막하다

형 at a loss

대부분의 기업들이 신규 채용을 줄이면서 취업을 준비하는 청년들이 막막해졌다.

As most companies cut back on hiring new workers, young people preparing for employment are at a loss.

12 면역력

명 immunity

바이러스에 감염되지 않으려면 면역력을 키워야 한다.

You need to build up your immune system to avoid contracting the virus.

면역 immunity　　면역 체계 immune system

13 몰두하다

동 be absorbed/engrossed

오랫동안 AI 연구에만 몰두한 결과 노벨상을 받았다.

He received the Nobel Prize after focusing only on AI research for a long time.

14 미각

명 taste

다른 사람에 비해 유난히 미각이 발달한 사람들이 있다.

Some people have a very developed sense of taste compared to others.

'감각'에는 또 어떤 것들이 있을까요?
What other sensations are there?
시각(sight), 청각(hearing), 촉각 (touch), 후각 (smell), 미각 (taste)

15 민망하다

형 embarrased, awkward

친구에게 돈을 빌리러 갔지만 이야기를 꺼내기가 민망해서 아무 말도 못하고 나왔다.

I went to borrow money from my friend, but I couldn't say anything because I felt embarrased.

16 방사능

명 radioactivity

그 지역에서 생산된 채소에서 방사능이 검출되었다.

Radioactivity was detected in vegetables grown in the area.

방사능 오염 radioactive contamination　방사능 유출 radioactive leak

17 방지

명 prevention

환자는 암 치료 후 재발 방지를 위해 노력하고 있다.

Patients are trying to prevent recurrence after cancer treatment.

방지하다 to prevent　방지되다 to be prevented

18 복합

명 complex, compound

이 곳은 젊은이들의 복합 문화 공간으로 거듭났다.

관련어

This place has been reborn as a complex cultural space for young people.

복합 기능 complex function　복합적 complex

DAY 26 ★★

19 안쓰럽다

형 pity, sorry

취업 준비 때문에 힘들어하는 아들을 보니 안쓰러운 마음이 든다.

I feel sorry for my son who is having a hard time preparing for a job.

20 역효과

명 adverse effect, backfire

아이를 너무 엄격하게 교육하면 오히려 역효과가 날 수 있다.

Educating your child too rigidly can backfire.

21 요소

명 factor, element

사람의 성격은 환경적인 요소에 의해 결정된다.

A person's personality is determined by environmental factors

22 용의자

명 suspect

이번 범죄 사건의 용의자는 옆집에 살고 있는 20대의 대학생이었다.

The suspect in the crime was a college student in his 20s living next door.

23 원본

명 original (text/document)

졸업증명서 사본을 제출했는데 원본을 다시 제출해 달라는 요구를 받았다.

I submitted a copy of my graduation certificate but was asked to resubmit the original.

사본 copy

24 유비무환

명 Better safe than sorry

우리 학교에서는 유비무환의 자세로 매달 재난 대피 훈련을 시행하고 있다.

In our school, we are conducting disaster evacuation drills every month because we think it's better safe than sorry.

25 음원

명 song, track, music

그 아이돌의 신곡 음원이 다음 달 1일에 발표된다.

The idol's new song will be released on the 1st of next month.

관련어 음원 차트 music charts

26 이끌다

동 to lead

그는 리더로 그의 팀을 성공적으로 이끌어 이번 경기에서 승리할 수 있었다.

As the leader, he successfully led his team to win this match.

27 일리

명 point

찬성과 반대편 주장 모두 일리가 있었다.

Both pros and cons had a point.

28 입장

명 position, stance

서로 입장이 다르면 생각도 다를 수 밖에 없다.

If we have different positions, we can't help but think differently.

29 재난

명 (natural) disaster

갑작스러운 홍수로 재난을 당한 주민들을 위한 임시 대피소를 운영 중이다.

A temporary shelter is in operation for residents who suffered under natural di aster because of the sudden flood.

관련어 재난지원금 emergency relief grant

30 전화위복

명 blessing in disguise

그때 대학교 입시에 실패한 것이 전화위복이 된 것 같아요.

I think failing the college entrance exam at that time was a blessing in disguise.

DAY 26 ★★

31 정서

명 emotion

정서가 불안할 때 다리를 떠는 경우가 많다.

I often shake my legs when I am emotionally unstable.

정서적 emotional

32 지적하다

동 to point out

친한 친구 사이라도 서로 잘못을 지적하기는 쉽지 않다.

It is difficult to point out another's mistake even if you are close friends.

지적 point out　　지적을 당하다 to be called out

33 추구하다

동 to strive for, to pursue

과도하게 신체적인 편안함을 추구하면 건강이 나빠질 수 있다.

Excessive pursuit of physical comfort can be detrimental to your health.

34 학대

명 abuse

아동 학대는 신체적 폭력뿐만 아니라 정신적 폭력도 해당한다.

Child abuse includes not just physical but emotional abuse as well.

35 환기하다

동 to ventilate

하루에 2번 정도 창문을 열어서 환기하고 있다.

I open the windows twice a day to ventilate.

환기 ventilation　　환기구 ventilation system

TOPIK에서 혼동하기 쉬운 단어

다의어 Polysemy

입장

❶ 당면하고 있는 처지나 상황

예 서로 입장이 다르면 생각도 다를 수 밖에 없다.

If we have different positions, we can't help but think differently.

❷ 행사나 공연 등이 열리는 장소 안으로 들어감.

예 지금부터 콘서트장 입장이 가능합니다.

Enterance into the concert is now available.

반의어 Antonym

독립적 independent ↔ 의존적 dependent

예 독립적인 아이가 사회성도 뛰어나다고 한다.

Independent children are said to have excellent social skills.

예 그는 의존적인 성격이라 혼자서 뭔가를 도전하지 않는다.

He has a dependent personality, so he doesn't try out anything by himself.

유의어 Synonym

끝맺다 finish ≒ 마치다

예 일을 시작하는 것도 중요하지만 잘 끝맺는 것도 중요하다.

일을 시작하는 것도 중요하지만 잘 마치는 것도 중요하다.

It's important to start a job, but it's also important to finish it well.

DAY 26 ★★

복습해 보세요

자연스러운 문장이 되도록 완성해 보세요.
Try to complete the sentence in a natural way.

1. 일을 시작하는 것도 중요하지만 잘 ㄲㅁㄴ 것도 중요하다.
   It's important to start a job, but it's also important to finish it well.

2. 전쟁이 끝나고 사람들은 평화로운 생활을 ㄴㄹㄱ 되었다.
   After the war, people were able to enjoy a peaceful life.

3. 다음달부터 음주 운전에 대한 특별 ㄷㅅ이 시작된다고 한다.
   It is said that special crackdowns on drunk driving will start from next month.

4. 대부분의 기업들이 신규 채용을 줄이면서 취업을 준비하는 청년들이 ㅁㅁㅎㅈㄷ.
   As most companies cut back on hiring new workers, young people preparing for employment are at a loss.

5. 사람의 성격은 환경적인 ㅇㅅ에 의해 결정된다.
   A person's personality is determined by environmental factors

6. 그때 대학교 입시에 실패한 것이 ㅈㅎㅇㅂ이 된 것 같아요.
   I think failing the college entrance exam at that time was a blessing in disguise.

다음 빈 칸에 알맞은 단어를 〈보기〉에서 골라 쓰세요.
Choose the appropriate word from <Example> to fill in the blanks below.

〈보기〉
a. 역효과가　b. 일리가　c. 지적하기는　d. 추구하면

7. 과도하게 신체적인 편안함을 (　　　　) 건강이 나빠질 수 있다.
   Excessive pursuit of physical comfort can be detrimental to your health.

8. 찬성과 반대편 주장 모두 (　　　　) 있었다.
   Both pros and cons had a point.

9. 아이를 너무 엄격하게 교육하면 오히려 (　　　　) 날 수 있다.
   Educating your child too rigidly can backfire.

10. 친한 친구 사이라도 서로 잘못을 (　　　　) 쉽지 않다.
    It is difficult to point out another's mistake even if you are close friends.

정답

1. 끝맺는　2. 누리게　3. 단속　4. 막막해졌다　5. 요소　6. 전화위복　7. d　8. b　9. a　10. c

DAY 27

확인해 보세요

빨간 시트지로 가리고 단어의 뜻을 알면, □에 ✓ 해 보세요.

After covering up the words with red cover, please check(✓) the box (□) when you know the meaning of the word.

□ 01	가다듬다	to calm, to straighten	□ 13	면제되다	to be exempt	□ 25	유사하다	similar
□ 02	개설	contruct	□ 14	몰아가다	to drive	□ 26	음질	sound quality
□ 03	고학력	highly educated	□ 15	무해하다	harmless	□ 27	이력	career, background
□ 04	국토	country, national land	□ 16	민주	democracy	□ 28	일반화하다	generalize
□ 05	나르다	transport, carry	□ 17	방수	waterproof	□ 29	자극적	stimulating, provoking
□ 06	논란	controversy	□ 18	방치되다	neglected	□ 30	재발하다	to reoccur
□ 07	단적	prime/ direct(example)	□ 19	본격적	in earnest	□ 31	절정	peak, climax
□ 08	대담	formal conversation	□ 20	압도적	overwhelming	□ 32	출시되다	released
□ 09	대외	foreign, external	□ 21	연간	annual	□ 33	지정되다	designated
□ 10	독선적	self-righteous	□ 22	요인	cause	□ 34	추세	trend
□ 11	동호인	members of a club	□ 23	유언	will	□ 35	한가롭다	leisurely, relaxed
□ 12	막바지	final stage, end of (road)	□ 24	원산지	origin			

DAY 27

 are the words that appeared in the former tests, and you may get a higher grade if you study them together.

01 가다듬다

동 to calm/collect, to straighten

그 가수는 공연을 앞두고 마음을 가다듬었다.

The singer calmed her mind ahead of the performance.

'가다듬다'는 어떤 단어와 같이 사용할까요?
What word would you use with '가다듬다'?

마음 mind
머리 head
호흡 breath
\+ **가다듬다**

02 개설

명 contruct

환경 단체는 새로운 도로 개설에 반대하고 있다.

Environmental groups oppose the construction of new roads.

개설하다 to construct　　　개설되다 to be constructed

03 고학력

명 highly educated

최근에 실업률이 높아지면서 고학력 실업자도 증가하는 추세이다.

With the recent increase in the unemployment rate, the number of highly educated unemployed is also increasing.

04 국토

명 country, national land

전쟁으로 인해 국토의 많은 부분이 파괴되었다.

Much of the country was destroyed by the war.

국토 개발 national land development

05 나르다

동 transport, carry

자동차가 없던 시절에는 소나 말을 사용하여 물건을 날랐다.

In the days when there were no cars, cows and horses were used to transport goods.

06 논란

명 controversy

최근 청소년의 흡연 문제가 논란이 되고 있다.

Smoking among adolescents has been a controversial topic recently.

출제 경향 how this word appears in the test

논란이 되는 사건들이 출제되는 경우가 많습니다. 특히 듣기에서 논란이 되는 이슈에 대해 토론하는 문제들은 계속 출제되고 있습니다.
사회적, 환경적, 과학적, 윤리적으로 논란이 되고 있는 주제를 미리 알아두는 것이 좋습니다.

Controversial cases are often asked. Questions that discuss controversial issues, especially in the istening secion, continue to be asked.
It's good to know ahead of time the topics of social, environmental, scientific and ethical contention.

DAY 27 ★★

07 단적

명 prime/direct(example)

가짜 뉴스에 대한 단적인 예를 들어 보겠습니다.

Let me give you a prime example of fake news.

08 대담

명 formal conversation

이 책은 교수와 제자의 대담 형식으로 만들어졌다.

The format of this book is written as a formal conversation between a professor and a student.

출제 경향 how this word appears in the test

대담을 듣고 푸는 문제가 듣기에서 항상 출제되고 있습니다.
질문에서 '대담'과 '담화'를 같은 의미로 사용하고 있습니다. 담화의 내용과 일치하는 것, 또는 담화 앞이나 뒤에 이어지는 내용이 무엇인지를 묻는 경우가 많습니다.

The question of listening to and solving the dialogue is always asked in listening. In the question, '대담' and '담화'' are used interchangeably. Questions often ask what matches the content of the conversation, or what follows before or after the conversation.

09 대외

명 foreign, external

이 항구는 일찍부터 대외 무역을 위해 개방되었다.

This port was open to foreign trade from an early age.

대외적 foreign, outwardly, publicly

10 독선적

명 self-righteous

자기 혼자만이 옳다고 생각하는 그의 독선적인 성격이 문제다.

The problem is his self-righteous personality, who thinks that only he is right.

11 동호인

명 members of a club, members with the same taste

주말이면 교외로 나가는 자전거 동호인이 증가하고 있다.

There is an increasing number of cyclist club members going out to the suburbs on weekends.

12 막바지

명 final stage, end of (road)

영화 개봉을 앞두고 막바지 편집 작업에 들어갔다.

The film entered the final editing stage as the premier date approached.

13 면제되다

동 to be exempt

수석 입학한 학생은 대학 4년 등록금이 면제된다고 한다.

It is said that the high-ranking students are exempted from the 4-year college tuition.

면제 exemption   면제하다 to exempt

면제를 받다 to receive exemption

'면제되다'는 어떤 단어와 같이 사용할까요?

What word would you use with the word '면제되다'?

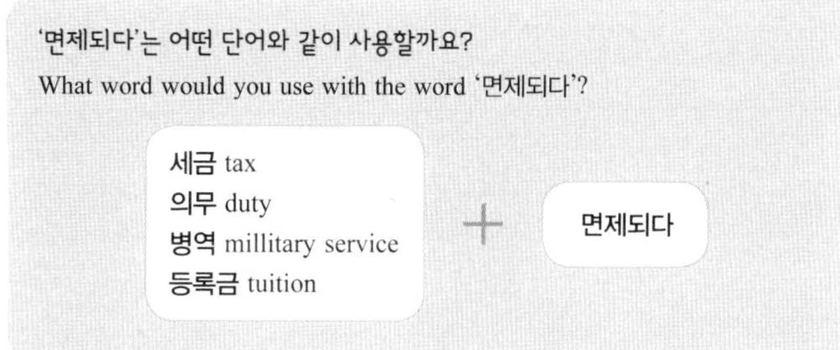

세금 tax

의무 duty

병역 millitary service

등록금 tuition

+ 면제되다

14 몰아가다

동 to drive

최근 이 드라마의 시청률이 상승했으므로 계속 이 기세를 몰아가야 한다.

The ratings for this drama have recently risen, so we have to keep driving this momentum.

'몰아-'는 "어떤 대상을 바라는 대로 움직여 가게 하다"라는 뜻을 가지고 있고, 다음의 단어들을 만나 사용돼요.

'몰아-' means "to make something move as desired", and is used in meeting the following words.

몰아내다(drive out), 몰아넣다(drive in), 몰아붙이다(drive in), 몰아쉬다(drive out), 몰아치다(drive out)

15 무해하다

형 harmless

인체에 무해하다는 광고를 보고 샀는데 유해 물질이 들어 있다는 보도를 보고 기가 막혔다.

I bought it after seeing an advertisement saying it was harmless to the human body, but I was shocked to see the report that it contained harmful substances.

무해 harmlessness

반) 유해하다 harmful

16 민주

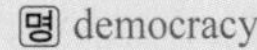
명 democracy

지금의 민주 국가를 만들기 위해 많은 사람들이 희생되었다.

Many people made sacrifices to make the democracy we have today.

민주적 democratic　　민주주의 democracy
민주화 democratization

17 방수

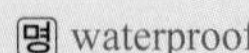
명 waterproof

이 시계는 방수 기능이 있어서 물에 차고 들어가도 괜찮다.

This watch is waterproof so it can be worn in water.

방수 처리 waterproofing　　방수 효과 waterproof effect
방수가 되다 to be waterproof

18 방치되다

동 neglected

제대로 된 돌봄을 받지 못하고 방치되는 아이들에 대한 대책이 필요하다.

There is a need to take measures against children who are neglected without proper care.

방치 neglection　　방치하다 to neglect

19 본격적

명 in earnest

그 공사는 다음주부터 본격적으로 시작할 예정이다

That construction is planned to start in earnest next week.

20 압도적

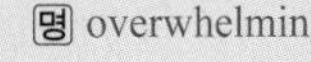
명 overwhelming

그는 90% 이상의 표를 얻어 압도적으로 당선되었다.

He was overwhelmingly elected with over 90% of the votes.

압도 overwhelm　　압도하다 to overwhelm
압도되다 to be overwhelmed

21 연간

명 annual

이상기온으로 인해 이 지역의 포도 연간 생산량이 급격하게 줄었다고 한다.

It is said that the annual production of grapes in this region has drastically decreased due to the abnormal temperature.

관련어

월간 monthly　　주간 weekly　　일간 daily

22 요인

명 cause

물가 상승의 요인은 수요의 증가와 공급의 감소이다.

The cause of inflation is an increase in demand and a decrease in supply.

23 유언

명 will

할아버지께서는 한 마디의 유언도 남기지 않으셨다.

Grandpa never left a single will.

관련어

유언장 will　　유언하다 leave a will

DAY 27 ★★

24 원산지

명 origin

모든 식당은 재료의 원산지를 표기할 의무가 있다.

All restaurants are obliged to indicate the origin of their ingredients.

25 유사하다

형 similar

이번 작품은 그의 전 작품들과 너무 유사하다.

This work is very similar to his previous works.

유사제품 similar product

26 음질

명 sound quality

깨끗한 음질을 원하시면 조금 더 비싼 이어폰을 추천드립니다.

If you want clear sound quality, we recommend a slightly more expensive ear phone.

27 이력

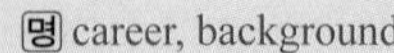
명 career, background

이번 강의를 맡은 강사의 이력이 화려했다.

The instructor in charge of this lecture had an impressive career.

이력서 resume

28 일반화하다

동 generalize

한 명의 외국인을 만난 후 그 나라 사람들은 모두 그럴 것이라고 일반화하면 안 된다.

After meeting one foreigner, you shouldn't generalize that everyone in that country will.

일반화 generalization

29 자극적

명 stimulating, provoking

요즘 자꾸 맵고 짠 자극적인 음식이 먹고 싶네요.

These days, I want to eat spicy, salty and stimulating food.

자극 stimulation 자극하다 to stimulate

자극되다 to be stimulated

30 재발하다

동 to reoccur

이런 아동 학대 사건이 재발하지 않도록 처벌을 강화해야 한다.

Punishments should be strengthened to prevent such incidents of child abuse from reoccurring.

재발 reoccurence

31 절정

명 peak, climax

지난 주에 설악산에 가니까 단풍이 절정이었어요.

I went to Seoraksan Mountain last week and the autumn leaves were at their peak.

인기 절정 height of popularity

32 출시되다

동 released

이번에 출시된 스마트폰은 특히 젊은 여성들에게 인기를 끌고 있다.

The newly released smartphone is especially popular among young women.

출시 release 출시하다 to release

33 지정되다

동 designated

쓰레기는 지정된 장소에 버려야 한다.

Garbage must be disposed of in designated areas.

지정 designation 지정하다 to designate

34 추세

명 trend

한국 사회에서는 1인 가구 수가 계속 증가하는 추세이다.

In Korean society, the number of single-person households continues to be on a rising trend.

35 한가롭다

형 leisurely, relaxed

오랜만에 혼자서 책도 읽고 음악도 들으며 한가로운 시간을 보냈다.

I spent my free time leisurely reading books and listening to music alone which I haven't done in a while.

DAY 27 ★★

TOPIK에서 혼동하기 쉬운 단어

다의어 Polysemy

가다듬다

❶ 마음을 정리한다

예 그 가수는 공연을 앞두고 마음을 가다듬었다.

The singer calmed her mind ahead of the performance.

❷ 흐트러진 대열이나 조직 등을 정리하여 싸울 준비를 하다.

예 전투를 앞두고 사령관은 대열을 가다듬었다.

Ahead of the battle, the commander organized his ranks.

반의어 Antonym

무해하다 harmless ↔ 유해하다 harmful

예 이 제품은 인체에 무해한 것이다.

This product is harmless to human body.

예 이 제품은 인체에 유해한 성분이 들어 있다.

This product contains ingredients that are harmful to the human body.

유의어 Synonym

나르다 transport, carry ≒ 옮기다

예 수레를 이용해 물건을 나르고 있다.

수레를 이용해 물건을 옮기고 있다.

I'm carrying the items using a cart.

복습해 보세요

서로 어울리는 단어를 찾아 연결해 보세요.

Find words that go with each other and connect them.

1. 호흡	a. 가다듬다
2. 독선적	b. 면제되다
3. 병역	c. 유사하다
4. 제품	d. 절정
5. 인기	e. 행동

자연스러운 문장이 되도록 둘 중에서 알맞은 단어를 고르세요.

Try to complete the sentence in a natural way by choosing the correct word.

6. 자동차가 없던 시절에는 소나 말을 사용하여 물건을 (a. 날랐다. / b. 몰아갔다.)

   In the days when there were no cars, cows and horses were used to transport goods.

7. 그는 90% 이상의 표를 얻어 (a. 본격적으로 / b. 압도적으로) 당선되었다.

   He was overwhelmingly elected with over 90% of the votes.

8. 이번에 (a. 지정된 / b. 출시된) 스마트폰은 특히 젊은 여성들에게 인기를 끌고 있다.

   The newly released smartphone is especially popular among young women.

9. 한국 사회에서는 1인 가구 수가 계속 증가하는 (a. 추세 / b. 이력)이다.

   In Korean society, the number of single-person households continues to be on a rising trend.

DAY 27 ★★

정답

1.a 2.e 3.b 4.c 5.d 6.a 7.b 8.b 9.a

Memo

DAY 28

확인해 보세요

빨간 시트지로 가리고 단어의 뜻을 알면, □에 ✓ 해 보세요.

After covering up the words with red cover, please check(✓) the box (□) when you know the meaning of the word.

□ 01	가구	household	□ 13	멸망시키다	to destroy	□ 25	음치	tone deaf
□ 02	개정	revisement, amendment	□ 14	몰입	immersion	□ 26	이례적	unusual
□ 03	고혈압	high blood pressure	□ 15	못마땅하다	displeased (with), dissatisfied (with)	□ 27	일방적	one-sided
□ 04	궁극적	ultimate	□ 16	민첩하다	quick, agile	□ 28	자기중심적	self-centered
□ 05	나열	list	□ 17	방어하다	defend	□ 29	재촉	urging
□ 06	논의	discussion	□ 18	방침	policy	□ 30	접근성	accessibility
□ 07	단절되다	to be cut off	□ 19	본성	true nature	□ 31	정책	policy
□ 08	대우	treatment	□ 20	양상	condition, aspect	□ 32	지지하다	to support
□ 09	독성	toxic	□ 21	연관되다	to be involved	□ 33	출산율	fertility rate
□ 10	되새기다	reflect	□ 22	요청하다	to request	□ 34	한결같다	consistent
□ 11	뒤덮다	cover	□ 23	원색적	crude, vulgar	□ 35	회의적	skeptical
□ 12	막상막하	neck-and-neck, be equally matched	□ 24	유세	campaign			

DAY 28

 are the words that appeared in the former tests, and you may get a higher grade if you study them together.

01 가구

명 household

1인 가구 수가 증가함에 따라 소형 가전 제품들이 많이 출시되고 있다.

As the number of single-person household increases, many small home appliances are being launched.

02 개정

명 revisement, amendment

기존 교과서에 대한 비판이 계속되면서 교과서 개정을 위한 연구가 시작될 예정이다.

As criticism of existing textbooks continues, research for revisement of textbooks will begin.

개정하다 to revise   개정되다 be revised

03 고혈압

명 high blood pressure

어머니는 고혈압 때문에 매일 약을 복용하신다.

My mother takes medicine every day because of high blood pressure.

반) 저혈압 low-blood pressure

출제 경향 how this word appears in the test

질병에 관련한 문제가 출제되는 경우가 많습니다. 질병과 관련된 단어를 정리해 두세요.

A lot of the questions are related to disease. Organize the words related to the disease: 유전적(genetic), 선천적(congenital), 후천적(acquired), 감염(infection), 치료(treatment), 입원(hospitalization), 수술(surgery)

04 궁극적

명 ultimate

종교의 궁극적인 목적은 마음의 평화라고 할 수 있다.

It can be said that the ultimate goal of religion is peace of mind.

05 나열

명 list

좋은 글은 단순한 사실의 나열만으로 되는 것이 아니다.

Good writing is not just a list of facts.

나열하다 to list

06 논의

명 discussion

교통 문제를 개선하기 위한 논의가 한창 진행 중이다.

Discussions to improve the traffic problem are in full swing.

논의하다 to discuss　논의되다 to be discussed

07 단절되다

동 to be cut off

상대방과 대화가 단절되지 않도록 꾸준히 노력해야 한다.

You have to constantly try not to cut off conversation with the other person.

단절시키다 to cut off

08 대우

명 treatment

나는 직장을 옮기면서 파격적인 대우를 받았다.

When I changed jobs, I was treated unconventionally.

차별 대우 discriminative treatment

09 독성

명 toxic

폐수로 인해 독성 물질이 바다로 흘러 들어갔다.

The wastewater caused toxic substances to flow into the sea.

10 되새기다

동 reflect

앞으로의 미래가 중요하므로 힘든 과거는 되새기지 않는 것이 좋다.

Because the future is important, it is better not to reflect on the difficult past.

11 뒤덮다

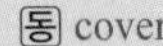
동 cover

비구름이 온통 하늘을 뒤덮고 있다.

Rain clouds cover the entire sky.

'뒤-'는 2가지의 의미를 가지고 있고 다음의 단어들을 만나 사용돼요.

'뒤–' has two meanings and is used with the following words.

① 몹시 예) 뒤섞다, 뒤흔들다
very Ex) mix up, shake fiercely

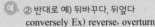

② 반대로 예) 뒤바꾸다, 뒤엎다
conversely Ex) reverse, overturn

12 막상막하

명 neck-and-neck, be equally matched

두 팀의 실력이 비슷하므로 막상막하의 접전을 벌일 것으로 예상된다.

The two teams are expected to have a neck-and-neck match because they are similar in performance.

13 멸망시키다

동 to destroy

결국 바이러스가 세계를 멸망시킬 것이다.

Eventually, the virus will destroy the world.

멸망 destruction　　멸망하다 to be destroyed
멸망되다 to be destroyed

14 몰입

명 immersion

그 배우는 어떤 상황에서도 감정 몰입을 잘한다.

The actor is good at immersing emotions in any situation.

15 못마땅하다

형 displeased (with), dissatisfied (with)

아이의 행동이 못마땅하더라도 참고 기다려줘야 한다.

Even if you are displeased with the child's behavior, you have to endure it and wait.

16 민첩하다

형 quick, agile

군인들은 민첩하게 이동을 시작했다.

The soldiers began to move with quick agility.

민첩성 quickness, agility

17 방어하다

동 defend

해킹을 방어하기 위해 전문가를 불러 시스템을 구축했다.

To defend against hacking, an expert was called in to build a system.

방어 defense　　방어적 defensive

18 방침

명 policy

우리 학교는 학생들의 스마트폰 사용을 금지하는 교육 방침을 계속 유지하고 있다.

Our school maintains an educational policy that prohibits students from using smartphones.

DAY 28 ★★

19 본성

명 true nature

상황이 악화되자 그의 본성이 드러났다.

As the situation worsened, his true nature was revealed.

20 양상

명 condition, aspect

국제 정세는 자국의 이익을 우선시하면서 복잡한 양상을 띠었다.

The international sphere took on a complex condition as each country prioritized one's own interest.

21 연관되다

동 to be involved/connected/related (with)

경찰은 이번 사건과 연관된 사람들을 모두 조사할 예정이라고 발표했다.

Police have announced that they will investigate all those connected in the incident.

관련어
연관 connection/relation　　연관성 connection
연관하다 to connect/relate

22 요청하다

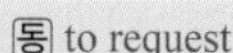

경제 위기로 인해 주변국에게 도움을 요청했다.

Due to the economic crisis, it requested for help from neighboring countries.

요청 request

23 원색적

명 crude, vulgar, raw

선거를 며칠 앞두고 상대 후보에 대한 원색적 비난이 이어졌다.

A few days before the election, crude criticism of the opposing candidate continued.

24 유세

명 campaign

대통령 선거를 위한 유세가 시작되었다.

The campaign for the presidential election has begun.

유세장 campaign rally

25 음치

명 tone deaf

저는 음치라서 사람들 앞에서 노래 부르는 게 정말 싫어요.

I'm tone deaf, so I hate singing in front of people.

26 이례적
명 unusual

그 나라에서 여성이 대통령이 된 것은 매우 이례적인 일이었다.

It was very unusual for a woman to become president in that country.

이례적 조치 unusual measure   이례적 상황 unusual situation

27 일방적
명 one-sided

그녀는 갑자기 나에게 다가와 일방적으로 화를 내고 사라졌다.

She suddenly approached me, became angry one-sidely, and disappeared.

일방 one side/way   일방적 주장 one-sided argument/claim

28 자기중심적
명 self-centered

어릴 때 자기중심적으로 생각하던 아이들은 성장하면서 다른 사람의 입장을 이해하게 된다.

Children who were self-centered when they were young develop an understanding of other people's point of view as they grow older.

DAY 28 ★★

29 재촉
명 urging

돈을 갚으라는 재촉이 이어지자 그녀는 파산 신청을 했다.

After being urged to pay the money, she filed for bankruptcy.

재촉하다 to urge

30 접근성
명 accessibility

이 곳은 서울까지 접근성이 좋아서 젊은 사람들한테 인기가 많다.

This place is popular with young people because it has easy access to Seoul.

접근 approach   접근하다 to approach

31 정책
명 policy

환경 문제를 해결하기 위한 다양한 정책이 마련되었다.

Various policies have been prepared to solve environmental problems.

32 지지하다

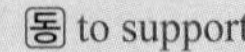

최근 조사에서는 지지하는 정당이 없다는 사람의 비율이 굉장히 높았다.

In a recent survey, the percentage of people who did not support a political party was very high.

지지 support　　지지자 supporter

'지지하다'는 어떤 단어와 같이 사용할까요?

What word would you use with the word '지지하다'?

정책 policy 발언 statement 주장 claim	+	지지하다

33 출산율

명 fertility rate

2021년 기준으로 한국의 출산율은 세계 최저 수준이다.

As of 2021, Korea's fertility rate is the lowest in the world.

출제 경향 how this word appears in the test

'인구'와 관련하여 변화를 나타내는 그래프 문제나, 저출산, 고령화 사회와 연결된 문제들이 출제되고 있습니다.

There are problems related to graphs showing changes in 'population' and problems related to low fertility and an aging society.

34 한결같다

형 consistent

남자친구는 연애하는 3년 동안 늘 한결같은 모습으로 나를 대했다.

My boyfriend has consistently treated me with the same attitude during the three years of dating.

'한결같다'는 어떤 단어와 같이 사용할까요?

What word would you use with the word '한결같다'?

마음 mind 자세 position 태도 attitude	+	한결같다

35 회의적 명 skeptical

사고 시 책임 소재와 관련해 자동 운전에 대해 회의적인 시각을 가진 전문가도 있다.

Some experts are skeptical of automatic driving when it comes to who is responsible in the event of an accident.

DAY 28 ★★

TOPIK에서 혼동하기 쉬운 단어

다의어 Polysemy

되새기다

❶ 지난 일을 다시 떠올리다

예 지나간 일은 너무 되새기지 않는 것이 좋다.

It is better not to reflect too much on the past.

❷ 소나 동물이 음식을 다시 씹다

예 소가 여물을 계속 되새기고 있다.

The cow is repeatedly chewing over the fodder.

반의어 Antonym

민첩하다 quick, agile ↔ 둔하다 sluggish, dull

예 군인들은 민첩하게 이동을 시작했다.

The soldiers began to move with quick agility.

예 계속되는 행군에 군인들의 움직임이 둔해졌다.

As the march continued, the movement of the soldiers became sluggish.

유의어 Synonym

단절되다 cut off ≒ 끊어지다

예 상대방과 대화가 단절되지 않도록 꾸준히 노력해야 한다.

상대방과 대화가 끊어지지 않도록 꾸준히 노력해야 한다.

You have to constantly try not to cut off conversation with the other person.

복습해 보세요

자연스러운 문장이 되도록 완성해 보세요.
Try to complete the sentence in a natural way.

1. 종교의 ㄱㄱㅈ인 목적은 마음의 평화라고 할 수 있다.
   It can be said that the ultimate goal of religion is peace of mind.

2. 좋은 글은 단순한 사실의 ㄴㅇ만으로 되는 것이 아니다.
   Good writing is not just a list of facts.

3. 나는 직장을 옮기면서 파격적인 ㄷㅇ를 받았다.
   When I changed jobs, I was treated unconventionally.

4. 상황이 악화되자 그의 ㅂㅅ이 드러났다.
   As the situation worsened, his true nature was revealed.

5. 경제 위기로 인해 주변국에게 도움을 ㅇㅊㅎㄷ.
   Due to the economic crisis, it requested for help from neighboring countries.

6. 최근 조사에서는 ㅈㅈㅎㄴ 정당이 없다는 사람의 비율이 굉장히 높았다.
   In a recent survey, the percentage of people who did not support a political party was very high.

DAY
28
★★

다음 빈 칸에 알맞은 단어를 〈보기〉에서 골라 쓰세요.
Choose the appropriate word from <Example> to fill in the blanks below.

〈보기〉

a. 일방적으로 b. 재촉이 c. 방어하기 d. 방침을

7. 돈을 갚으라는 (   ) 이어지자 그녀는 파산 신청을 했다.
   After being urged to pay the money, she filed for bankruptcy.

8. 우리 학교는 학생들의 스마트폰 사용을 금지하는 교육 (   ) 계속 유지하고 있다.
   Our school maintains an educational policy that prohibits students from using smartphones.

9. 그녀는 갑자기 나에게 다가와 (   ) 화를 내고 사라졌다.
   She suddenly approached me, became angry one-sidely, and disappered.

10. 해킹에 (   ) 위해 전문가를 불러 시스템을 구축했다.
    To defend against hacking, an expert was called in to build a system.

정답

1. 궁극적 2. 나열 3. 대우 4. 본성 5. 요청했다 6. 지지하는 7. b 8. d 9. a 10. c

Memo

DAY 29

확인해 보세요

빨간 시트지로 가리고 단어의 뜻을 알면, □에 ✓ 해 보세요.

After covering up the words with red cover, please check(✓) the box (□) when you know the meaning of the word.

	No.	Word	Meaning
□	01	가급적	possible
□	02	강세	strength, accent
□	03	거르다	to skip
□	04	골치	trouble, nuisance
□	05	궁금증	curiosity
□	06	낙천적	optimistic
□	07	논증	argument
□	08	단정하다	conclude
□	09	대응하다	respond
□	10	독자적	independent, unique
□	11	누각	stand out
□	12	들끓다	to boil
□	13	막연하다	vague
□	14	멸종	extinction
□	15	무궁무진하다	endless
□	16	밀도	density
□	17	방영	airing, broadcast
□	18	배기가스	exhaust gas
□	19	부각되다	to be highlighted
□	20	양성	training, nurturing
□	21	연구하다	research
□	22	용량	capacity
□	23	원활하다	smooth
□	24	유심히	carefully
□	25	음향	sound
□	26	이론적	theoretical
□	27	일방통행	one-way
□	28	자산	assest
□	29	재충전	recharge
□	30	정체	congestion, stagnation
□	31	직면하다	confront
□	32	정중하다	polite
□	33	한계	limit
□	34	하찮다	trivial
□	35	획득	acquisition, win

DAY 29

  are the words that appeared in the former tests, and you may get a higher grade if you study them together

01 가급적

 possible

정부는 가급적이면 세금을 늘리지 않는 정책을 만들기 위해 노력해야 한다.

The government should work to make policies that do not increase taxes if possible.

02 강세

명 strength, stress, accent

최근 IT분야 주식이 강세를 보이고 있다.

Stocks in the IT sector have been strong recently.

03 거르다

동 to skip

끼니를 거르는 불규칙한 식사 습관은 건강에 매우 안 좋다.

Irregular eating habits of skipping meals are very bad for health.

04 골치

명 trouble, nuisance, the head

사장님은 아르바이트생을 구하는 문제로 골치가 아팠다.

The boss was troubled by the problem of finding part-timers.

골칫거리 trouble, nuisance

05 궁금증

명 curiosity

시간이 지날수록 그 사람에 대한 궁금증은 더해 갔다.

As time passed, my curiosity about that person increased.

06 낙천적

명 optimistic

내 친구는 성격이 낙천적이라서 항상 웃는 얼굴이다.

My friend has an optimistic personality and always has a smile on his face.

출제 경향 how this word appears in the test

사람의 성향을 묻는 문제는 계속 출제되고 있습니다. 다음 단어를 같이 공부하세요.

Questions about people's disposition continues to be asked. Study the following words together.

비관적(pessimistic), 냉소적(cynical), 회의적(skeptical), 중립적(neutral), 주체적(subjective), 이해타산적(self-interested)

07 논증

명 argument

구체적인 예를 들어 자기 주장에 대한 논증을 제시하는 것이 좋다.

It is better to provide an argument for your assertion with concrete examples.

논증하다 to prove 논증되다 to be proven

DAY 29 ★★

08 단정하다

동 conclude

보이스피싱이 노인들만 대상으로 한다고 쉽게 단정하기는 어렵다.

It is difficult to conclude easily that voice phishing only targets the elderly.

09 대응하다

동 respond

생태계는 환경의 변화에 대응하지 못한 결과 파괴되었다.

Ecosystems are destroyed as a result of not responding to changes in the environment.

대응 response

10 독자적 명 independent, unique

문화는 나라마다 독자적인 성격을 가진다.

Each country has its own unique culture.

11 두각 명 stand out

그는 IT업계에서 두각을 나타내어 최고 연봉을 받고 있다.

He stands out in the IT industry, earning the highest salaries.

12 들끓다 동 to boil

진실을 외면하는 언론에 대한 비난 여론이 들끓고 있다.

Criticism of the media for ignoring the truth is boiling.

'들-'이는 '막', '몹시'의 뜻을 가지고 있고 다음과 같이 사용돼요.
'들–' has meanings like '막 (carelessly)' or '몹시 (very)' and is used like the following.

들뛰다, 들쑤시다
run hurriedly, to poke around

13 막연하다 형 vague

막연한 기대감만으로 투자를 하면 실패할 확률이 높다.

Investing with only vague expectations is highly likely to fail.

14 멸종 명 extinction

지구 온난화로 인해 멸종 위기에 처한 동물을 보호해야 한다.

We should protect endangered animals due to global warming.

멸종하다 to become extinct 멸종 동물 extinct animal
멸종 위기 endangered

15 무궁무진하다

형 endless

그 앱의 활용도는 무궁무진하다.

The uses of the app are endless.

16 밀도

명 density

서울의 인구 밀도가 지속적으로 높아지고 있다.

The population density of Seoul is continuously increasing.

17 방영

명 airing, broadcast

주연 배우가 촬영 중 사고가 나면서 드라마의 방영이 연기되었다.

The airing of the drama was delayed because the lead actor had an accident while filming.

방영하다 to air　　방영되다 to be aired

DAY 29 ★★

18 배기가스

명 exhaust gas

전기차 이용으로 자동차 배기가스의 양이 많이 줄어들었다.

The use of electric vehicles has significantly reduced the amount of vehicle exhaust gas.

19 부각되다

동 to be highlighted

실업 문제가 가장 큰 사회 문제로 부각되고 있다.

Unemployment is emerging as the biggest social problem.

이미지 부각 emerging image/highlighted image

부각하다 to highlight　　부각시키다 to highlight something

20 양성

명 training, nurturing

그 선생님은 은퇴 후에도 인재 양성에 힘쓰고 있다.

Even after his retirement, the teacher is working hard on nurturing talent.

양성하다 to train/nurture

21 연구하다

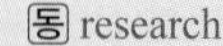
동 research

불치병을 치료하기 위해 다방면으로 연구하고 있다.

Various researches are being conducted to treat incurable diseases.

연구자 researcher　　연구실 laboratory
연구비 researching funds

22 용량

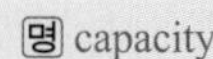
명 capacity

이것보다 용량이 조금 더 큰 USB가 필요하다.

You will need a USB with a slightly larger capacity than this.

대용량 large capacity

23 원활하다

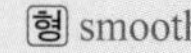
형 smooth

서로 다른 세대가 원활하게 의사소통 하기 위해서는 많은 노력이 필요하다

It takes a lot of effort for different generations to communicate smoothly.

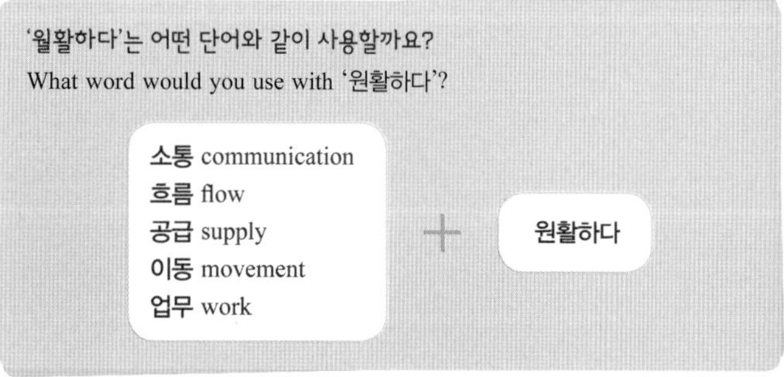

'월활하다'는 어떤 단어와 같이 사용할까요?
What word would you use with '원활하다'?
소통 communication
흐름 flow
공급 supply
이동 movement
업무 work
+
원활하다

24 유심히

부 carefully

경찰은 그 남자의 표정을 유심히 살피보았다.

The police looked carefully at the man's expression.

25 음향

명 sound

이 분은 카메라 담당이고, 저 분은 음향 담당입니다.

This person is in charge of the camera, and that person is in charge of the sound.

음향 효과 sound effect

26 이론적

명 theoretical

회사를 잘 운영하기 위해서는 이론적 지식도 중요하지만 실제적 감각도 필요하다.

In order to run a company well, theoretical knowledge is important, but also practical sense.

관련어

이론적 접근 theoritical approach

이론적 근거 theoritical evidence

이론적 배경 theoritical background

DAY 29 ★★

27 일방통행

명 one-way

저 길은 일방통행이기 때문에 들어가면 안 된다.

Do not enter that road as it is a one-way street.

28 자산

명 assest

은행에서 자산 관리를 모바일로 간단하게 할 수 있는 서비스를 내놓았다.

A bank has launched a service that makes asset management simple through mobile.

관련어

자산 관리 asset management 자산 증식 asset growth

자산 가치 asset value

29 재충전

명 recharge

재충전을 위해 오랜만에 여행을 가려고 한다.

I'm going on a trip after a long time to recharge.

재충전하다 to recharge

30 정체

명 congestion, stagnation

연휴 첫 날부터 고속도로 정체가 시작되었다.

Highway congestion began on the first day of the holiday.

정체되다 to be stalled to be in traffic　　정체기 stagnant period

31 직면하다

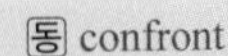

자신이 직면한 현실을 제대로 보고 대처해 나가야 한다.

You have to confront the reality you are facing and deal with it.

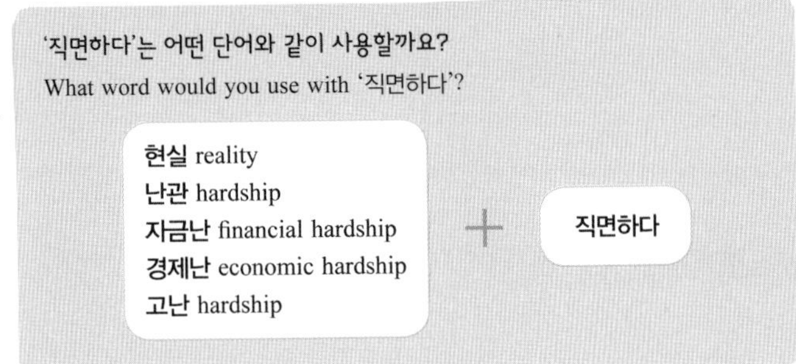

'직면하다'는 어떤 단어와 같이 사용할까요?
What word would you use with '직면하다'?
현실 reality
난관 hardship
자금난 financial hardship
경제난 economic hardship
고난 hardship
+
직면하다

32 정중하다

형 polite

나는 그의 정중한 사과에 화가 풀렸다.

I was relieved by his polite apology.

33 한계

명 limit

5시간 앉아서 일했더니 집중력의 한계가 왔다.

After sitting and working for 5 hours, I hit my limit of concentration.

한계점 uppermost limit, maximum

34 하찮다

형 trivial

중학교 때 제일 친했던 민주와는 하찮은 오해로 멀어졌다.

Minju, who was my best friend in middle school, drifted apart due to a trivial misunderstanding.

35 획득

명 acquisition, win

올림픽에서 메달 획득을 목표로 열심히 연습하고 있다.

He is practicing hard with the goal of winning a medal at the Olympics.

획득하다 to win/aquire

DAY 29 ★★

TOPIK에서 혼동하기 쉬운 단어

다의어 Polysemy

거르다

❶ 끼니를 건너 뛰다

예 끼니를 거르는 불규칙한 식사 습관은 건강에 매우 안 좋다.

Irregular eating habits of skipping meals are very bad for health.

❷ 망에 걸러 내다

예 좋은 막걸리를 얻기 위해서는 여러번의 거르는 작업이 필요하다.

In order to obtain a good makgeori (rice wine), several filtering operations are required.

반의어 Antonym

정중하다 polite ↔ 무례하다 rude

예 나는 그의 정중한 사과에 화가 풀렸다.

I was relieved by his polite apology.

예 나는 그의 무례한 행동에 화가 났다.

I got angry at his rude actions.

유의어 Synonym

유심히 carefully ≒ 자세히

예 경찰은 그 남자의 표정을 유심히 살펴보았다.

경찰은 그 남자의 표정을 자세히 살펴보았다.

The police looked carefully at the man's expression.

복습해 보세요

서로 어울리는 단어를 찾아 연결해 보세요.
Find words that go with each other and connect them.

1. 골치	a. 썩이다
2. 멸종	b. 근거
3. 흐름	c. 동물
4. 이론적	d. 원활하다
5. 현실	e. 직면하다

자연스러운 문장이 되도록 둘 중에서 알맞은 단어를 고르세요.
Try to complete the sentence in a natural way by choosing the correct word.

6. 경찰은 그 남자의 표정을 (a. 정중히 / b. 유심히) 살펴보았다.
   The police looked carefully at the man's expression.

7. 실업 문제가 가장 큰 사회 문제로 (a. 부각되고 / b. 대응하고) 있다.
   Unemployment is emerging as the biggest social problem.

8. 문화는 나라마다 (a. 독자적인 / b. 낙천적인) 성격을 가진다.
   Each country has its own unique culture.

9. 이것보다 (a. 음향이 / b. 용량이) 조금 더 큰 USB가 필요하다.
   You will need a USB with a slightly larger capacity than this.

DAY 29 ★★

정답

1.a 2.c 3.d 4.b 5.e 6.b 7.a 8.a 9.b

Memo

DAY 30

확인해 보세요

빨간 시트지로 가리고 단어의 뜻을 알면, □에 ✓ 해 보세요.

After covering up the words with red cover, please check(✓) the box (□) when you know the meaning of the word.

□ 01	가계	household budget	□ 13	막중하다	important, great	□ 25	응답자	respondent
□ 02	거부하다	refuse	□ 14	명단	list	□ 26	이면	background, hidden side
□ 03	거창하다	grand	□ 15	무난하다	easy, passable	□ 27	일탈	deviation
□ 04	공간	space	□ 16	밀려나다	to be pushed out	□ 28	자신만만하다	confident
□ 05	권력	authority	□ 17	방음	soundproof	□ 29	재치	wit
□ 06	난감하다	difficult	□ 18	배상	compensation	□ 30	정화	purification
□ 07	논평	comment	□ 19	부과하다	to impose	□ 31	중력	gravity
□ 08	단조롭다	monotonous	□ 20	양육	nurture, care	□ 32	중산층	middle class
□ 09	대조적	contrast	□ 21	연금	pension	□ 33	충족시키다	satisfy
□ 10	독재	dictatorship	□ 22	용품	goods	□ 34	한심하다	pathetic
□ 11	둔하다	dull	□ 23	위급하다	urgent	□ 35	확산되다	spread
□ 12	들이닥치다	to storm, drop in	□ 24	우발적	accidental			

DAY 30

are the words that appeared in the former tests, and you may get a higher grade if you study them together.

01 가계

명 household budget

가계에 도움이 되기 위해 맞벌이를 하는 부부가 증가하는 추세이다.

There is an increasing trend in the number of couples both working to help their household budget.

02 거부하다

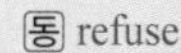

동 refuse

자존심이 강한 그 친구는 힘든 상황임에도 불구하고 나의 도움을 거부했다.

The proud friend refused my help despite the difficult situation.

거부 rejection　　거부 반응 adverse reaction
거부감 repulsion　　거부감이 들다 to be repulsed

03 거창하다

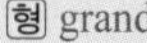

형 grand

거창한 계획보다는 현실성이 있는 계획을 세워야 한다.

You should have realistic plans rather than grand plans.

04 공간

명 space

요즘에는 작은 공간을 활용하여 넓게 사용할 수 있게 하는 인테리어가 유행이다.

Nowadays, using a small space to make the interior more spacious is popular.

공간적 spatial 가상 공간cyber space

05 권력

명 authority

권력만 추구하다 보면 오히려 가지고 있던 권력마저 잃을 수 있다.

If you pursue only authority, you can lose even the authority you already had.

06 난감하다

형 difficult

친구가 곤란한 부탁을 했는데 거절하지도 못하고 난감한 상황이다.

A friend made a difficult request, but I can't refuse it and I'm in a difficult situation.

07 논평

명 comment

신문이나 뉴스에서 정책에 대한 논평을 듣는 것은 매우 흥미롭다.

It is very interesting to hear comments about the policy in the newspaper or in the news.

시사 논평 comment on current events

08 단조롭다

형 monotonous

다양한 라이프 스타일을 추구하면 단조롭고 답답한 생활에 활력을 줄 수 있다.

Pursuing a diverse lifestyle can give vitality to a monotonous and stuffy life.

09 대조적

명 contrast

두 사람은 일하는 방식이 서로 대조적이었다.

The way the two worked was in contrast to each other.

대조 comparison　　대조하다 to compare

10 독재

명 dictatorship

국민들은 독재 정권에 대항하여 정권을 교체하였다.

The people changed the government against the dictatorship.

독재자 dictator

11 둔하다

형 dull

그는 머리가 좋은데 반해 운동 신경이 둔하다.

He is smart, but his motor nerves are dull.

12 들이닥치다

동 to storm, drop in

범인이 숨어있는 집에 갑자기 경찰들이 들이닥쳤다.

Police suddenly stormed the house where the criminal was hiding.

'들이-'는 '막', '갑자기'의 뜻을 가지고 있고 다음과 같이 사용돼요.
'들이–' includes meanings like '막 (just)' or '갑자기 (suddenly)' and is used as the following.

들이대다(to thrust/resist), 들이마시다(to inhale), 들이밀다(to shove in)

13 막중하다

형 important, great

여러분의 믿음에 막중한 책임감을 느낍니다.

I feel a great sense of responsibility for your faith.

14 명단

명 list

오늘 5시에 최종 합격자 명단을 발표했다.

The list of finalists was announced today at 5.

15 무난하다

형 easy, passable, safe

새로 나온 전기자동차는 색과 디자인이 무난한 편이다.

The new electric car has a passable color and design.

16 밀려나다

동 to be pushed out

직장에서 밀려나지 않기 위해 그는 주말에도 출근해 일을 하고 있다.

In order not to be pushed out of his job, he goes to work even on weekends.

17 방음

명 soundproof

우리 아파트는 방음이 잘 안 돼서 옆집의 소리가 너무 잘 들린다.

Our apartment is not well soundproofed, so you can hear the neighbors next door very well.

방음 시설 soundproof facilities

18 배상

명 compensation

가벼운 접촉 사고였지만 배상 문제는 그리 간단하지 않았다.

Although it was a minor contact accident, the issue of compensation was not so simple.

배상하다 to compensate　　배상을 받다 to receive compensation

19 부과하다

동 to impose

다른 사람에게 자신의 책임을 부과하는 것은 옳지 않은 행동이다.

Imposing responsibility on others is wrong.

부과 imposition　　세금 부과 imposition of tax

부과되다 to be imposed　　부과시키다 to impose

20 양육

명 nurture, raise, care for

아이들의 성격은 부모의 양육 방식에 따라 달라진다.

Children's personalities depend on how their parents nurture them.

양육비 child support cost　　양육자 caregiver

양육하다 raise　　양육되다 to be raised up

21 연금

명 pension

연금 덕분에 노후를 걱정 없이 보낼 수 있게 되었다.

Thanks to the pension, you can spend your old age without worry.

관련어

노령 연금 old-age pension　　퇴직 연금 retirement pension

DAY 30 ★★

22 용품

명 goods

애완동물의 인기가 급증하면서 반려 동물 용품의 수요도 증가하였다.

As the popularity of pets has rapidly increased, the demand for pet goods has also increased.

23 위급하다

형 urgent

소방관들은 위급한 상황에서 침착하게 대처하는 법을 훈련한다.

Firefighters are trained to remain calm in urgent situations.

위급 urgency

24 우발적

명 accidental

이번 사건은 우발적으로 저질러진 게 아니라 미리 계획된 범죄라고 한다.

It is said that this was not an accidental crime, but a planned crime.

반) 계획적 planned

25 응답자

명 respondent

설문 응답자에게는 소정의 선물을 드립니다. 많이 참여해 주세요.

A small gift will be given to the survey respondents. Please participate a lot.

출제 경향 how this word appears in the test

토픽에서는 설문조사 결과를 묻는 질문이 많이 출제됩니다. 다음 단어를 같이 공부하세요.

A lot of questions are asked about the results of the survey in Topik. Study the following words together:

조사기관(survey agency), 전체 응답자(all respondents), 대다수(majority), 절반 이상(more than half), 불과하다(only/just), 이르다(reach), 차지하다(take up), 달성하다(achieve), 급감하다(decline suddenly), 급증하다(increase suddenly), 추세(trend)

26 이면

명 background, hidden side

두 지역 사이의 계속되는 갈등 이면에는 역사적 원인이 있습니다.

In the background of the ongoing conflict between the two regions lies historical causes.

27 일탈

명 deviation

청소년들은 친구들과 어울려 음주와 같은 일탈 행동을 할 때가 있다.

Adolescents sometimes engage in deviant behaviors such as drinking with their friends.

일탈하다 to deviate

28 자신만만하다

형 confident

그 여배우는 신인 시절부터 자신만만한 태도로 유명했다.

The actress was known for her confident attitude from her rookie days.

29 재치

명 wit

그는 재치가 있는 농담으로 사람들의 기분을 좋게 만든다.

He makes people feel good with his witty jokes.

30 정화

명 purification

식물이 공기 정화에 도움이 된다고 해서 방에서 기르고 있다.

Plants are grown in rooms because they help purify the air.

정화하다 to purify　　정화되다 to be purified

DAY 30 ★★

31 중력

명 gravity

달의 중력은 지구 중력의 1/6이라고 한다.

The moon's gravity is said to be 1/6 of the Earth's gravity.

무중력 zero gravity

출제 경향 how this word appears in the test

'우주' 관련 주제는 읽기에서 자주 나오고 있습니다. 다음 단어들을 같이 공부하세요.

The topic of "space" comes up frequently in reading. Study the following words together.

행성 (Planets) - 화성 (Mars), 목성 (Jupiter), 지구 (Earth)

은하계 (galaxies), 블랙홀 (black holes), 빅뱅 (big bangs), 인공 위성 (satellites), 우주인 (astronauts), 외계인 (extraterrestrials), 탐사하다 (to explore), 탐사선 (space probes)

32 중산층

명 middle class

중산층이 많은 나라가 살기 좋은 나라라고 할 수 있다.

A country with a large middle class is a good country to live in.

상류층 upper class

33 충족시키다

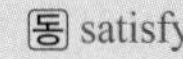

자동차 업계는 CO_2 배출에 대한 새로운 환경 기준을 충족시키기 위해 노력할 수 밖에 없는 상황이다.

The automotive industry is forced to strive to satisfy new environmental standards for CO_2 emissions.

충족 satisfaction　　충족되다 to be satisfied

충족하다 to satisfy

34 한심하다

형 pathetic

어머니는 집에서 하루종일 게임만 하는 아들을 한심하게 쳐다보았다.

The mother looked pathetically at her son, who played games all day at home.

35 확산되다

동 spread

젊은 세대를 중심으로 일과 생활의 균형을 중요시하는 움직임이 확산되고 있다.

A movement that places importance on work-life balance is spreading among the younger generation.

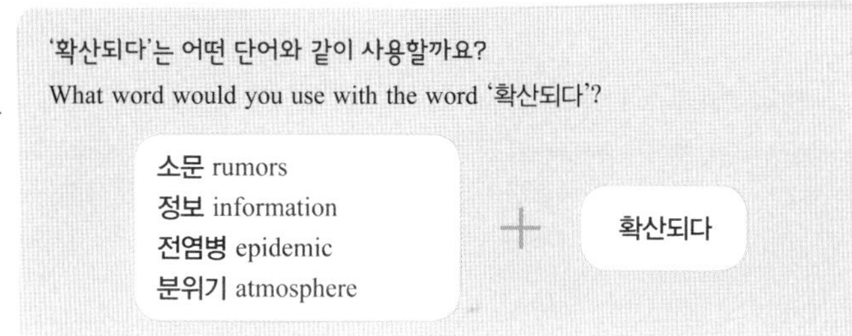

'확산되다'는 어떤 단어와 같이 사용할까요?
What word would you use with the word '확산되다'?
소문 rumors
정보 information
전염병 epidemic
분위기 atmosphere
확산되다

TOPIK에서 혼동하기 쉬운 단어

다의어 Polysemy

배상

❶ 다른 사람에게 입힌 피해를 물어주는 일

예 가벼운 접촉 사고였지만 배상 문제는 그리 간단하지 않았다.

Although it was a minor contact accident, the issue of compensation was not so simple.

❷ 격식을 갖춘 편지의 마지막에 자기 이름 뒤에 쓰는 말

예 보통 편지를 끝낼 때는 "ㅇㅇ 올림"이라고 인사하지만 장례 소식을 알리거나 단체로 소식을 전할 때는 "ㅇㅇ 배상"이라는 격식적인 높임 표현을 사용하는 경우가 많다.

Usually, at the end of a letter, we greet with "ㅇㅇ 올림", but when announcing a funeral or sending news to a group, we often use the formal exaltation of "ㅇㅇ 배상".

반의어 Antonym

우발적 accidental ↔ 계획적 planned

예 이번 살인 사건은 우발적으로 일어났다.

This murder case happened in an accidental way.

예 이번 살인 사건은 계획적인 것이었다.

This murder case was planned.

유의어 Synonym

난감하다 difficult ≒ 곤란하다

예 그의 질문에 어떻게 대답해야 할지 난감했다.

그의 질문에 어떻게 대답해야 할지 곤란했다.

It was difficult to answer his question.

복습해 보세요

자연스러운 문장이 되도록 완성해 보세요.

Try to complete the sentence in a natural way.

1. 자존심이 강한 그 친구는 힘든 상황임에도 불구하고 나의 도움을 ㄱㅂㅎㄷ.
   The proud friend refused my help despite the difficult situation.
2. 친구가 곤란한 부탁을 했는데 거절하지도 못하고 ㄴㄱㅎ 상황이다.
   A friend made a difficult request, but I can't refuse it and I'm in a difficult situation.
3. 국민들은 ㄷㅈ 정권에 대항하여 정권을 교체하였다.
   The people changed the government against the dictatorship.
4. 오늘 5시에 최종 합격자 ㅁㄷ을 발표했다.
   The list of finalists was announced today at 5.
5. 이번 사건은 ㅇㅂㅈ으로 저질러진 게 아니라 미리 계획된 범죄라고 한다.
   It is said that this was not an accidental crime, but a planned crime.
6. 두 지역 사이의 계속되는 갈등 ㅇㅁ에는 역사적 원인이 있습니다.
   In the background of the ongoing conflict between the two regions lies historical causes.

DAY 30 ★★

다음 빈 칸에 알맞은 단어를 〈보기〉에서 골라 쓰세요.

Choose the appropriate word from <Example> to fill in the blanks below.

〈보기〉

a. 방음이 b. 위급한 c. 들이닥쳤다 d. 부과하는

7. 범인이 숨어있는 집에 갑자기 경찰들이 (   ).
   Police suddenly stormed the house where the criminal was hiding.
8. 우리 아파트는 (   ) 잘 안 돼서 옆집의 소리가 너무 잘 들린다.
   Our apartment is not well soundproofed, so you can hear the neighbors next door very well.
9. 다른 사람에게 자신의 책임을 (   ) 것은 옳지 않은 행동이다.
   Imposing responsibility on others is wrong.
10. 소방관들은 (   ) 상황에서 침착하게 대처하는 법을 훈련한다.
    Firefighters are trained to remain calm in urgent situations.

정답

1. 거부했다 2. 난감한 3. 독재 4. 명단 5. 우발적 6. 이면 7. c 8. a 9. d 10. b

❶ 장(長) long, the firstborn

장거리 long distance

장기적 long-term

장남 one's eldest son

최장 the longest

장발 long hair

장녀 one's eldest daughter

❷ 단(短) short

단거리 short distance

단기적 short-term

최단 the shortest

단발 bobbed hair

▲장발 long hair

주간 복습 day 26 - day 30 

아래 단어를 보고 빈 칸에 뜻을 적어 보세요. 그리고 점선대로 접어서 적은 뜻이 맞는지 확인해 보세요. (만일 틀렸다면 뒷면의 단어 앞 □에 ✓ 하세요.)

Write down the meaning of the given word in the blank. Also, fold the page along a dotted line and check whether you got it right or wrong. (If you got it wrong tick the box in front of the word in next page.)

▼접는선

단어	뜻
난폭하다	
누리다	
독거노인	
재난	
추구하다	
면제되다	
본격적	
유사하다	
재발하다	
한가롭다	
단절되다	
못마땅하다	
연관되다	
정책	
회의적	
대응하다	
들끓다	
배기가스	
직면하다	
하찮다	
거부하다	
난감하다	
양육	
중산층	
확산되다	

※접어서 뜻이 맞는지 확인해보세요.

주간 복습 day 26 - day 30

빈 칸에 한국어 단어를 3번 적고 다시 외워 봅시다.

Write down the Korean word 3 times in the blank and try to memorize it again.

◀ 접는선

뜻
☐ violent, reckless
☐ to enjoy
☐ live alone
☐ (natural) disaster
☐ to strive for
☐ to be exempt
☐ in earnest
☐ similar
☐ to reoccur
☐ leisurely, relaxed
☐ cut off, sever
☐ displeased (with)
☐ to be involved (with)
☐ policy
☐ skeptical
☐ respond
☐ to boil
☐ exhaust gas
☐ confront
☐ trivial
☐ refuse
☐ difficult
☐ nurture, raise
☐ middle class
☐ spread

단어		
난폭하다		
누리다		
독거노인		
재난		
추구하다		
면제되다		
본격적		
유사하다		
재발하다		
한가롭다		
단절되다		
못마땅하다		
연관되다		
정책		
회의적		
대응하다		
들끓다		
배기가스		
직면하다		
하찮다		
거부하다		
난감하다		
양육		
중산층		
확산되다		

부록 Appendix

01 사동사

a causative verbs

02 피동사

a passive verbs

03 속담 및 관용 표현

proverbs, idomatic expressions

01 사동사 a causative verbs

끓이다 be boiled	기본형 끓다 boil	커피를 마시려고 물을 끓였어요. I boiled water to drink coffee.
높이다 increase	기본형 높다 high	가격을 높이면 물건 판매량이 줄어들 거예요. If you increase the price, the product will sell less.
먹이다 feed	기본형 먹다 eat	기침을 심하게 하면 아이에게 이 약을 먹이세요. When your kid severely coughs, feed him this medicine.
보이다 show	기본형 보다 see	신분증을 보여야 이 건물로 들어갈 수 있습니다. You should show your identification to enter the building.
붙이다 attach	기본형 붙다 stick	신청서에 꼭 사진을 붙여 주세요. Please attach a photograph on the application form.
속이다 trick	기본형 속다 be fooled	다른 사람을 자주 속이는 사람과는 친구가 되고 싶지 않아요. I do not want to be friends with the person who tricks others.
죽이다 kill	기본형 죽다 die	저는 벌레를 무서워해서 죽이지 못해요. I cannot kill bugs because I get scared of them.
줄이다 shorten	기본형 줄다 decrease	바지가 너무 길어서 길이를 좀 줄여야겠어요. The pants are too long so it should be shortened.
끝내다 finish	기본형 끝나다 be finished	이 일을 끝내면 좀 쉬고 싶어요. I want to take a break after this is finished.
넓히다 widen	기본형 넓다 broad	우리 집이 좁아서 집을 넓히는 공사를 했어요. Our house was small, so we built an extention to it.
눕히다 lay	기본형 눕다 lie	잠이 든 아이를 침대에 눕혔어요. I laid the sleeping baby on the bed.
맞히다 hit	기본형 맞다 be hit	아이에게 주사를 맞히기는 쉽지가 않네요. It is not easy to make the children get a shot.
앉히다 have one seated	기본형 앉다 sit	버스가 곧 출발하니까 아이를 자리에 앉혀 주세요. The bus will depart soon, so please have your child seated.

읽히다 have one read	기본형 읽다 read	선생님이 상희 씨에게 책을 읽혔어요. Teacher has Sang-hee read his book.
입히다 have one wear	기본형 입다 wear	이 옷이 잘 어울릴 것 같은데 아이에게 한번 입혀 보세요. This outfit seems to look good on your child, have him try this.
날리다 fly	기본형 날다 fly	종이 비행기를 만들어서 창 밖으로 날렸어요. I made an airplane out of paper and had it fly outside the window.
돌리다 operate	기본형 돌다 operate	저는 세탁기를 돌릴 테니까 혜경 씨는 청소를 해 주세요. I will do the laundry, Hea-Kyung please clean the apartment.
살리다 save	기본형 살다 live	의사가 물에 빠진 아이를 살렸어요. The doctor saved the drowning child.
알리다 notice	기본형 알다 know	새로운 소식이 있으면 꼭 저에게 알려 주세요. If you have any new information, please tell me what it is.
울리다 make one cry	기본형 울다 cry	저는 어렸을 때 동생을 자주 울렸어요. When I was young, I often made my younger brother cry.
감기다wash	기본형 감다wash	미용실에 가면 미용사가 제 머리를 감겨 줘서 참 편해요. When I visit hair salon, it is really comfortable since the hair dresser washes my hair.
남기다 leave (to remain)	기본형 남다 leave	밥을 남기지 말고 다 드세요. Do not leave any food on your plate and eat all of them.
맡기다 leave (to go)	기본형 맡다 take	그 옷은 세탁기에 빨지 말고 세탁소에 맡겨야 해요. You should take those clothes to the laundry instead of washing them yourself.
벗기다 take one's clothes off	기본형 벗다 take off	아이가 비를 맞고 집에 와서 젖은 옷을 벗겨 줬어요. My kid came back home soaked in rain, so I took his clothes off.
숨기다 hide	기본형 숨다 hide	그 사람 표정을 보니까 뭔가 숨기는 것이 있는 것 같아요. The look on his face says that he is hiding something.
신기다 have one wear	기본형 신다 wear	지금 나가야 하니까 얼른 아이에게 신발을 신겨 주세요. We have to go out now, so please have the child wear his shoes.

씻기다 wash	기본형 씻다 wash	강아지가 더러워서 좀 씻겨야겠어요. You should wash your dog.
웃기다 make one laugh	기본형 웃다 laugh	전 재미있는 말로 다른 사람들을 웃기는 것을 좋아해요. I like to make other people laugh with funny stories.
깨우다 wake one up	기본형 깨다 wake up	시간이 없으니까 빨리 상희 씨를 깨우세요. There's no time, so wake Sang-hee up.
비우다 be emptied	기본형 비다 empty	사무실 쓰레기통을 누가 비웠지요? Who emptied the trashcan in the office?
세우다 be stopped	기본형 서다 stop	친구 집 앞에 차를 세우고 기다렸어요. I stopped the car in front of my friend's house and waited.
씌우다 have one wear	기본형 쓰다 wear	밖이 추우니까 아이에게 모자를 씌워 주세요. It is cold outside so have your kid wear a cap.
재우다 have one sleep	기본형 자다 sleep	아기를 재워야하니 잠시만 조용히 해 주세요. Please be silent since I need to have the baby asleep.
태우다 have one ride	기본형 타다 ride	승준 씨는 여자 친구를 자전거에 태우고 소풍을 갔어요. Seung-Jun went on a picnic with his girlfriend, riding on the back of his bike.

02 피동사 a passive verbs

놓이다 be placed 기본형 놓다 place
저기 테이블 위에 놓여 있는 물건이 뭐예요?
What is that placed on the table?

바뀌다 be changed 기본형 바꾸다 change
혜경 씨가 이사를 가서 주소가 바뀌었어요.
Hea-Kyung moved and her address changed.

보이다 be seen 기본형 보다 see
창문을 열면 바다가 보이는 집에 살고 싶어요.
I want to live in the house where I can see the ocean.

쌓이다 be piled 기본형 쌓다 pile
한동안 청소를 안 했더니 집에 먼지가 쌓여 있네요.
There is a pile of dust in the house since I have not cleaned the place for a while.

쓰이다 be written 기본형 쓰다 write
책에 이름이 쓰여 있으니까 주인을 찾을 수 있을 거예요.
You may find the owner of the book since the name is written on it.

잠기다 be locked 기본형 잠그다 lock
가게 문이 잠겨 있는 것을 보니 아무도 없나 봐요.
There must be no one in the store since the door is locked.

닫히다 be closed 기본형 닫다 close
바람 때문에 문이 저절로 닫혔어요.
The door closed by itself because of the wind.

막히다 be blocked 기본형 막다 block
출퇴근 시간에는 길이 많이 막혀요.
The traffic jam is serious every morning and evening when people are going and coming back from work.

먹히다 be eaten 기본형 먹다 eat
쥐가 고양이에게 먹혔어요.
The rat was eaten by the cat.

밟히다 be stepped 기본형 밟다 step
지하철에 사람이 많아서 계속 발을 밟혔어요.
Too many people were in the subway and my foot was constantly stepped on.

업히다 carry somebody or something on one's back 기본형 업다 ride on somebody's back
어젯밤에 혜경 씨는 취해서 친구에게 업혀서 집에 왔어요.
Last night Hea-Kyung was so drunk that she was carried here on her friend's back.

읽히다 be read 기본형 읽다 read
책 내용이 어려워서 잘 읽히지 않네요.
The book's content is too challenging, so it is hard to read.

잡히다 be caught 기본형 잡다 catch
지난주에 일어난 살인사건의 용의자가 잡혔대요.
The suspect of the homicide was caught last week.

걸리다 be hanged	기본형 걸다 hang	우리 집에는 가족 사진이 걸려 있어요. There is a family picture hanging on our house wall.
날리다 fly	기본형 날다 fly	봄에는 바람이 불면 꽃잎이 날려서 참 예뻐요. It is beautiful in the spring to see the petals fly in the wind.
들리다 hear	기본형 듣다 hear	소리가 잘 안 들리는데 소리를 좀 크게 해 주세요. I cannot hear the sound, so can you please turn up the volume?
물리다 be bitten	기본형 물다 bite	여름철에 창문을 열고 자면 모기에게 많이 물려요. If you let your window open in the summer while you are sleeping, you will get many bites from mosquitoes.
열리다 be opened	기본형 열다 open	집에 와 보니 문이 열려 있어서 깜짝 놀랐어요. I was shocked to see my window being opened when I came back from work.
팔리다 be sold	기본형 팔다 sell	이 옷이 요즘 잘 팔리는 옷이에요. These clothes are the ones that are being sold well these days.
풀리다 be solved	기본형 풀다 solve	이 수학 문제는 너무 어려워서 잘 풀리지 않네요. This math problem is too challenging to be solved.
끊기다 stopped operating	기본형 끊다 disconnect	너무 늦어서 마지막 지하철마저 끊겼어요. I was too late that the last subway already left.
담기다 be filled with	기본형 담다 put something in	식탁 위에 있는 소금이 담긴 통을 갖다 주세요. Can you please take the jar filled with salt on the kitchen table and bring it to me?
빼앗기다 be robbed	기본형 빼앗다 rob	집에 오는 길에 나쁜 사람에게 돈을 빼앗겼어요. While I was coming back home, I had a bad man rob me.
안기다 be in one's arm	기본형 안다 hug	아이가 엄마에게 안겨서 자고 있는 모습이 참 귀엽네요. The child sleeping in his mother's arms is just too cute.
쫓기다 be chased	기본형 쫓다 chase	그 도둑은 경찰에게 쫓기다가 넘어졌다. The thief tripped while he was chased by the police.

03 속담 및 관용표현 proverbs, idomatic expressions

■ 가는 날이 장날

As luck would have it

This expression is used when you end up with something unexpected while you were doing something.

■ 가는 말이 고와야 오는 말이 곱다

What goes around comes around

It means that in order to hear good things from the counterpart, you should tell him good things first.

■ 갈수록 태산이다

Out of the frying pan into the fire

You use this expression when you face work that becomes harder and harder as it proceeds.

■ 겉 다르고 속 다르다

Appearances are deceptive

It means that the expression that is revealed outside is totally different from what is in one's mind.

■ 계란으로 바위 치기

Beat one's head against the wall

This expression is used when you are too weak so that you will never win no matter how hard you try.

■ 공든 탑이 무너지랴

A man's labors will be crowned with success

It means that the work with paintaking care will always create positive results.

■ 그림의 떡

Pie in the sky

It describes an object that one will never get and almost impossible to reach.

■ 긁어 부스럼 만들기

Let sleeping dog lie

This expression is used when someone is unecessarily involed with the work and even make it worse than before.

■ 꿩 대신 닭

Something is better than nothing

This is used when something is needed but you don't have it, you use different but similar thing instead that is usually not good enough than the original thing that you needed in the first place.

■ 남의 떡이 더 커 보인다

The grass is greener on the other side of the fence

You use this expression when the thing that other people have looks better than your's.

■ 도토리 키 재기

A miss is as good as a mile

This exepression is used when two people argue that he is better than the other, but actually both of them has no big of a difference.

■ 돌다리도 두들겨 보고 건너라

Look before you leap

It means that you should be careful of doing whatever you do.

■ 등잔 밑이 어둡다

A beacon does not shine on its own base

It means that it is rather hard for you to know what happens close to you than what happens far from you.

■ 땅 짚고 헤엄치기

Swimming while touching the ground.
= it's a piece of cake

It means that the thing that you are trying to do is easy.

■ 말 속에 뼈가 있다

Many a true word is spoken in jest

You use this expression when you hear a normal expression but it has a sarcasm behind the apparent meaning.

■ 모르는 게 약

Nothing hurts like the truth

It means that it may be better for you to not know about it since knowing will only make you worse.

■ 믿는 도끼에 발등 찍힌다

(get) Stabbed in the back

You use this expression when the work that you believed will turn out fine but not or you were betrayed by the person you believed in.

■ 밑 빠진 독에 물 붓기

All that is put in a riven dish is lost

This expression is used when there is no positiv outcome of what you are doing or you cannot c anything about it.

■ 배보다 배꼽이 크다

It is the tail wagging the dog

This is used when the basic thing needs mo attention or cost that is spent while doing th main task.

■ 보기 좋은 떡이 먹기에도 좋다

Names and natures do often agree

It means that there is a moment when a goo appearance is also important.

■ 산 넘어 산

Out of the frying pan into the fire

It is an expression that used when after gettin out of a bad situation you end up in the wors one.

■ 쇠귀(소귀)에 경 읽기

Talking to the wall.

This expression is used when the person tha you are teaching does not anderstand what yo are saying no matter how many times you repea what you tell him.

■ 수박 겉 핥기

Scratching the surface

This expression is used when someone does a lazy work and does not do the important thing that hc should do.

■ 시간은 금

Time is gold

It means that the time is invaluable as gold is.

■ 시간이 약

Time heals all wounds

It means that even though you have gone through a devastating thing or heart breaking thing, time will always make the pain heal.

■ 식은 죽 먹기

Something is a breeze = it's a piece of cake

It means that the thing that you are trying to do is easy.

■ 실패는 성공의 어머니

Failure is but a stepping stone to success

This means that in order to succeed in the longrun, it is necessary for you to fail first, and you should not be afraid of failing.

■ 싼 게 비지떡

You get what you pay for

It means that the cheap product is bad.

■ 아는 길도 물어서 가라

Look before you leap

It means that you should be cautious even while you are doing the thing that you are familiar with.

■ 아니 땐 굴뚝에 연기 날까

Where there's smoke, there's fire

It means that when there is a result, there must be a cause that made that result.

■ 앓던 이가 빠진 것 같다

Feel sudden relief

This expression is used when someone finally solved a big problem that had been bothering him greatly

■ 어깨가 무겁다

Feeling a big burden on my shoulders

This is an expression that describes the status that is highly stressed with heavy responsibility.

■ 열번 찍어 안 넘어가는 나무 없다

Little strokes fell great oaks

This means that even the hardest work can be done when you constantly try to do it.

■ 오르지 못할 나무는 쳐다 보지 마라

Don't bite off more than you can chew

It means that you should never try to do the thing that is hard for you to do with your ability.

■ 윗물이 맑아야 아랫물이 맑다

The fish always stinks from the head downwards

This means that the elder should act well, so that the young can learn from that and do well in the future.

■ 입에 쓴 약이 병에는 좋다

A good medicine tastes bitter

This means that even though the course of doing a certain work can be hard, the result will pay off after you endure the pain and accomplish it.

■ 자식 이기는 부모 없다

There's no parent who win their children.
= No parent win their children

This means that when the child seriously decides to do certain thing, no parents can prevent them from doing that.

■ 천 리 길도 한 걸음부터

Step by step one goes a long way

It means that no matter how fast you want to finish a certain job, you should never be hasty but be patient by slowly doing the proper things step by step starting from the beginning.

■ 티끌 모아 태산

Many a little makes a miracle

This means that you can get a big thing in the long run after gathering the smallest things.

■ 하늘의 별 따기

Catching a star in the sky

It is an expression that shows that the goal that you are trying to achieve is beyond your ability so that the possibility that you will succeed is low.

■ 원숭이도 나무에서 떨어진다

Even homer sometimes nods

It means that even an expert can sometimes make a mistake in the field where he specialize.

단어장

self-vocabulary booklet

day 01 – day 30

Now, cheer up until you reach the mid-level of TOPIK!

DAY 01 | 일일 단어 리스트

☐ 01 가해자	perpetrator	☐ 13 막대하다	huge	☐ 25 은퇴	retirement
☐ 02 감시	monitoring	☐ 14 머금다	hold/keep/with (something) on one's face	☐ 26 의혹	suspicion
☐ 03 개량	improvement	☐ 15 목격하다	witness	☐ 27 일관성	consistency
☐ 04 고소득	high income	☐ 16 민간	general public	☐ 28 일대일	one-on-one
☐ 05 국산	domestic	☐ 17 방관적	bystander attitude	☐ 29 재개발	redevelopment
☐ 06 꺼리다	disincled	☐ 18 복제	copying	☐ 30 적발되다	be caught
☐ 07 냉전	cold war	☐ 19 심경	feeling/mind/ mood	☐ 31 접촉	be contact
☐ 08 노후	old age	☐ 20 여정	journey	☐ 32 지연되다	delay
☐ 09 단련	training	☐ 21 오작동	malfunction	☐ 33 초과	exceed
☐ 10 대세	tide	☐ 22 요건	requirement	☐ 34 하마터면	almost
☐ 11 도피하다	escape	☐ 23 원료	ingredient	☐ 35 확률	probability
☐ 12 동참	participation	☐ 24 유발하다	motivate		

DAY 02 | 일일 단어 리스트

☐ 01 개방적	open	☐ 13 면모	aspect/side	☐ 25 음성	audio
☐ 02 개선하다	improve	☐ 14 목차	table of contents	☐ 26 이견	disagreement
☐ 03 고용	employment	☐ 15 미화하다	glamorize	☐ 27 일깨우다	remind
☐ 04 국정	state affairs	☐ 16 민감하다	sensitive	☐ 28 입소문	word of mouth
☐ 05 끌어올리다	pull up	☐ 17 방범	crime prevention	☐ 29 재고	stock
☐ 06 노리다	target	☐ 18 복지	welfare	☐ 30 전력	electricity
☐ 07 녹지	greenery	☐ 19 심화하다	deepen	☐ 31 정년	retirement age
☐ 08 단서	clue	☐ 20 역경	adversity	☐ 32 지장	harm/disrupt
☐ 09 대수롭다	big deal	☐ 21 왕래	interaction/ come and go	☐ 33 촉박하다	to be tight on/ pressed for (something)
☐ 10 동향	to trend	☐ 22 요령	trick/hang of it	☐ 34 회피하다	avoid
☐ 11 동행	accompany	☐ 23 원망	resentment	☐ 35 획일적	uniform
☐ 12 막론하다	regardless	☐ 24 유보하다	to withhold		

DAY 03 | 일일 단어 리스트

No.	단어	Meaning
☐ 01	가부장적	patriarchal (something)
☐ 02	가하다	put
☐ 03	격려하다	encourage
☐ 04	공권력	law enforcement
☐ 05	규제	regulation
☐ 06	남용하다	abuse
☐ 07	농산물	agricultural/ farm products
☐ 08	달리하다	be different(from)
☐ 09	닳다	to run/ wear out/down
☐ 10	돈독하다	close/friendly
☐ 11	득점	score
☐ 12	만사	everything
☐ 13	무료하다	bored
☐ 14	무안하다	to be embarrassed
☐ 15	무중력	zero gravity
☐ 16	밀접하다	close
☐ 17	배제하다	to exclude/ rule out
☐ 18	분쟁	conflict/ dispute
☐ 19	불황	recession/ depression
☐ 20	역대	best/ worst ever
☐ 21	열등감	sense of inferiority
☐ 22	위반하다	to violate/ break (a law)
☐ 23	유일무이	the one and only/sole
☐ 24	의료	healthcare/ medical care
☐ 25	이왕이면	might as well
☐ 26	임종	death/passing
☐ 27	자초지종	full account
☐ 28	재활	rehabilitation
☐ 29	제도적	institutional (something)
☐ 30	제멋대로	as one pleases
☐ 31	진열되다	on display
☐ 32	친환경	eco-friendly (something)
☐ 33	해당하다	be applicable(to)/ be considered
☐ 34	휩쓸리다	to be swept
☐ 35	흡족하다	to be satisfied

DAY 04 | 일일 단어 리스트

No.	단어	Meaning
☐ 01	가사	household chores
☐ 02	간결하다	concise
☐ 03	격리	quarantine/ isolation
☐ 04	공사장	construction site
☐ 05	균형	balance
☐ 06	납득하다	accept/ understand
☐ 07	누리꾼	netizen
☐ 08	달구다	heat (up)
☐ 09	담담하다	unruffled/calm
☐ 10	돋보이다	to stand out
☐ 11	들락거리다	frequently went in and out
☐ 12	만연하다	be pervasive/ rampant
☐ 13	무릅쓰다	risk
☐ 14	무언	unspoken (something)
☐ 15	무한	infinity
☐ 16	밀착시키다	to bring closer
☐ 17	배출	emission/ discharge
☐ 18	분해하다	to disassemble/ take (sth) apart
☐ 19	비관적	pessimism
☐ 20	역량	capability
☐ 21	열성	enthusiasm (for)
☐ 22	위법	illegal
☐ 23	유입	inflow/influx
☐ 24	의류	clothing
☐ 25	이윤	profit
☐ 26	임하다	assume
☐ 27	자본주의	capitalism
☐ 28	작심삼일	a short-lived resolve
☐ 29	쟁점	(controversial) issue
☐ 30	제시하다	to propose/ present
☐ 31	제한하다	to restrict/limit
☐ 32	진출	advancement/ inroad
☐ 33	침체	recession/ depression
☐ 34	해박하다	comprehensive/ extensive
☐ 35	휴전	ceasefire/truce

DAY 05 | 일일 단어 리스트

□ 01 가상 virtuality	□ 13 무모하다 reckless	□ 25 이전하다 to relocate/move
□ 02 갈다 replace	□ 14 무용지물 uselessness	□ 26 이직 change of job
□ 03 격식 formality	□ 15 무형 intangible	□ 27 입시 entrance exam
□ 04 공산품 industrial products	□ 16 밀폐되다 be sealed/enclosed	□ 28 잡음 static
□ 05 극단적 extreme	□ 17 배타적 exclusive/intolerant/	□ 29 저리다 to ache/to be numb
□ 06 납부 payment	□ 18 비례하다 be proportional	□ 30 제작하다 produce
□ 07 누비다 travel, go around	□ 19 양해 understanding/excuse	□ 31 조난 distress
□ 08 담보 guarantee	□ 20 열악하다 poor/inadequate	□ 32 진취적 enterprising
□ 09 대책 (counter) measure	□ 21 우세하다 superior/exceed	□ 33 침해 invasion/violation
□ 10 돌발 unexpected/burst	□ 22 위상 status/position	□ 34 해약하다 to cancel/terminate
□ 11 들추다 expose/lift	□ 23 유전 heredity/genetic	□ 35 흐릿하다 cloudy/blurry
□ 12 만장일치 unanimity	□ 24 의약품 medical supplies	

DAY 06 | 일일 단어 리스트

□ 01 가식적 pretentious	□ 13 말단 end/terminal	□ 25 유지하다 maintain
□ 02 감소 decline/reduction	□ 14 맞대다 put together/face	□ 26 의외 surprise
□ 03 격차 gap/disparity	□ 15 무효 void	□ 27 이점 advantage/benefit
□ 04 공식적 official	□ 16 밑거름 (figurative) foundation	□ 28 입양 adoption
□ 05 극대화 maximization	□ 17 배포하다 distribute	□ 29 장거리 long-distance
□ 06 낭패 trouble/failure	□ 18 범주 category	□ 30 저마다 each
□ 07 누출 leak	□ 19 부재 absence	□ 31 제한하다 to limit
□ 08 단축 shortneing	□ 20 비중 importance/weight	□ 32 죄책감 guilt
□ 09 답례품 goodie bag	□ 21 어리둥절하다 puzzled	□ 33 질기다 tough/durable
□ 10 대처하다 to manage/respond	□ 22 열의 enthusiasm	□ 34 타격 blow/hit
□ 11 돌연변이 mutation	□ 23 예리하다 keen/sharp	□ 35 행정부 administration
□ 12 등장인물 characters	□ 24 위생 hygiene/sanitation	

DAY 07 | 일일 단어 리스트

☐ 01	가정하다	assume/suppose	☐ 13	명료하다	clear/articulate	☐ 25	이를테면	for example/ such as
☐ 02	개인주의	individualism	☐ 14	묵직하다	heavy	☐ 26	이정표	road sign/ milestone
☐ 03	견디다	endure/withstand	☐ 15	바짝	extremely (close/dry/crisp)	☐ 27	입증하다	to prove
☐ 04	공유하다	to share	☐ 16	배회하다	to wander	☐ 28	장유유서	the younger should give precedence to the elder/elders first
☐ 05	근로	work/labor	☐ 17	범하다	make (a mistake)	☐ 29	저버리다	to betray
☐ 06	낱낱이	in detail/fully	☐ 18	비참하다	tragic/miserable	☐ 30	조급하다	in a hurry
☐ 07	눈살	frown between one's eyebrows	☐ 19	어설프다	sloppy/clumpy	☐ 31	주도적	proactive
☐ 08	당당하다	to be confident	☐ 20	염두	mind	☐ 32	질리다	be frightened, be sick of
☐ 09	대체하다	replace	☐ 21	온난화	warming	☐ 33	타당성	validity
☐ 10	동감하다	agree	☐ 22	위조	forgery	☐ 34	허기	hunger
☐ 11	등재되다	be registered	☐ 23	유치하다	host	☐ 35	흥청망청	lavishly/ extravagantly
☐ 12	말문	speech	☐ 24	의지하다	rely			

DAY 08 | 일일 단어 리스트

☐ 01	간과하다	overlook	☐ 13	명목	cause/pretext	☐ 25	이르다	to reach/arrive
☐ 02	거슬리다	to be irrating	☐ 14	문득	suddenly/ all of a sudden	☐ 26	이주하다	to migrate/move
☐ 03	견제하다	check, hold in check	☐ 15	박람회	fair/exhibition	☐ 27	입지	conditions, position
☐ 04	공정하다	fair/impartial	☐ 16	배후	someone behind the action	☐ 28	재개발	redevelopment
☐ 05	근무지	workplace	☐ 17	범행	crime	☐ 29	저작권	copyright
☐ 06	내면	inner side	☐ 18	상당하다	significant/ considerable	☐ 30	조마조마하다	nervous/afraid
☐ 07	눈에 띄다	catch one's eye	☐ 19	어이없다	absurd	☐ 31	주되다	main/principal
☐ 08	당락	outcome	☐ 20	염려	worry/concern	☐ 32	질의	question
☐ 09	대폭	significantly/ sharply	☐ 21	온전하다	sane/sound	☐ 33	탄생	birth
☐ 10	동결되다	be frozen/ stopped	☐ 22	위축되다	be daunted/ intimidated	☐ 34	허둥지둥	hurriedly, in a hurry
☐ 11	등지다	turn one's back on	☐ 23	유통되다	to be circulated/ distributed	☐ 35	흥행	hit/success
☐ 12	말미암다	due to	☐ 24	이기심	selfishness			

DAY 09 | 일일 단어 리스트

☐ 01 간소하다	simple/plain	☐ 13 명백하다	to be clear	☐ 25 익명	anonymity
☐ 02 걷잡다	control	☐ 14 문명	civilization	☐ 26 자가	oneself
☐ 03 결단	decision	☐ 15 박탈하다	disqualify	☐ 27 재고	stock/ inventory
☐ 04 근원	root/cause/ source	☐ 16 번거롭다	inconvenient/ cumbersome	☐ 28 저조하다	low
☐ 05 급변하다	to rapidly change	☐ 17 법규	law	☐ 29 조만간	soon
☐ 06 내몰다	to drive/force	☐ 18 생소하다	unfamiliar	☐ 30 주목	attention
☐ 07 눈에 선하다	be fresh/live in one´s memory	☐ 19 어처구니	be absurb	☐ 31 주식	staple food
☐ 08 당면	current/ immediate	☐ 20 영광	honor/glory	☐ 32 터놓다	open one's heart
☐ 09 대피	evacuation	☐ 21 완쾌하다	recover completely	☐ 33 허름하다	shabby/poor
☐ 10 동경	admiration/ longing	☐ 22 위태롭다	risky/perilous	☐ 34 흐뭇하다	pleased
☐ 11 디디다	step on	☐ 23 유해	hazard, harm	☐ 35 희미하다	to be faint/ dim
☐ 12 맞아떨어지다	match	☐ 24 이득	profit		

DAY 10 | 일일 단어 리스트

☐ 01 간절하다	to be desperate	☐ 13 명분	cause/ justificiation	☐ 25 이름나다	to be famous for
☐ 02 겪다	to experience	☐ 14 문상	offer of condolences	☐ 26 인건비	labor costs
☐ 03 결말	ending	☐ 15 반감	hostility/ animosity	☐ 27 자각	self-awareness/ consciousness
☐ 04 공해	pollution	☐ 16 번번이	always, all the time	☐ 28 재난	natural disaster
☐ 05 금리	interest rate	☐ 17 법률	law	☐ 29 저하	fall, decline
☐ 06 내비치다	express	☐ 18 생계	livelihood	☐ 30 조율하다	to tune, to coordinate
☐ 07 눈여겨보다	pay attention to	☐ 19 억누르다	to suppress	☐ 31 질환	disease/illness
☐ 08 당부	request	☐ 20 영구적	permanent/ lasting	☐ 32 짐작하다	to assume
☐ 09 댓글	comments	☐ 21 완화하다	to relax	☐ 33 허물다	knock down
☐ 10 동등하다	equal (to)	☐ 22 위협	threat/harm	☐ 34 허용되다	to be allowed/ permitted
☐ 11 딜레마	dilemma	☐ 23 유형	type, category	☐ 35 희박하다	rare/sparse
☐ 12 맞장구	chime in	☐ 24 이르다	early		

DAY 11 | 일일 단어 리스트

- ☐ 01 간접 indirect
- ☐ 02 견문 knowledge/ experience/
- ☐ 03 결함 defect/fault
- ☐ 04 과감하다 to be daring/ decisive
- ☐ 05 금액 price
- ☐ 06 내역 breakdown
- ☐ 07 눈을 붙이다 get some sleep, take a little nap
- ☐ 08 당사자 the person/ party directly involved
- ☐ 09 덤벼들다 to lunge for
- ☐ 10 동력 driving force/ power source
- ☐ 11 딛다 step on, overcome
- ☐ 12 매기다 score, set
- ☐ 13 명상 meditation
- ☐ 14 문헌 literature/ references
- ☐ 15 반려견 pet dog
- ☐ 16 번식히다 to reporduce
- ☐ 17 법안 bill
- ☐ 18 생태계 ecosystem
- ☐ 19 언급 comment/ reference
- ☐ 20 연료 fuel
- ☐ 21 예산 budget
- ☐ 22 위화감 sense of incompatibility
- ☐ 23 유효 valid/available
- ☐ 24 이념 ideology/ideals
- ☐ 25 이산화탄소 carbon dioxide
- ☐ 26 인공위성 satellite
- ☐ 27 자금 fund
- ☐ 28 재능 talent
- ☐ 29 저해 hindrance/ impairment (to)
- ☐ 30 조작하다 to operate/ create
- ☐ 31 주장하다 to claim/ assert
- ☐ 32 집단 organization
- ☐ 33 통과되다 to be passed
- ☐ 34 허술하다 to be flimsy
- ☐ 35 희생하다 to sacrifice

DAY 12 | 일일 단어 리스트

- ☐ 01 간주하다 to regard/ consider
- ☐ 02 결합 union/ combination
- ☐ 03 계발 improvement
- ☐ 04 과대평가 overestimation
- ☐ 05 급등 jump, sharp rise
- ☐ 06 내쫓다 kick out
- ☐ 07 눈짓 look/glance
- ☐ 08 당선 election
- ☐ 09 덮치다 to hit/strike
- ☐ 10 동문서답 an irrelevant answer
- ☐ 11 따갑다 sting/prick
- ☐ 12 매달리다 to cling/hang (on)
- ☐ 13 명성 fame
- ☐ 14 물끄러미 to peer/gaze
- ☐ 15 반론 rebuttal
- ☐ 16 번창 prosperity, flourish
- ☐ 17 베테랑 veteran/expert
- ☐ 18 서먹하다 to feel awkward/ uncomfortable
- ☐ 19 언론 press/media
- ☐ 20 예상하다 to predict/ expect
- ☐ 21 욕구 desire/want
- ☐ 22 유교 Confucianism
- ☐ 23 육지 land/mainland
- ☐ 24 이상 기후 abnormal climates
- ☐ 25 인공적 artificial
- ☐ 26 자급자족 self-sufficient
- ☐ 27 재정적 financial
- ☐ 28 적발하다 to catch/ uncover
- ☐ 29 조장하다 encourage/ aggravate
- ☐ 30 주최 host
- ☐ 31 차단하다 to block
- ☐ 32 터뜨리다 to pop/burst
- ☐ 33 투덜거리다 to complain
- ☐ 34 홀가분하다 to be lighthearted/ carefree
- ☐ 35 희한하다 to be rare/ exotic

DAY 13 | 일일 단어 리스트

☐ 01 갈등	conflict	☐ 13 명심하다	keep in mind	☐ 25 이성적	rational
☐ 02 경기	economy	☐ 14 물량	supply/volume	☐ 26 인권	human rights
☐ 03 공산주의	communism	☐ 15 반목	hostility/feud	☐ 27 자립	self-reliance
☐ 04 과도하다	excessive	☐ 16 벤처	venture	☐ 28 재촉하다	to urge
☐ 05 급속	rapidity, swiftness	☐ 17 성취하다	to achieve/ accompany	☐ 29 적정	optimum
☐ 06 냉담하다	to be cold	☐ 18 얼떨떨하다	to be dazed/ bewildered	☐ 30 조정	adjustment
☐ 07 눈치를 보다	to be self-conscious, to read the room	☐ 19 예외	exception	☐ 31 중소	small and medium
☐ 08 대거	in a group, in great numbers	☐ 20 우선순위	priority	☐ 32 차분하다	to be calm
☐ 09 도	limit, degree	☐ 21 우여곡절	complications, twist and turns	☐ 33 투표권	right to vote
☐ 10 동반	company, together	☐ 22 원자력	nuclear power	☐ 34 허위	falsehood
☐ 11 딱하다	pitiful, sad	☐ 23 유권자	voters	☐ 35 힘겹다	hard, difficult
☐ 12 매듭	knot/tie	☐ 24 윤리	ethics		

DAY 14 | 일일 단어 리스트

☐ 01 감당하다	to handle	☐ 12 때우다	to fill/patch	☐ 24 유기견	abandoned dogs
☐ 02 경고하다	to warn	☐ 13 매료시키다	to captivate	☐ 25 융통성	flexibility
☐ 03 공평하다	to be fair	☐ 14 명예	reputation/ honor	☐ 26 이열치열	fight fire with fire
☐ 04 과소평가	underestimation	☐ 15 물려받다	to inherit/ succeed	☐ 27 인내심	patience
☐ 05 과언	exaggeration	☐ 16 반박하다	to refute	☐ 28 자수성가	self-made
☐ 06 냉혹하다	cold, harsh	☐ 17 벼르다	to eagerly wait	☐ 29 재충전하다	recharge
☐ 07 뉘우치다	to be remorseful, to repent	☐ 18 세균	bacteria	☐ 30 적합하다	to be appropriate/ suitable for
☐ 08 다그치다	to reprimand	☐ 19 얼버무리다	to speak vaguely	☐ 31 조치하다	to take measures/ actions
☐ 09 대견하다	to be proud of	☐ 20 여파	aftermath	☐ 32 중시하다	to consider important
☐ 10 도달	arrival, reaching	☐ 21 예측하다	to predict	☐ 33 차일피일	constantly procrastinate
☐ 11 동병상련	You can have compassion/ understanding for another when you experience the same situation as them	☐ 22 우열을 가리다	place above	☐ 34 파격적	shocking, unconventional
		☐ 23 운행	operation	☐ 35 헌법	constitution

DAY 15 | 일일 단어 리스트

☐ 01	감량	reduction, loss	☐ 13	매립	landfill	☐ 25	이외	besides, except
☐ 02	겸하다	to engage in	☐ 14	명확하다	clear	☐ 26	인상착의	description(look and dressing)
☐ 03	과연	indeed, really	☐ 15	뭉클하다	to be touched/ moved	☐ 27	자숙하다	to self-reflect
☐ 04	관세	duties, tariffs	☐ 16	반발심	resistance, rebellion	☐ 28	재치	wit
☐ 05	급락	plummet, sudden drop	☐ 17	변덕	whim	☐ 29	전무후무	unprecedented
☐ 06	넘보다	to covet	☐ 18	소송	lawsuit	☐ 30	조합	combination
☐ 07	느닷없이	abruptly, out of the blue	☐ 19	엄연하다	undeniable, clear	☐ 31	중점	a focus
☐ 08	다다르다	to reach	☐ 20	역부족	not enough	☐ 32	차질	disruption
☐ 09	대내적	internality	☐ 21	오류	error	☐ 33	파업	strike
☐ 10	도덕	ethics, morals	☐ 22	우직하다	to be simple and honest	☐ 34	허탈하다	dejected, let-down
☐ 11	동서고금	all times and places	☐ 23	유기농	organic	☐ 35	헐값	bargain price
☐ 12	떠밀리다	to be pushed into	☐ 24	융합하다	to combine			

DAY 16 | 일일 단어 리스트

☐ 01	감명	inspiration	☐ 13	매매	sales, trading	☐ 25	응모	application
☐ 02	경로	route	☐ 14	모방하다	to mimic/copy	☐ 26	이의	objection
☐ 03	관습	custom/practice	☐ 15	미달	insufficiency, shortfall	☐ 27	인색하다	to be stingy/ sparing
☐ 04	권위	authority, prestige	☐ 16	반전	twist, reversal	☐ 28	자아실현	self-acutalization
☐ 05	급증하다	to increase rapidly	☐ 17	변수	variable	☐ 29	재택	be (at) home
☐ 06	노골적	obvious/open	☐ 18	손실	loss	☐ 30	전성기	prime, best days
☐ 07	능동적	active	☐ 19	업적	achievement	☐ 31	조화	harmony
☐ 08	다수결	majority	☐ 20	역설적	irony	☐ 32	증가하다	to increase/rise
☐ 09	대대적	large- scale, extensive	☐ 21	오름세	upward trend	☐ 33	참고하다	to refer to
☐ 10	도도하다	haughty, arrogant, proud	☐ 22	우스꽝스럽다	ridiculous	☐ 34	판단하다	to judge/ consider
☐ 11	동식물	animals and plants	☐ 23	우호적	friendly	☐ 35	헛디디다	to miss one's step
☐ 12	떳떳하다	to have a clear conscience	☐ 24	유난히	especially/ particularly			

DAY 17 | 일일 단어 리스트

☐ 01	가공	process, manufacture	☐ 13	뜸하다	to be infrequent to lose touch (for)	☐ 25	의기소침하다	dispirited, down
☐ 02	감염	infection	☐ 14	매섭다	to be fierce/harsh	☐ 26	이익	profit/interest
☐ 03	경유	stopover	☐ 15	모범	model	☐ 27	인신공격하다	to make a personal attack
☐ 04	광범위하다	to be extensive/ broad	☐ 16	미덕	virtue	☐ 28	자외선	UV-light
☐ 05	극복하다	to overcome	☐ 17	반항	rebellion	☐ 29	재활	rehabilitation
☐ 06	기부금	donation	☐ 18	변천	change	☐ 30	전염되다	to spread a contagious disease
☐ 07	노령	old age	☐ 19	수용	accomodation, acceptance	☐ 31	종사자	worker
☐ 08	능률	efficiency	☐ 20	연연하다	to cling/ stick to	☐ 32	증상	symptom
☐ 09	다스리다	to manage/rule	☐ 21	온대	temperate (climates)	☐ 33	채용하다	to hire
☐ 10	대두되다	to come up, to be on the rise	☐ 22	올바르다	correct, right	☐ 34	팽팽하다	to be tense/ strained
☐ 11	도래하다	to come/arrive	☐ 23	우후죽순	spring up everywhere	☐ 35	헛수고	vain attempt/ effort
☐ 12	동요하다	to disturb/waver	☐ 24	유대감	bond			

DAY 18 | 일일 단어 리스트

☐ 01	각광	spotlight	☐ 13	마니아	mania, enthusiast	☐ 25	이타주의	altruism
☐ 02	감탄하다	to admire/ wonder	☐ 14	매입하다	to purchase, to buy	☐ 26	인위적	unnatural (something)
☐ 03	계기	chance, opportunity	☐ 15	모색하다	seek, find	☐ 27	작동하다	to work/ function
☐ 04	괘씸하다	disgusting/ disgraceful	☐ 16	미묘하다	subtle	☐ 28	저가	low-cost
☐ 05	금융업	financial business	☐ 17	발각되다	to be discover	☐ 29	전형적	typical
☐ 06	기압	atmospheric pressure	☐ 18	변형되다	to be modified	☐ 30	좌절	setback, frustration
☐ 07	노릇	role	☐ 19	수익	profit	☐ 31	지독하다	awful, terrible
☐ 08	능숙하다	to be skilled/ proficient at	☐ 20	염증	infection, inflammation	☐ 32	책정하다	to set
☐ 09	다지다	to brace oneself, determine to keep	☐ 21	옹호하다	to protect, to support	☐ 33	편견	prejudice
☐ 10	대들다	to challenge/defy	☐ 22	운송	transportation	☐ 34	허전하다	empty
☐ 11	도리	duty, right	☐ 23	유도하다	to induce/guide	☐ 35	혁신	revolution
☐ 12	동원하다	mobilize, gather	☐ 24	의례적	formal			

DAY 19 | 일일 단어 리스트

No.	단어	뜻	No.	단어	뜻	No.	단어	뜻
☐ 01	갑작스럽다	sudden	☐ 13	마다하다	resist	☐ 25	의식적	conscious
☐ 02	거치다	go through	☐ 14	맥	pulse, energy	☐ 26	이해관계	interest
☐ 03	고갈	depletion	☐ 15	모순	inconsistency	☐ 27	인재	talented person
☐ 04	교대하다	to change shift	☐ 16	미생물	microbe	☐ 28	작용하다	apply, action
☐ 05	급여	wages	☐ 17	발굴되다	to be excavated	☐ 29	저물다	get dark
☐ 06	기여하다	contribute	☐ 18	병행하다	combine, do	☐ 30	전환	transformation
☐ 07	노사	labor and management	☐ 19	습득	acquisition	☐ 31	죄책감	guilt
☐ 08	능통하다	fluent in/at	☐ 20	열풍	fever, craze	☐ 32	지방 자치단체	local government
☐ 09	다채롭다	to be colorful/ diverse	☐ 21	영리	profit	☐ 33	처벌	punishment
☐ 10	대등하다	equal	☐ 22	완곡하다	euphemistic	☐ 34	편파적	partial
☐ 11	도모	to promote/plan	☐ 23	웃돌다	exceed	☐ 35	현저하다	marked, noticeable
☐ 12	동일하다	same	☐ 24	유독	especially			

DAY 20 | 일일 단어 리스트

No.	단어	뜻	No.	단어	뜻	No.	단어	뜻
☐ 01	강력하다	strong, powerful	☐ 13	마일리지	mileage	☐ 25	의식주	basic necessities of life; food, clothing, shelter
☐ 02	고령화	aging	☐ 14	맥락	context	☐ 26	인상적	memorable, impressive
☐ 03	구독	subscription	☐ 15	모욕적	insult	☐ 27	인종	race
☐ 04	기막히다	unbelievable	☐ 16	미세	micro, fine	☐ 28	잔인하다	cruel, merciless
☐ 05	기상	weather	☐ 17	발급	issue, get	☐ 29	저서	books
☐ 06	기증	donation	☐ 18	보건	health	☐ 30	장담	guarantee, assure
☐ 07	노숙자	homeless	☐ 19	시행착오	trials and errors	☐ 31	주거	living, residence
☐ 08	다국적	multinational	☐ 20	여간	ordinarily, normally	☐ 32	지배적	majority, dominance
☐ 09	단가	unit price	☐ 21	완료하다	to complete	☐ 33	철저히	thoroughly, strictly
☐ 10	대략적	general/ outline	☐ 22	요양하다	to recuperate, nurse	☐ 34	폐지되다	to be abolished
☐ 11	도약하다	jump, leap	☐ 23	웅장하다	grand, magnificent	☐ 35	혐오	harted
☐ 12	동정하다	to have pity	☐ 24	유동적	flexible			

DAY 21 | 일일 단어 리스트

☐ 01 강렬하다	strong, intense	☐ 13 맥박	pulse	☐ 25 인성	character, personality
☐ 02 고르다	even, fair	☐ 14 모질다	harsh, heartless	☐ 26 인증하다	to certify
☐ 03 구성하다	to form/build	☐ 15 미숙하다	inexperienced	☐ 27 잡음	static noise
☐ 04 기한	deadline	☐ 16 발령	appointment, assignment	☐ 28 저소득	low-income
☐ 05 끔찍하다	terrible, grusome	☐ 17 보편적	common, universal	☐ 29 절차	procedure
☐ 06 내실	interior	☐ 18 실업	unemployment	☐ 30 주관하다	to be in charge of
☐ 07 노출	exposure	☐ 19 여건	condition	☐ 31 지불	payment
☐ 08 단결	unity, solidarity	☐ 20 완만하다	gentle, gradual	☐ 32 첨부	attachment
☐ 09 대립되다	be opposed to, competing	☐ 21 우선시하다	to prioritize	☐ 33 촉구하다	to call for, to demand
☐ 10 도입하다	to implement/ introduce	☐ 22 워낙	such	☐ 34 표절	plagiarism
☐ 11 동조하다	to agree	☐ 23 유래	origin	☐ 35 형편없다	poor, terrible
☐ 12 마케팅	marketing	☐ 24 의외로	unexpectedly, surprisingly		

DAY 22 | 일일 단어 리스트

☐ 01 가늠	estimate	☐ 13 맵시	appearance, style	☐ 25 유행가	pop songs
☐ 02 강제적	forced	☐ 14 모형	model	☐ 26 의욕	will
☐ 03 고립	isolation	☐ 15 미약하다	weak, slight	☐ 27 인종	race
☐ 04 구직	job hunting	☐ 16 발신자	sender	☐ 28 인지	cognition, recognition
☐ 05 기호	symbol, sign	☐ 17 벅차다	overwhelming, difficult	☐ 29 절감	reduction
☐ 06 낙관적	optimistic	☐ 18 보수적	conservative	☐ 30 저조	low, poor
☐ 07 노폐물	waste	☐ 19 실용	utility, practicality	☐ 31 점검하다	to inspect
☐ 08 단계적	in stages/ step-by-step	☐ 20 여론	public opinion	☐ 32 지속	continuance
☐ 09 대변하다	to talk on behalf of	☐ 21 여지	room, margin	☐ 33 체감	sense, feel
☐ 10 도처	everywhere	☐ 22 완치	full recovery	☐ 34 필수품	necessity
☐ 11 동종업계	same field/ industry	☐ 23 원격	remote	☐ 35 혜택	benefit
☐ 12 마취	anesthesia	☐ 24 유력하다	strong, dominant		

DAY 23 | 일일 단어 리스트

☐ 01 가속	acceleration	☐ 13 맹렬하다	fierce	☐ 25 육류	meat
☐ 02 강조하다	to emphasize	☐ 14 모호하다	ambiguous	☐ 26 의존도	dependency
☐ 03 고소	sue	☐ 15 미정	undefined	☐ 27 인파	crowd
☐ 04 구체화	materialization, specification	☐ 16 민낯	true/naked face	☐ 28 일거양득	killing two birds with one stone
☐ 05 기호	taste, preference	☐ 17 발휘하다	demonstrate, show	☐ 29 잦다	frequent
☐ 06 내딛다	to set foot on (to start/begin)	☐ 18 복원	restoration	☐ 30 저하	decline, deterioration
☐ 07 노화	aging	☐ 19 실행	implementation, execute	☐ 31 접종	vaccination
☐ 08 단념하다	give up	☐ 20 여전하다	still	☐ 32 지수	index, quotient
☐ 09 대북	(towards)North Korea	☐ 21 연일	day after day, everyday	☐ 33 체결하다	to sign/enter into
☐ 10 도태되다	to die out, to be selected out	☐ 22 왜곡	distortion, twist	☐ 34 하락	fall, decline
☐ 11 동질성	homogeneity	☐ 23 원동력	driving force	☐ 35 혹평	criticism
☐ 12 막다르다	dead end	☐ 24 유망	promising, bright		

DAY 24 | 일일 단어 리스트

☐ 01 가라앉다	to settle/subside	☐ 13 무력	armed/ military force	☐ 25 이산가족	separated families
☐ 02 가열하다	to heat	☐ 14 무분별하다	thoughtless, indiscriminate	☐ 26 임기	term, tenure
☐ 03 거세다	strong, harsh	☐ 15 무인	self service, unmanned	☐ 27 자영업	self-employment
☐ 04 공공시설	public facilities	☐ 16 밀어붙이다	push (ahead)	☐ 28 정체성	identity
☐ 05 권유하다	to recommend, suggest	☐ 17 배설물	waste, excretion	☐ 29 제기하다	to raise/bring up
☐ 06 난처하다	in a dilemma, awkward	☐ 18 분담	division of labor	☐ 30 조퇴	early leave
☐ 07 논하다	to discuss	☐ 19 불경기	recession	☐ 31 직위	position
☐ 08 단합하다	to unify	☐ 20 연령	age	☐ 32 취지	purpose
☐ 09 달성하다	to reach/achieve	☐ 21 우려하다	to worry	☐ 33 한창	the height, full bloom
☐ 10 독점하다	to have a monopoly	☐ 22 위독하다	critical	☐ 34 효력	effect, power
☐ 11 뒤풀이	afterparty	☐ 23 유언비어	wild/groundless rumor		
☐ 12 만료되다	to be expired	☐ 24 응하다	respond to, accept		

DAY 25 | 일일 단어 리스트

- ☐ 01 가려내다 to distinguish/determine
- ☐ 02 가파르다 steep
- ☐ 03 건의 suggestion/proposal
- ☐ 04 공교육 public education
- ☐ 05 귀하다 rare, precious
- ☐ 06 남녀평등 gender equality
- ☐ 07 농경 agriculture, farming
- ☐ 08 단호하다 stern, firm
- ☐ 09 달아오르다 to heat up, to blush
- ☐ 10 독창성 uniqueness, originality
- ☐ 11 뒷받침 backing, support
- ☐ 12 만만하다 easygoing, insignificant
- ☐ 13 무례 disrespect, rudeness
- ☐ 14 무상 free
- ☐ 15 무작정 blindly, recklessly
- ☐ 16 밀어주다 to support, to back (up)
- ☐ 17 배열 arrangement
- ☐ 18 분배 distribution, division
- ☐ 19 불과하다 just, only
- ☐ 20 열광하다 to go wild, to get excited
- ☐ 21 우수성 superiority, excellence
- ☐ 22 위력 power
- ☐ 23 유용하다 useful
- ☐ 24 의도 motive/intention
- ☐ 25 이색적 unusual, unique
- ☐ 26 임대하다 to rent (out)
- ☐ 27 자존심 pride, self-respect
- ☐ 28 재테크 investment techniques
- ☐ 29 적도 equator
- ☐ 30 제공하다 to provide
- ☐ 31 제대하다 to be discharged from the military
- ☐ 32 진단하다 to diagnose
- ☐ 33 치안 public security
- ☐ 34 합리적 logical
- ☐ 35 후유증 aftermath

DAY 26 | 일일 단어 리스트

- ☐ 01 고위 high-ranking
- ☐ 02 국제적 international
- ☐ 03 끝맺다 to end/finish
- ☐ 04 난폭하다 violent, reckless
- ☐ 05 녹초 utterly exhausted
- ☐ 06 누리다 to enjoy
- ☐ 07 단속 crackdown, enforcement
- ☐ 08 대안 alternative
- ☐ 09 독립적 the elderly independent
- ☐ 10 독거노인 the elderly people living alone
- ☐ 11 막막하다 at a loss
- ☐ 12 면역력 immunity
- ☐ 13 몰두하다 be absorbed/engrossed
- ☐ 14 미각 taste
- ☐ 15 민망하다 embarrased, awkward
- ☐ 16 방사능 radioactivity
- ☐ 17 방지 prevention
- ☐ 18 복합 complex, compound
- ☐ 19 안쓰럽다 pity, sorry
- ☐ 20 역효과 adverse effect, backfire
- ☐ 21 요소 factor, element
- ☐ 22 용의자 suspect
- ☐ 23 원본 original (text/document)
- ☐ 24 유비무환 Better safe than sorry
- ☐ 25 음원 song, track
- ☐ 26 이끌다 to lead
- ☐ 27 일리 point
- ☐ 28 입장 position, stance
- ☐ 29 재난 (natural) disaster
- ☐ 30 전화위복 blessing in disguise
- ☐ 31 정서 emotion
- ☐ 32 지적하다 to point out
- ☐ 33 추구하다 to strive for, to pursue
- ☐ 34 학대 abuse
- ☐ 35 환기하다 to ventilate

DAY 27 | 일일 단어 리스트

☐ 01 가다듬다	to calm, to straighten	☐ 13 면제되다	to be exempt	☐ 25 유사하다	similar
☐ 02 개설	contruct	☐ 14 몰아가다	to drive	☐ 26 음질	sound quality
☐ 03 고학력	highly educated	☐ 15 무해하다	harmless	☐ 27 이력	career, background
☐ 04 국토	country, national land	☐ 16 민주	democracy	☐ 28 일반화하다	generalize
☐ 05 나르다	transport, carry	☐ 17 방수	waterproof	☐ 29 자극적	stimulating, provoking
☐ 06 논란	controversy	☐ 18 방치되다	neglected	☐ 30 재발하다	to reoccur
☐ 07 단적	prime/ direct(example)	☐ 19 본격적	in earnest	☐ 31 절정	peak, climax
☐ 08 대담	formal conversation	☐ 20 압도적	overwhelming	☐ 32 출시되다	released
☐ 09 대외	foreign, external	☐ 21 연간	annual	☐ 33 지정되다	designated
☐ 10 독선적	self-righteous	☐ 22 요인	cause	☐ 34 추세	trend
☐ 11 동호인	members of a club	☐ 23 유언	will	☐ 35 한가롭다	leisurely, relaxed
☐ 12 막바지	final stage, end of (road)	☐ 24 원산지	origin		

DAY 28 | 일일 단어 리스트

☐ 01 가구	household	☐ 13 멸망시키다	to destroy	☐ 25 음치	tone deaf
☐ 02 개정	revisement, amendment	☐ 14 몰입	immersion	☐ 26 이례적	unusual
☐ 03 고혈압	high blood pressure	☐ 15 못마땅하다	displeased (with), dissatisfied (with)	☐ 27 일방적	one-sided
☐ 04 궁극적	ultimate	☐ 16 민첩하다	quick, agile	☐ 28 자기중심적	self-centered
☐ 05 나열	list	☐ 17 방어하다	defend	☐ 29 재촉	urging
☐ 06 논의	discussion	☐ 18 방침	policy	☐ 30 접근성	accessibility
☐ 07 단절되다	to be cut off	☐ 19 본성	true nature	☐ 31 정책	policy
☐ 08 대우	treatment	☐ 20 양상	condition, aspect	☐ 32 지지하다	to support
☐ 09 독성	toxic	☐ 21 연관되다	to be involved	☐ 33 출산율	fertility rate
☐ 10 되새기다	reflect	☐ 22 요청하다	to request	☐ 34 한결같다	consistent
☐ 11 뒤덮다	cover	☐ 23 원색적	crude, vulgar	☐ 35 회의적	skeptical
☐ 12 막상막하	neck-and-neck, be equally matched	☐ 24 유세	campaign		

DAY 29 | 일일 단어 리스트

□ 01 가급적	possible	□ 13 막연하다	vague	□ 25 음향	sound
□ 02 강세	strength, accent	□ 14 멸종	extinction	□ 26 이론적	theoretical
□ 03 거르다	to skip	□ 15 무궁무진하다	endless	□ 27 일방통행	one-way
□ 04 골치	trouble, nuisance	□ 16 밀도	density	□ 28 자산	assest
□ 05 궁금증	curiosity	□ 17 방영	airing, broadcast	□ 29 재충전	recharge
□ 06 낙천적	optimistic	□ 18 배기가스	exhaust gas	□ 30 정체	congestion, stagnation
□ 07 논증	argument	□ 19 부각되다	to be highlighted	□ 31 직면하다	confront
□ 08 단정하다	conclude	□ 20 양성	training, nurturing	□ 32 정중하다	polite
□ 09 대응하다	respond	□ 21 연구하다	research	□ 33 한계	limit
□ 10 독자적	independent, unique	□ 22 용량	capacity	□ 34 하찮다	trivial
□ 11 두각	stand out	□ 23 원활하다	smooth	□ 35 획득	acquisition, win
□ 12 들끓다	to boil	□ 24 유심히	carefully		

DAY 30 | 일일 단어 리스트

□ 01 가계	household budget	□ 13 막중하다	important, great	□ 25 응답자	respondent
□ 02 거부하다	refuse	□ 14 명단	list	□ 26 이면	background, hidden side
□ 03 거창하다	grand	□ 15 무난하다	easy, passable	□ 27 일탈	deviation
□ 04 공간	space	□ 16 밀려나다	to be pushed out	□ 28 자신만만하다	confident
□ 05 권력	authority	□ 17 방음	soundproof	□ 29 재치	wit
□ 06 난감하다	difficult	□ 18 배상	compensation	□ 30 정화	purification
□ 07 논평	comment	□ 19 부과하다	to impose	□ 31 중력	gravity
□ 08 단조롭다	monotonous	□ 20 양육	nurture, care	□ 32 중산층	middle class
□ 09 대조적	contrast	□ 21 연금	pension	□ 33 충족시키다	satisfy
□ 10 독재	dictatorship	□ 22 용품	goods	□ 34 한심하다	pathetic
□ 11 둔하다	dull	□ 23 위급하다	urgent	□ 35 확산되다	spread
□ 12 들이닥치다	to storm, drop in	□ 24 우발적	accidental		

INDEX

ㄴ